Burrhus F. Skinner

Other titles in the Mind Shapers Series

Burrhus F. skinner
The Shaping of Behaviour

Frederick Toates
Professor of Biological Psychology, The Open University

Mind Shapers – Key Psychologists and their impact
Series Editor: Richard Stevens

First published 2009 by
PALGRAVE MACMILLAN

Palgrave Macmillan in the UK is an imprint of Macmillan Publishers Limited, registered in England, company number 785998, of Houndmills, Basingstoke, Hampshire RG21 6XS.

Palgrave Macmillan in the US is a division of St Martin's Press LLC, 175 Fifth Avenue, New York, NY 10010.

Palgrave Macmillan is the global academic imprint of the above companies and has companies and representatives throughout the world.

Palgrave® and Macmillan® are registered trademarks in the United States, the United Kingdom, Europe and other countries.

ISBN-13: 978–0–230–21866–6

This book is printed on paper suitable for recycling and made from fully managed and sustained forest sources. Logging, pulping and manufacturing processes are expected to conform to the environmental regulations of the country of origin.

A catalogue record for this book is available from the British Library.

A catalog record for this book is available from the Library of Congress.

10   9   8   7   6   5   4   3   2   1
18   17   16   15   14   13   12   11   10   09

Printed and bound in Great Britain by
CPI Antony Rowe, Chippenham and Eastbourne

Contents

Acknowledgements

I would like to acknowledge the role of several people in the creation of the present book. Dr. Richard Stevens, the editor of the Mindshapers series, provided the motivation and persistence in getting me to write it and provided invaluable advice throughout. I appreciate the comments received from Kent Berridge, Bob Boakes, Angus Gellatly, Geoff Hall, Julie Hargreaves, Sue Koger, Graham Mitchell, Russell Stannard and Madeline Watson.

I would like to acknowledge the help received from Neha Sharma of Palgrave Macmillan and Shirley Tan of Expo Holdings.

Preface

So, there is yet another contribution on Skinner to add to the many books and countless article pages already written! Have we not long ago 'done to their death' the arguments about reinforcement, Beyond Freedom and Dignity and free will versus determinism? Surely all this work has simply attained a point of stalemate, which, at best, only serves to generate more heat than light. Isn't Skinner passé now; merely a distant memory from the history of a past age that has been swept aside by more recent developments in psychology? One might quite reasonably wonder whether there can be anything left to say about Skinner. Although he was probably the most controversial scientist since Darwin and was (maybe, still is) the most famous scientist in America, that might not be enough to justify yet more pages.

My guiding principle in writing this book is that there is still much left to be said. Skinner was more than 'just' a psychologist but rather also a philosopher and, above all, a social reformer. In some ways he was ahead of his time. To my knowledge, he was the first scientist to anticipate the current crises of ecology and pollution in the world. Furthermore, he suggested a radical solution to them. In the present global crisis, that, in itself, would justify taking another and very careful look at him. In my view, survival itself could well depend upon a better understanding and application of the science of human behaviour.

The Skinnerian perspective has tended to stand somewhat aloof from mainstream psychology, probably not least because Skinner himself seemed not to wish to be part of the mainstream as it was then. The present book represents an attempt to integrate Skinner into the mainstream of psychology by indicating where bridges can be built (e.g. with cognitive, social and biological perspectives). It will show where Skinnerian ideas are alive and well. So, the book is neither a eulogy for Skinner nor a dismissal of his ideas. Rather, it aims for a compromise position that sets him into a broader context and in a key place in the development of psychology.

The present book makes no attempt to go into the details of Skinnerian schedules, which are well described elsewhere or into the more detailed philosophical aspects of behaviourism, which are described and debated extensively elsewhere.

Frederick Toates
Milton Keynes
2008

1 Who was B.F. Skinner?

Why such fame?

When the Vice-President of the United States uses the expression "very dangerous" about a man's utterances, what image does this trigger in your mind? Most likely, it is that of an international terrorist, the President of a hostile power or a Mafia Godfather, whose menacing features stare out from the pages of the FBI's 'Most Wanted' rogues' gallery.

When someone is blamed almost single-handedly for America losing the Vietnam War, what image does this evoke for you? It is probably safe to guess that the image would be of a Russian or Chinese spy at the heart of the Pentagon, a failed President or a highly-incompetent general.

Surely, amongst the last candidates to come to mind in either role would be a bespectacled highbrow professor, who spent much of his time in the genteel atmosphere of Harvard University, observing pigeons as they pecked keys and rats as they pressed levers. Yet, Vice-President Spiro Agnew[1] gave the "most dangerous" description to the Harvard professor of psychology, Burrhus Frederic Skinner*.

So, what kind of sinister double life was the famous professor leading in order to earn such a rare and unenviable distinction? After all, his devotion to observing laboratory animals might be regarded as somewhat eccentric but that in itself is hardly sufficient to cause the FBI to open a file on him (as indeed they did). Similarly, why did US Congressman Cornelius Gallagher propose that the US government should stop the research support that it was giving to Skinner?

What earned his negative reputation was the *extrapolation* that Skinner made from experiments on animals in laboratory cages to explaining the

---

*Of course, given the subject of the book, you might well have guessed already that it was Skinner but the argument remains true.

1

human behaviour that he observed around him in the 'land of the free'. The determinants of the behaviour of laboratory rats and pigeons have, it was suggested, some fundamentally common features with the determinants of the behaviour of so-called free citizens. In the words of Congressman Gallagher, steps need to be put in place[2]:

> ... to deal specifically with the type of threats to our Congress and our Constituents which are contained in the thoughts of B.F. Skinner.

Skinner argued that the behaviour of a person, whether tramp, saint, sinner or whoever, is the product of the history of what *has been done to* him or her during a life-time. What cannot be accounted for by this *environmental* factor ('nurture'), past and present, is left to the *genes* ('nature') as an explanation. So, the individual is squeezed inextricably between these two sets of determining factors. Differences in genes and environment would be seen as the determinants of differences between individuals.

The role of a person's life-time experience is comparable to how the key-pecking of the pigeon can be explained 'historically' by what *has been done* to the pigeon. In the pigeon's case, it is usually in terms of how the experimenter arranged for the delivery of food pellets to be triggered by the hungry bird's pecks on a key.

Such an unflattering analogy might seem to run counter to the most cherished ideals of an individualistic and democratic culture, in which people are thought to decide freely their own destiny and whereby they should be held responsible for their own actions. So, when these latter and grander terms are applied to American society, behaviour is said to be *spontaneously* and *purposively* generated as a result of prior conscious reflection and sometimes even in opposition to the push and pull of life-time circumstances. This is a culture in which the rugged individual, who asserts personal responsibility, is something of a hero. Unlike that of Skinner's pigeon, it is argued, human behaviour has an element of *inscrutability* about it: its determinants might be known only to the individual showing the behaviour. Thereby, human behaviour merits its fair share of praise or blame, and corresponding reward or punishment, not only in this life but, according to some, for all eternity. The law of the land is based upon the assumption of personal responsibility and the right to apply punishment for violation, except where there is evidence that the freedom of choice is impaired.

Skinner's offence was to give an account that 'takes away' from humankind this quality of freedom and autonomy, with its associated personal responsibility (To keep you, I hope, captivated, the exact logic of why he was blamed for America losing the Vietnam War will have to wait until later!). The notions of freedom and autonomy, he argued, were the useless and superstitious remnants of a pre-scientific age, to be discarded along with the belief in a flat earth, demonic-possession and six-day creation. To use his favourite term, 'autonomous man'*- was to be relegated merely to a place in the history books of psychology and culture. But history has taught us that so-called useless and superstitious remnants can die hard, as Skinner was quick to discover for himself.

In the first major dethroning of the scientific era, Copernicus and Galileo had found that old ideas, in their case that the earth has a special astronomical place at the geometric centre of cosmological creation, are not to be painlessly discarded. Next, Darwin appeared to have dislodged humankind from its unique place at centre-stage in an act of biological creation, a move that still encounters passionate resistance. Freud is sometimes credited with the third major dethroning of humankind, which would make Skinner's the fourth. A vociferous part of humankind was to hit back at any such heresy.

Platt[3] writes:

Darwin, like Skinner, was accused of unjustified extrapolation from birds to dogs to man, and of treating man as a mere animal. And in both cases, in spite of the scientific clarification and the technical successes, there were loud protests from the defenders of humanism and morality.

Skinner told us that our near-universal intuition and feeling that we have free will to consciously decide our actions is merely an illusion. This is somewhat like Copernicus telling people that what was obvious before their eyes, i.e. that the sun rotates around the earth, is in truth an illusion[4].

It was not only right-wing Conservative politicians, such as Spiro Agnew, and religious people who considered Skinner to be outrageous in making his claims. He also earned the wrath of liberals, humanists and left-wing radicals, most famously the linguist Noam Chomsky. In addition, a large

---

*I use the gendered term where it was used in this way by Skinner.

number of psychologists were incensed by what they considered grossly over-simplified claims concerning what made people act as they do.

Surely, rang the counter-argument, it must count that humans have a sophisticated language, free will and conscious insight into their behaviour. Their actions bear evidence of a self-generated purpose; something not yet achieved (a goal in the mind) is playing a role in controlling their current behaviour. Behaviour is said to be *purposive*, guided by goals that might be idiosyncratic and evident only to the individual in question. These goals can be articulated by the individual, if he or she freely chooses to do so. Despite the best (or worst!) intentions of the psychologist, people being studied have minds of their own and can spring surprises. This means that very little could be usefully extrapolated from the tractable behaviour of the laboratory rat to that of the priest or street mugger.

Skinner countered that the language of 'inner states', such as thoughts and conscious goals as a means of explanation, is not one that is useful to a science of behaviour. We are still left with the task of explaining how these goals and other mental states arise in the first place. The contents of the conscious mind as reported by introspection were rejected as a basis for explanation in psychology. Rather, to understand thinking and behaviour, we need to focus on the causes of both of these within the environment.

A development of psychology, termed 'cognitive psychology', put on a more formal scientific footing such internal processes as goal-direction, memory, attention and decision-making. However, this did nothing to placate Skinner, who reiterated that this was looking in the wrong place for the determinants of behaviour.

Foundations of behaviourism

The *behaviourist* school of psychology argued that behaviour itself should form the subject-matter of psychology. In a branch of this that became known as 'radical behaviourism', Skinner and his followers[5] took this as its frame of reference but argued that the study of conscious states is permitted in a science of psychology. Indeed, they suggested that they might have some very useful things to say about how these states arise. It is simply that we are not permitted to *explain* behaviour in terms of such states of mind. To try to do so is called 'mentalism' by Skinnerians and this is definitely a pejorative expression. Any explanation based on mentalism is said to be fictional since it immediately raises the issue of what caused the mental state.

Suppose, for example, that one asks a child why he hit another and the child answers "Just because I felt like it"[6]. The mental state of 'just feeling like it' is itself in need of an explanation in terms of a cause, which to a Skinnerian would be in terms of the aggressive child's life history. Similarly, for a Skinnerian, to suggest that the child was offensive 'because he has low self-esteem' explains nothing. Where is this mysterious thing, which is called 'self-esteem', located? What evidence do we have for its existence, apart from the *behaviour* that we are trying to explain by means of it? The argument in terms of such mental causes is a circular one, even though, in popular discourse, low self-esteem is seen as the culprit for explaining a variety of personal failings.

As a philosophical foundation for his whole approach, Skinner noted that we are all the product of a process of evolution, in which, survival, in effect, poses a number of similar 'problems' for any species. Skinner's favourite species for research were rats, pigeons and humans and he emphasized certain general features. Each must find food, water and shelter, and each is attracted to engage in sexual behaviour.

Why use rats and pigeons? They are simpler organisms to study than humans are. For practical and ethical reasons, it is obviously easier to maintain them under controlled laboratory conditions, in which interference from outside is minimized. In this sense, Skinner was little different from other scientists, such as biologists, physicists or chemists, who also start by studying the most simple systems[7]. He argued that insights arising from non-humans can give important clues as to how human behaviour operates and sometimes suggest research that can be applied to humans.

The notions of reinforcement and punishment

Positive reinforcement

Skinner suggested that nature provides a range of what he termed *positive reinforcers*, such things as food, shelter, sex and water. These reinforcers shape the behaviour of the animal, i.e. they change the future probability of showing the behaviour that was occurring just before the reinforcer appeared. The term 'reinforcer' describes the fact that behaviour is strengthened in this process. The link with evolutionary thinking is that the contact with positive reinforcers tends to help the animal to survive and reproduce.

The most fundamental pillar of Skinnerian psychology is really so basic that it could be described on the back of a postcard. If a *positive reinforcer* follows a particular behaviour, then that behaviour will increase in frequency (or, as it is sometimes expressed, 'rate'). For example, suppose an experimenter deprives a rat of water for some hours. The rat is then placed in a maze, where, after running along an arm, it comes to a T-junction and encounters the choice of turning into a left or right arm. If the rat turns to the left, it finds a small quantity of water. If the rat turns right, it finds nothing. In psychological jargon, there exists what is termed a *contingency* between the behaviour of turning left and obtaining water. A 'contingency' is the arrangement of events as organized by the experimenter, in this case the link between behaviour and finding water. At first, the rat's choice is apparently random but, after a number of experiences in the maze, it almost invariably turns to the left. So, the favoured jargon of behaviourism is as follows. Water is said to be a 'positive reinforcer' for the behaviour of a thirsty animal, in this case, turning left; water is 'positively reinforcing' and the behaviour of turning left has been 'positively reinforced'.

For another demonstration of the same principle, suppose a hungry pigeon is placed in a *Skinner box* – a piece of apparatus consisting of a key, which, if pecked, causes a pellet of food to appear. The experimenter has arranged a 'contingency' between pecking and food. At first, the pigeon might show little inclination to peck the key. So, the experimenter would try the 'generous criterion' of giving pellets simply when the pigeon's beak is in the vicinity of the key. Subsequently, the experimenter becomes less generous by giving pellets only when the bird shows pecking anywhere near the key. By careful observation of its behaviour and by the giving of pellets, successively closer approximations to key-pecking can be reinforced, such that the bird comes to reliably peck the key and earn food pellets.

Such changing of behaviour and establishing a new behaviour is known as 'operant conditioning', the animal is said to emit 'operants', that is to say, effects which *operate* on the environment. These operants can then be reinforced. The initial phase of the experiment, which guides the behaviour by small increments in the direction of the desired response, is known as 'shaping'. The term 'successive approximations' applies here: the criterion for gaining the pellet is made slightly more difficult by small steps, each requirement being a closer approximation to the final criterion of behaviour: key-pecking. This is by analogy with a potter shaping by small steps an unformed piece of clay (untrained or 'naïve' rat/pigeon) into the final product, the vase (trained rat/pigeon).

In a Skinnerian analysis, in this regard what goes for rats goes equally well for humans. For example, a child is praised for his or her hard work in completing homework and, in the future, there is an increase in time spent with this activity[8]. A comedian is applauded for a particular joke, which then tends to be repeated at future venues.

It is important to note that Skinner is not asserting that the controls underlying human and rat behaviour are identical. Rather, he is saying that there are some important principles in common. By comparison, no one would say that the rat kidney and human kidney are identical. However, medical science has advanced enormously by investigating features that are similar across species.

Food, water and sex have a broad application as positive reinforcers across species but some positive reinforcers are more peculiarly human. For example, a wide range of different expressions of gratitude for a particular action is one such, and this tends to increase the frequency (rate) of showing the behaviour that the expressions follow, but it is obviously limited to humans.

It will hardly have escaped your notice that food, water, praise and sexual contact are all things that we tend to find pleasant. So, in the Skinnerian glossary, is the term 'positive reinforcement' synonymous with 'pleasure' or, as it might be expressed, 'positive hedonic consequence'? Strictly speaking it is not and this is for two reasons.

First, as noted already, Skinner was part of a school within psychology termed 'behaviourism', more precisely a brand termed 'radical behaviourism'. Just to remind you of one of the school's fundamental premises: radical behaviourism did not rule out mental terms, such as feelings, from the discussion. However, these terms were not permitted to be part of the *explanation* of behaviour. This school believed in a purely *objective* explanation, one that tried hard to purge 'mentalistic' terms as the basis of the explanation. In strictly objective terms, pleasure is unobservable, i.e. we cannot say whether the rat enjoys eating or having sex. Therefore, we are not permitted to say that the rat is pressing the lever in a Skinner box because, for example, it *wants* food or *enjoys* food. That would be mentalistic. We are permitted only to say that 'food is reinforcing to it'. Indeed, by these rigorous criteria, we cannot even say for sure that another person is actually ever enjoying a hedonic experience! Most people would probably risk the leap of speculation that a hungry rat does enjoy such activities, just as most of us would tend to believe other people to be experiencing pleasure, based upon their facial reactions and spoken accounts. However, we cannot directly observe or measure pleasure as such and so Skinner did not define positive reinforcement in terms of pleasure.

Secondly, the objective definition allows for a somewhat counter-intuitive possibility: a person might show an increase in frequency of a particular behaviour as a result of the action of a reinforcer even when there was good reason to doubt the existence of any conscious hedonic effect. For example, it might be that a reinforcer acts at an unconscious level. Indeed, in one experiment, people with a history of addiction to morphine were found to increase their frequency of pressing a lever to obtain very small quantities of this drug injected into them, even though they could not consciously detect the drug that was being used as reinforcer, as compared to a neutral substance, a 'placebo'[9]. A similar effect occurs with cocaine. Hence, by the criterion of increasing lever-pressing, the drug was positively reinforcing but it was not consciously detectable, let alone consciously pleasurable.

For a more natural example, consider unreciprocated love. If the great poets and novelists, as well as agony aunts, are right, this must surely involve a very great deal of misery with little or nothing in the way of hedonism and yet often the suitor's ardour seems to be only strengthened by the experience.

A positive reinforcer is defined not by its intrinsic properties but by its *effect*. If a particular behaviour is followed by something that causes this behaviour to increase in frequency, then that is all that there is to it – the 'something' is defined as a positive reinforcer[10]. So a claim of the kind – "I have been positively reinforcing my husband for years but I can't get him to change his ways" represents a contradiction in terms. Whatever the wife was doing one cannot say. However, we can be certain that, in Skinnerian terms, she was not positively reinforcing the behaviour in question. Otherwise, she would have changed his behaviour in the desired direction.

Negative reinforcement

Positive reinforcement is not the only means of changing behaviour, according to Skinner. Amongst other processes, there are also negative reinforcement and punishment (next section). These two often get confused but there is no need to do this, since they are quite distinct. Negative reinforcement refers to a procedure whereby some event is *terminated* following a particular behaviour. This termination serves to strengthen behaviour and so the expression 'reinforcement' is equally appropriate here.

Imagine that a rat is placed in a Skinner box with a loud noise present. A lever-press switches off the noise. Suppose that the rat learns to lever-press as a result of this arrangement of events. In this case, the loud noise is acting as a negative reinforcer. Somewhat symmetrical with positive reinforcement, those things that can be recruited as negative reinforcers would generally be termed 'aversive'. However, in strict Skinnerian language, the definition is in terms of the effect on behaviour, rather than any associated psychological feeling. In evolutionary terms, it helps an animal's survival chances to terminate contact with such things as excesses of heat or cold, pain-producing objects and loud noises.

Punishment

The term 'punishment' refers to something that follows a particular behaviour and which has the effect of *decreasing* the frequency (rate) of showing the behaviour. For example, suppose that a blast of loud noise is given every time a rat turns into one arm in a maze. The frequency with which the animal takes that turn is observed to decrease. Hence, the loud noise is acting as a punisher. Note that the same physical stimulus might be used as either a negative reinforcer or a punisher. The difference is not in the stimulus itself but in the arrangement of its occurrence: negative reinforcement, where behaviour *terminates* the stimulus, and punishment, where behaviour *is followed by* the stimulus. It is not difficult to appreciate the value of punishment in terms of survival: by lowering the tendency to act in a way that leads to aversive events, such as damaging sounds, dogs that bite or excessive heat, we lower the probability of encountering such threats to our survival.

Punishment is particularly good for revealing the unique, and, some opponents might say, least offensive, features of a Skinnerian world view. Skinner opposed the use of punishment both for ethical and practical reasons. Where and how ethics arise in a Skinnerian world is a subject that we must defer until later but the practical issue of punishment is perhaps one that puts Skinner in a light that is more acceptable to the humanist. He noted that it is possible to reduce the frequency of a particular behaviour by the use of certain punishing ('aversive') stimuli. Indeed, punishment is often immediately effective. However, over the longer term, punishment of an *undesired* behaviour can be much less effective than positive reinforcement of an incompatible *desired* behaviour.

General principles and comparison of processes

Positive reinforcement, negative reinforcement and punishment all have an important feature in common: in each case, behaviour has a consequence, which changes the future probability of showing the behaviour in question.

Suppose, for example, that a child is misbehaving in school. It might be possible to lower the frequency of this by rapidly following each instance of misbehaviour with an aversive event. However, organisms can have a nasty habit of hitting back. The punishment might only be effective in the presence of the teacher; when teacher's back is turned, the undesirable behaviour reappears. Worse still, the child might subsequently go truant. A broad guilt and fear might form in association with the school. Punishment at best teaches someone what *not to do* but does not necessarily teach them what he or she *should do*. It is far better, Skinner argued, to find an alternative and desired behaviour that is incompatible with the undesired one and try to positively reinforce this alternative. There is a rather obvious point here but none-the-less it is frequently missed: positive reinforcement tends to keep the child at the site where the reinforcement is applied[11]. For example, the child who is positively reinforced in school will tend to stay there rather than playing truant.

A similar logic applies to attempts to exploit negative reinforcement[12]. Suppose that a child is nagged incessantly for laziness and incompetence. The nagger might be convinced that the child will learn to escape the aversion by working hard but, of course, so often the child does not react in this way. Rather, he or she might, say, attack the source of aversive stimulation physically or run from the situation.

Control by aversive stimuli can take the form not only of actual painful events but threats of such future events, e.g. the threat of the soul's eternal damnation as a result of earthly misbehaviour. Punishers can also take the form of spoken taunts and insults.

One might speculate that, if Skinner had been employed as a consultant for the writing of *The Ten Commandments*, their character would have been radically different. As they stand, most of the ten are prohibitions on what *not* to do, inviting punitive sanctions for their violation. For example, "Thou shalt not commit adultery" might have been restructured in Skinnerian terms as "Thou shalt honour fidelity". This would then invite positive reinforcement for such desired behaviour. Whether the outcome would have been a greater compliance is, of course, something we shall never know!

In Skinnerian terms, punishment, like positive and negative reinforcement, is defined in terms of its consequences. It is here that the strength of a Skinnerian argument is apparent: by objective analysis, many so-called punishments do not act to lower the frequency of showing the undesirable behaviour. What might be thought to be 'punishment' by the person applying it does not in fact serve this role by the Skinnerian criterion of a decreasing tendency to exhibit the 'punished' behaviour. People often have their own views of what *must* constitute punishment, based not so much on a careful observation of behaviour but on personal hunches. Smacks (or a threat of them when back home), shouts or words of censure often fail to lower the frequency of the undesired behaviour *over the long term*, in spite of the punisher's firm conviction that they just have to achieve this. If it fails, the reaction can be one of increasing the intensity of the supposed punishment.

Such failure of aversive intervention links to an important foundation of the Skinnerian view[13]: we need to be more scientific in our approach. So often, interventions are made simply on the assumption that they will work. Careful checking of the results of any intervention is essential.

It is important to note another qualification to the use of the term 'reinforcement'. It is often said that "one man's meat is another man's poison", and presumably the same applies to women. Although such things as water to a thirsty person are universal reinforcers, in other cases what is a positive reinforcer for one person might well be a punisher or negative reinforcer for another. Again, this emphasizes that the nature of reinforcement is an *interaction* between the external world and the individual. An obvious example of this is the difference between different people in their reactions to popular music.

Another term that is needed in order to understand Skinner's world view is 'extinction'. If a reinforcer is removed from a situation, then the behaviour that has been reinforced will typically decline in frequency and might cease entirely. For example, if the pellets of food are removed from the delivery apparatus in the Skinner box, then after a while the frequency of lever-pressing will reduce. Ultimately, the rat will quit pressing. Something might be worrying you, along the following lines. So far I have described the use of positive and negative reinforcement, as well as punishment, in terms of sequences of events ('contingencies') deliberately arranged by someone. The apparatus is organized so that a pellet of food falls into the delivery tray every time that the rat presses a lever or a blast of loud noise occurs every time that it takes a certain turn in a maze. Surely, you might wonder, so much of human life is not normally like that, except in such cases as being smacked around the ear, sentenced to jail or being given a prize in school. The answer is that, in life, contingencies of reinforcement *naturally* occur, some programmed but many quite unintentional.

For example, very few families would surely set out to turn their children into nervous wrecks, delinquents or hardened criminals by the deliberate and optimal use of reinforcement. However, the Skinnerian argument is that, by means of subtle and unplanned reinforcers and punishers, behaviour might be quite inadvertently drawn in such undesired directions. Similarly, most people who get married would probably be mortified to be told that they were applying contingencies of reinforcement such as to lead to marital break-up but this can happen.

Take a child who is not reinforced for socially-acceptable actions, e.g. no reciprocal smiling for his or her own reaction of smiling. Such a child might withdraw from social contact. The child might obtain reinforcement from watching violent video games, which then develops into a gang culture and violence. So, a criminal might be said to exhibit violence because of a life-time's inadvertent reinforcement of violent behaviour and a failure to have more socially-acceptable behaviour reinforced. Perhaps, as a child, the criminal found that he could gain attention only by outbursts of anger. The times the child was behaving in an acceptable way were ignored.

Skinnerian freedom seen in terms of reinforcers

With the help of the notion of reinforcement, the use of the word 'freedom' in Skinnerian terms might be illustrated as follows[14]. Consider the case of a woman who takes some money out of her purse to give to another person. Suppose she goes out of her way to move towards a collection point for the needy and, with joy, hands it over. She is generally assumed to be acting 'freely' since, for amongst other reasons, she *feels* that she is acting freely. Behaviour conforms to her wishes. Despite the feeling of freedom, Skinner would suggest that her behaviour is the outcome of a history of having been *positively* reinforced for the behaviour of giving. Contrast this with when she hands it over to a street mugger at gunpoint. In the latter case, she is acting to escape aversion (a case of being *negatively* reinforced) and against her wishes – she might or, or more likely, might *not* feel much in the way of a free choice. However, in both cases, according to a Skinnerian view, ultimate causation lies in the history of environmental events to which she was exposed. Her behaviour was inevitably written into the historical script.

In Skinner's sense of 'freedom', Skinnerian methods can increase one's freedom[15]. For example, individuals with severe learning difficulties can be taught basic coping skills such as to give them a degree of autonomy from their carers. Some children only communicate by their self-injurious behaviour, whereas reinforcement can open up the possibility of communication through language. By keeping children on the straight and narrow and thereby preventing them from coming into conflict with the law, they might well be spared prison. Someone with an addiction to hard drugs is hardly free in any normally accepted sense of the word and yet behavioural interventions can help to get the addict 'clean'. The freedom opened up to someone by gaining literacy is immeasurable. One could go on with numerous similar examples.

Assessing Skinner

So much for the basic principles – how would we go about assessing the ideas of Skinner? Could we do a series of experiments that would show that people really are deluded into believing that their behaviour is one of expressing spontaneous purposive choices, whereas in reality it is inescapably a reflection of their history of reinforcement? As doubtless you will appreciate, this presents insurmountable ethical and practical obstacles. In principle, you would need to take a human from the time of conception as a single cell within the womb and observe everything that it does and is done to it. One would need some way of cataloguing the behaviour that the growing child shows and the possible reinforcing events that follow such behaviour. One would need to monitor the changes in frequency of different behaviours and thereby be in a position to predict what the infant would do at some subsequent stage of life.

In the absence of such an experimental programme, we must be content to speculate using less rigorous criteria, based upon the accumulation of bits of evidence. For example, the behaviour of laboratory animals kept under controlled conditions shows quite convincingly how behaviour can be brought under the control of reinforcers. Are we prepared to extrapolate to humans on the basis of such results?

Further evidence can be gained on the basis of carefully-controlled and measured interventions made into the environment of humans. For example, school children can be observed and reinforced for desirable behaviours. In practice, such studies do indeed show convincingly that praise can act as a reinforcer such that desired behaviour increases in frequency[16]. So, there is good evidence to believe that some human behaviour can be altered as a result of reinforcement. Evidence for the centrality of the principle of reinforcement will be presented in subsequent chapters. However, it will also be argued that reinforcement is only *one* process amongst others that can play a role in determining behaviour, not that it is necessarily the only process.

Some implications

How would the abandonment of explanations in terms of spontaneous purposive choice, in favour of one based upon a life-time's history, fit into a lay understanding of behaviour? The answer is a clear 'very mixed'; it depends largely on the person whose behaviour is the target of the explanation.

On the one hand, people commonly have an immediate gut reaction of hostility to any such dethroning of autonomous man[17]. On the other hand, our culture already accepts that a life-time's history of 'what is done to' an individual must play a profound role in shaping behaviour. For example, people often express the opinion that female sex workers have no real choice in their occupation, as this is inevitably the result of circumstances not of their own making, such as lack of parental love, alienation, powerlessness, poverty or drugs. Feminists often use such an argument to suggest the unfairness of legal sanctions.

Many people tend to excuse a degree of bad behaviour where there exists evidence of mitigating circumstances. For example, a child growing up in a disturbed and violent family might be expected to show some tendency to exhibit maladaptive behaviour when adult. Such a child is perhaps more likely to earn sympathy than one who 'goes off the rails' after a pampered middle-class upbringing. The justice system also provides for the notion of mitigating circumstances: for example, a woman who is the victim of consistent domestic abuse is likely to expect a relatively light sentence for killing her spouse, or, if not, there is often public outrage. Could the reaction be a question of degree? Many people might see some mitigating circumstances, i.e. some belief in environmental determining factors. However, they would be reluctant to go as far as Skinner in writing personal agency and responsibility entirely out of the script.

A striking asymmetry arises here and it forms a central pillar of the Skinnerian message. Most of us like to believe in our own capacity for informed and inscrutable purposive choices when the consequences of these choices are ones that others might be expected to admire. By contrast, when the consequences are ones that others would deplore, we tend to launch a desperate search for mitigating circumstances. The defence plea takes the form of disturbing bodily states, such as stress, pain or premenstrual tension, or life-time events in terms of personal history, such as abuse, thwarting, lack of rewards and opportunities.

I have witnessed a particularly illuminating and amusing example of such asymmetry in teaching Skinnerian principles. Students were instructed on how they should go about forming a skilled bar-pressing rat by the optimal use of food pellets as reinforcement. They were then given an untrained ('naïve') rat and a Skinner box and left to get on with it. When checking up on the students an hour or so later, attribution of responsibility often depended upon the success of the session. The sight of a skilled bar-pressing rat would typically be accompanied by the remark "Look – we have done very well", whereas, when the rat was totally ignoring the lever, the students tended to remark "You seem to have given us a dud rat". At another level in this situation, the same asymmetry tends to repeat itself: tutors are more likely to take credit for any successful students, whereas the less successful can be blamed for their own failings. Skinner exposed such illogical asymmetries to the full in advancing his message.

Skinner as missionary: social, ethical and global issues

Skinner viewed himself not just as a scientist discovering the laws governing behaviour but also as a missionary and ambassador, whose role it was to convert the world to the cause of studying behaviour as a science and implementing its results. When he reviewed the problems of the world, such as crime, poverty, prejudice, discrimination and conflict, Skinner argued passionately that their solution demanded the application of such a science. By analogy, no one would seriously consider trying to solve the problems of global disease without exploiting the insights of medical science or trying to cure crop failures without first engaging agricultural science. The science of behaviour that Skinner advanced was based firmly in the principles of behaviourism, with the notion of positive reinforcement at centre-stage. He saw maladaptive behaviour as being the inevitable outcome of a maladaptive history of reinforcement, e.g. inadvertent reinforcement of undesirable behaviour and failure to reinforce desirable behaviour.

So, what was the philosophical foundation for Skinner's argument? It was based upon the imperative of the survival of humankind. On this topic, he wrote[18]:

> Do not ask me why I want mankind to survive. I can tell you why only in the sense in which the physiologist can tell you why I want to breathe.

As early as 1948, Skinner published a utopian novel, *Walden Two*, which described a community organized on the basis of positive reinforcement. Indeed, years before the terms 'sustainability', 'climate change' and 'global warming' came into the headlines, in this novel Skinner made a green proclamation. Just consider the following, which was in the preface to the 1976 edition, i.e. long before the world was aware of climate change[19]:

> Not only can we not face the rest of the world while consuming and polluting as we do. We cannot for long face ourselves while acknowledging the violence and chaos in which we live.

A number of commentators outside the behaviourist school have been impressed by such efforts of Skinner and his followers to solve social problems. One such was the distinguished British historian Arnold Toynbee[20], who wrote:

> Manifestly, we ought to give the most serious consideration to a doctrine whose exponents see in it a means of saving mankind from imminent catastrophe and a means of guarding ourselves against being treated by each other with cruel injustice.

Not surprisingly, Skinner also triggered a strong counter-reaction from those who saw him as a threat to freedom and democracy. The idea that a culture could be engineered, involving the application of reinforcement principles, was seen by some, including the United States Vice President, Spiro Agnew, as totalitarian and anti-American. In this climate, the title of Skinner's 1971 book *Beyond Freedom and Dignity* might well have been a calculated provocation[21]. How could one improve on the cherished ideals of freedom and dignity, which are enshrined in the US constitution, and what brand of audacity is revealed by even trying to do so? What sort of dictatorship was in prospect – the dreaded and feared Communist variety?

Skinner had a powerful and well-developed counter-attack: freedom, as normally conceived, is an illusory concept in any case, depending, as it does, on the pre-scientific notion of autonomous man. One cannot take away what is not already there. Rather, he was designing a culture based upon a radically different and scientifically realistic notion of freedom, defined as a lack of *aversive* control. Skinner argued that society is already controlling people but often by the use of aversive means, through which so many of its problems arise. Skinner did not *invent* operant conditioning but merely articulated its optimal use and advanced the cause of the *positive* reinforcement aspect of it.

As Wheeler[22] notes:

> ...behaviour is, and always has been, strongly affected by environmental factors composed of both aversive and reinforcing elements and that, for certain types of performance, the most powerful conditioners are the positive reinforcers. Humans now live, and always have lived, in a world of positive reinforcement: that is the fact, and it is a fact with sound scientific underpinning. Therefore, there can be no question of deciding whether or not to *believe* in operant conditioning, or whether or not to introduce

it, much as we may decide whether or not to introduce the computer...

Similarly, concerning the ubiquity of operant conditioning, Platt[23] observes:

> It is not a method of manipulation that is simply turned on or off by a wicked dictator or a good fairy.

So, if we wish to change society to improve the human condition, we have to change the nature of the contingencies of reinforcement that underlie the behavioural control that the environment exerts. All else is naïve dreaming and is doomed to failure. For example, to reform criminals, we need to carefully reinforce their good behaviour and take the emphasis away from punishing the bad. If we want to improve the quality of our education, we need to design education programmes in such a way that they are stimulating and learners are reinforced for their learning.

To his supporters, Skinner had obtained the most reproducible and lawful results in the history of psychology. In trying to apply these results scientifically to human behaviour, he was something of a secular messiah, who could lead the way to the prevention of global catastrophe and towards a more fulfilling life for all.

According to Skinner's opponents, he was a threat to freedom and liberty, the author of manifestos that, if taken seriously, would lead to tyranny, if not hell on earth. By making comparisons with rats and pigeons, humans were degraded and their most sacred and uniquely human attributes were ridiculed. To critics who were familiar with non-human species, his psychology demeaned not only humans but rats and pigeons too, since it revealed only stereotyped responses in a very restricted environment. As observed by his admirer, Richelle[24], some portrayed him as:

> ...the last representative of the behaviourist school, and as such, presented as a sort of fossil, or, in the last 25 years of his life, as the obsolete and unique surviving specimen of an otherwise extinct species...

So, which of these 'two Skinners' was he *really*?

A possible compromise position

At this point and before going into the details in the subsequent chapters, I would like to stand back a bit and take something of an overview, while trying to introduce some balance into the discussion. I will give some signposts as to where the following chapters will be going.

Skinner was profoundly radical to the point of being outrageous but it would be foolish to ignore someone who was the most famous scientist in America. Similarly, it would seem to be a big mistake not to do justice to the author of a prescient green manifesto written in 1945, long before the world was even aware of a looming global energy and pollution crisis.

First, let us consider Skinner the scientist. Broadly speaking, given such a radical argument, there appear to be three possible responses, as follows.

The first of these is to read and try to understand the message and then to reject it (or, as in many cases, to reject it merely on gut reaction and hearsay!). The logic might be that Skinner's methods can be applied to rats pressing levers for food but either (1) they are quite irrelevant to human behaviour or (2) they are entirely and highly dangerous. In principle, either (1) or (2) might be the case but surely they could not both be true. I will argue that a blanket rejection by taking either of these positions would be a great mistake.

The second possibility is to accept the message whole-heartedly and become a fundamentalist Skinnerian. One might then campaign for the victory of a Skinnerian world. This would mean throwing out, or at least down-playing, some 99.9% of what psychologists have ever written. This is because, to the dedicated Skinnerian, the existing body of psychology is either fundamentally wrong or, at best, a distraction in answering the needs of survival. The argument will be developed that neither is this the best way forward.

The third type of reaction, the one to be developed here, is that characterized by compromise. There are various forms that such compromise might take. In principle, one might believe in determinism but feel that Skinner has over-emphasized the role of operant conditioning. After all, Skinner did not invent determinism as a philosophical position.

The argument to be developed here is that Skinner accurately described some fundamental and often grossly underestimated and misunderstood determinants of human behaviour[25]. However, these need to be integrated with a range of other processes that together make up a human. In such integration, the processes that Skinner described have a prior claim to special importance since we can, relatively painlessly, do something about them. For example, we can redesign an educational or penal system. There is little or nothing we can do as yet to improve the human condition by targeting the genes that we inherit. Indeed, even to suggest trying to do so is the trigger to even more outrage than Skinner's environmentally-directed solutions. So this is an obvious reason why the Skinnerian message is crucially important.

If we pursue this approach, further questions then arise. How do we integrate a Skinnerian approach into a broader picture? Since it seems that no one can ever either prove or refute Skinner's argument that we are totally determined, the issue must remain one of metaphysical speculation and belief. This raises the prospect that we might follow a kind of pragmatic middle-line, where some kind of autonomy is thought to exist side-by-side with a belief in the efficacy of operant conditioning[26]. Of course, the questions remain as to *what* kind of autonomy and how it intermeshes with deterministic processes!

Where a belief in at least some degree of autonomy seems to be the optimal solution to a problem, we might act on the assumption that it is a feature of humankind. In other situations, a belief in the dominance of environmental determinism could prove the most useful way forward. This of course raises the most mind-boggling philosophical dilemmas but they appear to be a part of the human condition that we need to live with. Subsequent chapters will explore such a possible compromise in the hope that it is not merely fudging the issue!

People tend to see themselves as setting goals that they can consciously articulate. Could it be that those goals that we set are themselves largely the product of our history of exposure to reinforcers or are there idiosyncratic goals that arise in ways not open to public scrutiny? Such issues will be explored in the subsequent chapters. Evidence will be presented that to a very considerable extent we are under the control of determining factors located in the environment, hence pointing to the appropriateness of the methods of traditional science to their understanding. However, not all of these factors are of the kind emphasized by Skinner.

When it comes to the application of Skinnerian methods, it would be logically consistent to fully embrace these as a very effective means of changing society for the better, without thereby accepting the full Skinnerian package with its total rejection of the notion of autonomy[27]. Neither need we reject the notion that cognitive processes can play a role in the explanation of behaviour. It will be suggested that we can usefully study mental processes while still seeing that a principal determinant of the content of our mental life and behaviour is the kind of process described by Skinner. The notion of a limited and constrained autonomy might be intellectually justifiable.

Having set the scene by reviewing the position of Skinner and why it is so controversial, the next chapter will look at the events in his life and the historical development of his ideas.

B.F. Skinner (right) and the author (left).

2 Biography, Background and Impact

Childhood in Susquehanna

Burrhus Frederic Skinner was born on March 20th 1904 in the Pennsylvania railroad town of Susquehanna, to a mother who had worked as a secretary but gave this up to become a housewife, and to a father who was a small-town lawyer. Home life was, for the most part, simple, predictable and peaceful, being described by Skinner as "sympathetic".

The Skinners formed part of the congregation of the local Presbyterian Church and were teetotal. As a child, Burrhus Frederic attended Sunday school and soon absorbed the ecologically and ethically valued imperative of "Waste not, want not", which was to stand him in good stead for life. His autobiography reveals a strait-laced, even Puritan, upbringing[1]. At the prospect of any violation of respectability, Skinner's mother would pre-dictably exclaim "Tut-tut" followed by "What will people think?"[2]. Sex was not on the agenda of family conversation; the evidence points to it being considered mainly an undesirable feature of the human condition. Skinner's mother and some friends once observed two children in a nearby yard as they explored each other's bodies and the young Skinner eavesdropped on her reaction: "If I caught my children doing that, I would skin them alive".

True to behaviourist philosophy, feelings are not to the forefront of Skinner's autobiographical writings, though they are far from being excluded – the ups and downs of life are mainly described in terms of observable behaviour and what are assumed to be its determinants in the environment.

Skinner's grandmother taught him, at an early age, about the prospect of eternal damnation in hell, which triggered much anxiety. To illustrate her teaching, she opened the oven door to reveal the heat and flames to the frightened young boy, as a vivid model of the punishment contingency that awaits the sinner[3]. The experience gave him nightmares. One could speculate that this early exposure to punitive control played a crucial role in his later unreserved opposition to aversive methods. Years later, he wrote of the suffering that such teaching caused him[4]. His autobiography describes *feelings* of prolonged guilt, triggered by what might objectively be considered only minor transgressions. In around 1945, of course well before climate change was an issue, Skinner documented his guilt at owning a car[5].

The boy was to produce a morality play *Christmas Spirit*, with characters named Greed, Youth, Gluttony, Adventure and Jealousy, a possible hint of messianic directions to be followed later! Another such hint is revealed in the way that he described his experience in learning mathematics[6]:

...the delight to be found in bringing order out of chaos.

In those days of the first decades of the 20th century, life in small-town Susquehanna, of course, had little in the way of mass commercial entertainment of the kind encountered these days. Stupefied audience passivity was yet to hit the world, people being required to contribute something to their own entertainment by means of physical, or at least mental, effort. Susquehanna had the occasional performances of theatre and opera, while visiting singers, magicians and lecturers would also entertain its inhabitants. A large degree of self-sufficiency was called for; the citizens were left to their own creative devices, as in music-making, amateur theatre, writing long letters and appreciating classical literature, or even the occasional clever prank and practical joke (Skinner was later to excel at all of these activities).

The young Skinner showed a keen and well-developed fascination with the various features of the social and physical world around him and spent time designing and building mechanical and electrical gadgets. This experience was to prove invaluable in his later life as a psychologist. Susquehanna was set in beautiful countryside and he was never far from contact with nature. Skinner – known to friends as 'Fred' and having red hair – engaged in camping, fishing, collecting various fruits and nuts for eating and animals for observation. Boredom seems not to have featured in his life.

Years later, after becoming famous and having tasted *avant-garde* Greenwich Village and the intellectual heights of Harvard, Skinner would reflect on life in early 20th century small-town Susquehanna with somewhat mixed feelings. On the one hand, the town was indeed small – just a few thousand souls – and people knew each other. In some ways, it was rather like the kind of utopian community he would later come to champion so ardently. In Susquehanna, Skinner was able to lock into safe patterns of reciprocal (positive) social reinforcement and could explore the natural world freely. There was much opportunity to 'learn by doing'; expressed in his favoured terms, the environment provided rich reinforcement in return for Fred's active manipulation of it. Susquehanna had not yet been corrupted by mass consumerism. On the other hand, he also found life there to be somewhat narrow, claustrophobic and Philistine, dominated by considerations of "what will people think?"

Boxes of various shapes, sizes and functions make regular and milestone appearances in Fred's life, starting from age ten[7]. The first 'Skinner box', constructed from a packing case, was intended for housing Fred himself rather than a rat or a pigeon. Therein, he arranged books on a shelf to form a study and he placed a candle for illumination. A curtain was drawn across the entrance for privacy.

A reviewer of the first volume of Skinner's autobiography noted that, if the identity of the author were to be kept disguised from the reader, then, up to about page 60, no decisive give-away clue could be found. We might equally well be glimpsing the childhood of a future statesman, inventor, lawyer or actor. But from page 60 onwards, the reader familiar with psychology could surely be left in little doubt as to who is the author. The entry here gives as good a feel for Skinner's inimitable style as any of his writing[8]:

> I learned the technique of masturbation quite by accident, when
> I was perhaps eleven. Up to that point sexual play had consisted of
> undirected handling of genitalia. One day another boy and I had
> gone out of town on our bicycles and walked up a creek, beside which
> we were later to build a shack. We were sitting in the sun engaged in
> rather idle sex play when I made several rhythmic strokes which had
> a highly reinforcing effect. I immediately repeated them with even
> more reinforcing results.

Note the absence of any reference to a subjective state of pleasure, a common feature of Skinner's writing. To all but the fundamentalist Skinnerian, the term 'reinforcing' as used here would probably be taken as technical jargon for 'pleasure' but this might well not have been the author's intention. Rather, the Skinnerian account is in terms of the apparently objective process of *reinforcement*, presumably to be evidenced only by the subsequent observations of a repetition of this behaviour!

Later in his life, sometimes the term 'reinforcement' appeared to be used to describe a situation where, at the time the behaviour was performed, Skinner anticipated that it would be repeated in the future. This was presumably based on a history of reinforcement of similar behaviour. For example, I was once with him at the Open University in England (see page 21), when, after being thanked for his lecture, he told one of my female students that he found the sight of her smile in the audience to be "very reinforcing".

College life

After leaving school, Skinner attended Hamilton College, in New York State, where he studied languages and literature, with a course in psychology. His autobiography would surprise greatly any reader who, not entirely unreasonably, imagined the author to be somewhat 'cold' and mechanically controlled. It records that, whilst at Hamilton, his grandmother's death "touched me deeply"[9]. There is even considerable evidence of a tormented romantic. Consider, for example, the statement that, because of having no girlfriend, "I remember walking the streets in physical pain from the lack of someone to put my arms around"[10]. Still in a language probably surprising to some, he recorded "the sheer physical pain" that was triggered by unreciprocated love[11]. Much later, he was to record[12]:

I weep at movies, when listening to music, or just thinking about someone I love. And I'm not ashamed.

There is the revelation that, after being jilted by a woman named Nedda[13]:

For a week I was in almost physical pain, and one day I bent a wire in the shape of an N, heated it in a Bunsen burner, and branded my left arm. The brand remained clear for years.

Skinner does not try to explain this behaviour and it would seem to be particularly problematic to do so in his own favoured terms. The common sense explanation would most likely involve the assumption that the "almost physical pain" had a role in *causing* Skinner to act in this way, as a desperate plea for help. However, he ruled out explanations of this kind since they merely invited the question – from where did the psychological pain arise? The answer would presumably be that the pain arose from the environment, i.e. the loss of Nedda.

At this point Skinner might appear to be tying himself in knots. How do we explain the sudden production of an apparently novel behaviour? The reaction is presumably not innate and might be described as spontaneous and creative. What sort of history of reinforcement, if any, lay behind it? We need to ask whether it was shaped by a history of self-mutilation (the autobiography does not describe any such earlier events) and, if so, what served to reinforce such biologically maladaptive behaviour? An explanation along these lines would appear to get rather tortuous.

One of Skinner's notes, written *when he was still a young undergraduate*, records being "faint with ecstasy" at the touch of a woman's hand on his[14]. This is one of relatively few references to strong positive emotion.

It was close to his college campus that Skinner lost his innocence – in a brothel, during a visit with fellow students. How might we explain this event? A commonsense interpretation would most likely have much to do with a prior *conscious expectation* of both pleasure and the removal of fear, frustration and uncertainty. The anticipation of elevated status might also enter the equation. But in Skinnerian terms, such commonsense is within the forbidden cognitive explanatory framework. So, what might an explanation in the purely retrospective terms of reinforcement look like? We would need to ask about the similarity between cues present in this situation and those at earlier courting experiences, which would increase the probability of response production. Skinner's earlier sexual approach behaviours were thwarted by partner resistance before consummation. None-the-less, presumably they must have offered sufficient reinforcement to lead to this landmark visit. Clearly, if his early exposure to "Tut-tut – What will people think?" and to images of hell-fire still retained any aversive power, by now such vicarious punishment contingencies proved to be inadequate to counter the approach gradient of increasing reward.

That sex was later to form a powerful positive reinforcer for Skinner is suggested by the remark of Bjork[15] that:

> …indeed, Skinner would have a reputation as a womanizer.

Intellectual roots

After leaving college, Skinner was adrift and in despair for a year but then developed his interest in biology and behaviour. The world needs to thank (or blame, according to opinion!) the English philosopher Bertrand Russell for the future course of the young Fred. Russell's book *Philosophy*, which was published in 1927, described the work of the pioneer of behaviourism, John B. Watson. In response to his reading of Russell, Skinner purchased a copy of Watson's book *Behaviourism* and was fired by the prospect of a science of psychology that was based on the study of behaviour. These links led Skinner to study the research of Pavlov on what is termed 'conditioning'.

The influence of Pavlov

In Pavlov's most famous experiment, a hungry dog was observed not to salivate to a tone (for example, of a bell or metronome) but to produce saliva to the presentation of food. After a number of paired presentations of the tone and the food, the dog came to salivate to the tone in advance of the food and even on those occasions when the food was not given. The originally 'neutral stimulus' of the tone had become converted into what was termed a 'conditional stimulus', capable of triggering salivation (sometimes the term 'conditioned' is used here instead of 'conditional').

Why the adjective 'conditional'? It refers to the fact that there are *conditions* attached to the capacity of the sound to trigger salivation: it needs to have been paired with the food on a number of occasions. By contrast, the food was described as an 'unconditional stimulus': there are no prior conditions attached to its capacity to trigger salivation, assuming, of course, an intact and hungry dog. Hence, the term 'conditioning' was applied to this procedure. This specific type of conditioning later acquired the title of 'classical conditioning' or 'Pavlovian conditioning'. John Watson pioneered the study of classical conditioning in America.

Other influences

John Watson had urged that psychology should turn away from introspection (a person looking at his or her own conscious mind and reporting on its contents) as a method of investigation and turn to the study of behaviour in its own right. He argued that psychology had no more need of introspection than did physics.

Pavlov and Watson were not Skinner's only intellectual foundations. He was also inspired by the physiologist Jacques Loeb, who studied the behaviour of simple animals under carefully-controlled laboratory conditions.

Ernst Mach, the Austrian physicist and philosopher, provided some crucial philosophical foundations for Skinner. Mach had argued that science should concern itself with *observables* and avoid metaphysical speculation. Taking a very similar line and also powerfully influential was the physicist Percy Bridgman, whom Skinner later got to know personally.

The psychologist Edward Thorndike had made a study of how cats learn to escape from puzzle boxes by manipulating latches, documenting the latency (time delay) between being placed in the box and escaping to obtain food. Thorndike elaborated the 'Law of effect' a basic principle of reinforcement: a response that is followed by satisfaction to the animal is more likely to be repeated in the future, whereas one followed by discomfort is less likely to occur again. This set the scene for Skinner's own study of the principles of reinforcement. Note that Thorndike used such unobservable terms as 'satisfaction' in his theorizing. Later, in pursuit of behaviourist purity, Skinner was to depart from this explanatory framework.

Harvard – the making of a psychologist

Skinner sought a place doing postgraduate studies in psychology. Alas, by then, Watson, an obvious potential supervisor, had been fired from his university position at Johns Hopkins University, so he was unavailable to serve in this role. Skinner applied to Harvard and was accepted to start in the autumn of 1928. His first research was in both psychology and physiology, coloured by a belief in the principles of behaviourism. He investigated how nervous systems control behaviour in non-human species. Skinner gravitated to the study of rats running in mazes, attributing the rats' behaviour to a series of reflexes.

The stimulus-response link

At first, Skinner's intellectual framework was that provided by the notion of the 'stimulus-response link': during learning, a particular stimulus becomes associated with a particular response and complex behaviour could, at least in principle, be understood as the sum of a number of such links. The relation between each stimulus and its associated response could be documented in purely objective terms. Although he started from the study of biology, he advocated developing a psychological science of *behaviour* independent of the study of biology. Skinner favoured understanding behaviour as such, looking for the correspondence between events in the environment (stimuli) and the animal's reaction to those events (responses). Skinner[16] was later to write of this stage of his intellectual development:

I was convinced that the concept of the reflex embraced the whole field of psychology.

Mazes and boxes

The process of training a rat to run through a maze is termed 'instrumental conditioning'. The expression 'instrumental' indicates that the rat's behaviour determines (is 'instrumental in') the sequence of events, i.e. if it makes the correct turns, then it arrives at the goal box and gets the reward of, say, a food pellet. This stands in distinction to classical conditioning, as pioneered by Pavlov, in that, in classical conditioning, the animal does not play a role in the sequence of external events. For example, it was Pavlov, not the dog, who paired the tone with the arrival of food. In classical conditioning the animal is relatively passive in so far as the conditioning process goes, whereas in instrumental conditioning it is active.

There is an old joke showing one rat saying to another "I think that I got this guy conditioned. Every time I run to the end of this maze, he gives me a pellet of food". There is some truth in this: in any instrumental conditioning situation there is a dynamic interaction between animal and environment. The animal changes the environment and the environment changes the animal.

In a maze, of course, the rat must be picked up from the goal box and placed in the start box after each run. The timing is in the hands of the experimenter – quite literally so. This is a labour-intensive task for the experimenter. Skinner developed a labour-saving piece of apparatus, whereby an animal could earn food by making a particular single response, normally, in the case of a rat, lever-pressing. The lever-press would trigger the drop of a pellet into a small tray from which the rat could eat it. This is a form of instrumental conditioning in that the animal is instrumental in the sequence of events but it is a form given a particular name: 'operant conditioning'.

As noted in Chapter 1, the origin of the term 'operant' is that behaviour acts ('operates') on the environment to cause a consequence[17]. In turn, the consequence is such as to alter the future probability of showing this behaviour. So, for example, lever-pressing causes food to appear and the ingestion of food increases the future probability of lever-pressing. The defining feature of operant conditioning as a special form of instrumental conditioning is that the animal is self-pacing; it is entirely 'in the hands' of the animal as to when it responds. With a number of technical refinements, the piece of apparatus soon became familiar as the 'Skinner box', though Skinner himself resisted giving it this name.

In the restrained environment of the Skinner box, behaviour can be demonstrated to come *under the control of its consequences*. That is to say, the food increases the future probability of showing the behaviour, i.e. lever-pressing, that leads to food. Herein, according to Skinner, lies a microcosm of much that happens in the wider world, to rat and human alike.

A caution is needed here[18]. Skinner is not saying that the rat acts because of what it *expects* will happen. That would be to bring cognition into the picture, something forbidden in Skinnerian terms. Rather, according to Skinner, the rat acts now because of what *in the past* followed similar behaviours. The current rat is a changed rat relative to earlier in its life, because of what happened in the meantime.

When it is said that lever-pressing is reinforced and increases in frequency, this refers to behaviour defined in terms of its function: the lowering of the lever. If we were to examine the rat closely, we might well find that no two lever-presses are exactly alike. On one occasion, it could use its right front paw and on another occasion its left front paw but these are described as 'functionally equivalent' responses since they have the same effect of lowering the lever[19]. Similarly, if a person is rewarded for opening a window, this does not specify the exact means employed but the functional end-point of getting the window open.

Skinner discovered that, once responding by a rat or pigeon was established, he did not need to reinforce every response with food. Rather, only, say, every tenth response need be followed by food. This is known as 'partial reinforcement' and it became a topic of intense research in its own right. Skinner stumbled upon the effect by accident: the laboratory ran very short of food pellets and needed to economize on their use! Partial reinforcement makes the response 'resistant to extinction'. That is to say, rats that experience such a schedule keep going longer when extinction conditions (i.e. removal of food from the apparatus) are imposed in comparison to those who have experienced only continuous reinforcement. There is a moral to this story for rat and human alike – getting rewards too easily tends to undermine resilience[20]. The power of partial reinforcement might also help to explain why some people persist in unlikely romantic relationships when the benefits seem to be rather sparse.

Skinner also observed what was termed 'secondary reinforcement'. Suppose that every time the rat presses the lever and a pellet of food falls, a tone is sounded. The tone acquires some reinforcement value by virtue of its pairing with the 'primary reinforcement' of the food. This can be measured by observing that the rat will work to obtain the tone even in the absence of food. Of course, after a while the tone will lose its power unless it is again paired with food, i.e. extinction occurs.

So, to summarize briefly, Skinner distinguished between two different processes of conditioning, classical (sometimes termed 'respondent') and instrumental. His contribution was mainly to the study of the particular form of instrumental conditioning that is known as operant conditioning. Both types of conditioning are also sometimes described as examples of 'associationist learning', meaning that the animal comes to associate two events.

Revolutionary zeal

While still a research student, the young Skinner saw himself as spearheading a revolution in psychology. This stood in stark contrast to most postgraduate students, who plod the well-trodden path of their supervisors and make only a small incremental change to the *status quo*. Stubborn, determined and single-minded, we see the emergence of a more dogmatic Skinner of the kind that tended to perplex and annoy friend and foe alike. It must be very rare indeed, if not unique, that a postgraduate student within any subject makes a serious attempt to portray all of its major schools except his own as 'fruitless efforts'. Thereby, they are consigned to the dustbin of intellectual history. Turf wars in academia can be just as vitriolic as in any other sphere of life, with outcomes by no means sealed only by relative ability and achievement. Despite some people's touching belief that psychology must be above all such personal squabbles, alas this is far from the case. Colleagues described Skinner as 'brilliant' but also "argumentative, fanatical, and intolerant of other approaches"[21]. Brilliance is not always an unalloyed benefit, especially if it triggers a feeling of 'too clever by half'.

Consider, for an example of self-assertion[22]:

> ...I was now so much the complete behaviourist that I was shocked when people I admired used mentalistic terms.

As a good example of the attempt to expunge mental language, note Skinner's reaction to the seemingly innocuous 'throw-away' remark made by a colleague during a visit to the laboratory[23]:

> Watching one of my squirrels running in the squirrel cage, he chuckled and said, "He likes that", and I was shaken.

However, even Skinner was not yet fully immune from the mentalist virus, as he freely admitted[24]:

> I had trouble with my own speech, catching myself as I started to say "mind" or "think", like an atheist who finds himself saying "Thank God".

Mercifully, he was to find later a way of living with the virus[25]:

> It took me a long time to realize that in using the vernacular I was no more a traitor to my science than the astronomer who comments on a beautiful sunset knowing full well that the sun does not "set".

On one occasion, when Skinner reached a particular insight in developing the principles of operant conditioning as something distinct from classical conditioning, we witness a reaction that others have doubtless experienced but few would be so honest as to acknowledge in public[26]:

> ...I was terribly excited. It was a Friday afternoon and there was no one in the laboratory whom I could tell. All that weekend I crossed streets with particular care and avoided all unnecessary risks to protect my discovery from loss through death.

Quite how Skinner would account for this particular instance of behaviour in his own favoured terms is alas something we shall probably never know. However, it would seem to be problematic. Skinner[27] argues that the effect of strong positive reinforcement acts in opposition to that of an aversive stimulus. Let us assume that the traffic was at normal levels during the weekend in question. A powerful dose of positive reinforcement on the

Friday afternoon should therefore surely have made Skinner more, not less, likely to step off the pavement without looking. It would appear that the behaviour might be explained by permitting some cognitive terms into the analysis. The more that life has to offer, so the cognitive conflict ('dissonance') between the cognitions of life and death would be all the greater.

Moving on from stimulus-response

By 1931, Skinner was starting to have doubts as to the validity of the stimulus-response model as an all-embracing explanation of behaviour[28]. The principle of a stimulus-response link was logical as an explanation of, for example, the salivation of Pavlov's dog to the sound of a bell. The sound is a *distinct stimulus* presented over a short period of time and the salivation is the response that immediately follows this. The knee-jerk reflex to a tap on the knee is another example of a stimulus-response connection at work. By contrast, in the Skinner box, the lever did not appear to trigger pressing in any comparable way. The lever was not something to be presented 'on and off' like a bell or a hammer tap to the knee but rather was a constant feature of the environment, whether the rat pressed it or not.

This created something of a dilemma for Skinner. The terms 'stimulus' and 'response' are precisely part of the kind of objective language that is appealing to a behaviourist, involving observables. At first, this approach offered the promise of reducing complex behaviour to its identifiable component parts. However, to use this language, an extrapolation appeared to be necessary, since the meaning of 'stimulus' becomes problematic. One might speculate that the lever caught the rat's *attention* or became *attractive* (i.e. formed a stimulus) only at those specific times when the rat pressed it.

Alas, use of such terms as 'attention' and 'attractive' sounds decidedly non-behaviourist, since they have a distinct mentalistic feel to them. Worse still, the scientist has no objective way of defining them, forcing him or her to appeal to precisely the occurrence of the behaviour that these terms are supposed to be explaining. Furthermore, the rats were not passive prior to pressing the lever. They were constantly active, raising their bodies on the hind legs, sniffing and poking around. What are the particular stimuli that trigger each such bit of behaviour or should it be described as 'spontaneous'?

So, something radical had to happen. Should Skinner peer inside the rat's brain for evidence of objectively measurable events corresponding to when the response is shown? No. He rejected explanations in either mental or biological terms and found a quite different solution. If you ever thought that the principle of stimulus-response is too simple as an explanation of behaviour, you might like to think again. Skinner proposed a radical simplification of even this principle!

You might find the solution to be somewhat hair-splitting but it enabled Skinner to keep his behaviourist objectivity unsullied. He wrote the stimulus out of the story in so far as a *direct trigger* to a response is concerned. Rather, the lever is simply defined as something *in the presence of which* the rat tends to perform a pressing response. Training increases the probability that this response will occur when the rat is in the environment of the training, i.e. the box and the lever. This is all entirely observable and involves no theoretical speculation at all. Why the rat presses at exactly the times that it does is regarded as not really the business of a behaviourist psychologist.

Some conditioning terms

The term *elicited* (the stimulus 'elicits' the response) was adopted to describe the response that arises from classical conditioning, e.g. something such as salivation, where a distinct stimulus is present. In contrast to this, the term *emitted* was adopted to describe the response shown in operant conditioning, e.g. as in the Skinner box (the rat 'emits' lever-presses)[29]. As a semantic quibble, one might argue that 'response' implies a stimulus but Skinner was able to live with what was considered a slight linguistic anomaly.

Skinner found that once operant behaviour was established he could bring it under the control of what are termed 'discriminative stimuli'[30]. For example, take a pigeon that is pecking a key for food and shine a spot of light near to the key. Suppose that when the light is green the pigeon obtains reward as before but when it is red the pigeon receives no food for its key pecking. After a time, the pigeon will peck when the light is green but not when it is red. The colour of the light has become a discriminative stimulus.

At this point a distinction needs to be made between the terms 'reward' and 'reinforcement', as used in psychology. Rewards are things assumed to be of positive quality that are given without much reference to their timing or consequences. Thus, a Christmas present might be described as reward. It is not necessarily contingent upon any particular behaviour by the recipient and so there is not necessarily a change in the frequency of any behaviour. Similarly, simply to drop food pellets to a hungry rat without any requirement of a particular behaviour on the part of the rat might be described as 'reward'.

Skinner became a champion of the approach of studying *individual* animals, having little time for the grouping of data and the formation of statistical averages. This was equally true of the individual records of each lever-pressing rat as it was later to be for the progression or otherwise of individual pupils in school.

After his initial researches at Harvard, Skinner left to take up teaching positions at the University of Minnesota and then Indiana University.

Peculiarly human aspects

Skinner did not confine himself to the study of rats and pigeons. He developed a strong interest in human language, and performed careful observations of how sentences are structured and he attempted to understand this in behaviourist terms[31]. Words were said to be emitted because of a history of reinforcement in a particular environmental context, somewhat as lever-pressing is emitted. Thus, the person to whom one is speaking is supposed to be the reinforcing agent, using such reinforcers as smiles or praise. Skinner even analysed the verbal processing of Shakespeare by studying his works. Language, as much as any topic discussed by Skinner, provided fuel for his critics and it is not hard to see why (discussed in Chapter 4). Consider Skinner's claim[32]:

> When people spoke, wrote, or gestured, they were not expressing ideas or meanings or communicating information; they were behaving in ways determined by certain contingencies of reinforcement maintained by a verbal community.

Skinner[33] advanced the idea that, apart from histories of reinforcement, behaviour could also come under the control of rules, which are culturally transmitted. In this way, the individual can benefit from the experience of others, without necessarily having the corresponding direct experience.

This is termed 'rule-governed behaviour'. For example, the rule 'avoid the swamp over there' can be assimilated and acted upon following a verbal message and without necessarily having any direct earlier experience of sinking in swamps. Similarly, Skinner[34] also acknowledged that the individual can come under the control of verbal statements of contingencies, such as "if you do X, consequence Y will follow". The possession of language opens up new possibilities: humans can short-circuit lengthy learning that is based only on direct experience. However, Skinnerian followers would still see rules being maintained in part by the consequences of following them[35]. For example, being rescued from sinking in a swamp after disobeying the rule would be a powerful trigger to respect the rule.

Future directions

With the rise of Nazism in Germany and the depression at home in the United States, Skinner contemplated his future. Should he move into the study of politics? On reflection, he decided to remain with psychology and try to employ it for the improvement of humankind. After America entered the Second World War, Skinner had a plan for helping the war effort – he would train kamikaze pigeons to steer missiles onto targets such as enemy aircraft carriers. They would be rewarded for pecking at images of suitable targets and the pecks would orient the missile. Although the military looked into the idea, it was never put into practice and doubtless confirmed in the eyes of many the image of an eccentric genius.

Putting his well-honed DIY skills to work, another project was a baby-tender, a controlled environment in which his daughter was raised. Although he claimed with justification that Debbie was very healthy and happy, this invention, which earned the name of the air-crib or, as a pun, the 'heir-conditioner', never lifted off as a commercial project[36]. Skinner took a keen interest in his daughter's development and observed what would, these days, be seen as an instance of what is known as 'imitation' or 'mirroring'[37]:

> One day when I had opened the window of the baby-tender and was talking to Debbie, I wrinkled my nose. To my amazement she immediately wrinkled hers. At the time I was not convinced that there was any innate tendency to imitate, but it seemed impossible

that she could have learned that the muscles she moved produced an expression on her face like the one she had seen on mine.

Perhaps reflecting fears about Skinner's approach and ideas, rumours spread widely that the daughter became psychotic or committed suicide, whereas in reality she became a very successful artist, living in London[38].

A utopian visionary

At the end of the war in 1945, we see evidence of Skinner coming to the belief in a utopian solution to the world's problems, based on small communities working according to behaviourist principles. He felt regret that young soldiers returning from the war should go back to a humdrum and predictable existence defined by gaining job, child and car. Rather, "they should explore new ways of living, as people had done in the nineteenth century"[39]. Skinner was inspired by the Shakers and other religious perfectionist sects, having grown up near to the foundations of some such communities.

It was then that Skinner embarked on his novel *Walden Two*. This described a utopian community, living according to the principles of behavioural science and consistent mutual positive reinforcement, with an avoidance of competition and punishment. Many facilities that would otherwise be owned individually would become communal so that ecologically the community would be more viable. The book was a prescription for what Skinner desired to be achieved and thought was realistic. However, it appears that many readers took the book, not to be an act of advocacy, but rather as a very clever 'spoof', a dire warning as to what could happen if we abandon a belief in freedom and responsibility[40].

The book's name derived from the title of a book, *Walden*, by Henry David Thoreau, who had set up a one-man ecological community next to Walden Pond. Skinner made "an annual pilgrimage" to the pond, which is located near to Concord, Massachusetts[41]. The name of the star of *Walden Two* was Frazier, taken most probably from a family who dedicated a stained glass window in Fred's local church in Susquehanna. As a child, he had spent considerable time sitting below the window, near to the inscription acknowledging the family.

An important principle of Skinner's good life as described in the story would be provided by the instruction[42]:

Simplify your needs. Learn how to be happy with fewer possessions.

A crucial message of *Walden Two* and much of Skinner's subsequent writing was that, if the affluent were to consume less of the earth's resources, the potential for conflict would be very greatly reduced. However, without a source of alternative reinforcers, this will remain merely a pious hope. Small organic communities, in which there is a rich source of social and ecologically viable reinforcers, are the answer.

In some ways, *Walden Two* might be rightly seen as a return to a pre-industrial romantic and idyllic society, to a time of harmony before the fall of humankind with industrialization. However, in other ways, this would be misleading[43]. Such times were also characterized by ills of a sort that Skinner would wish to correct, such as gender inequality, drudgery and long hours of labour, as well as threats of conflict between groups. Also, Skinner intended that *Walden Two* should be based firmly in a scientific understanding of behaviour and the exploitation of a beneficial technology such as teaching machines. *Walden Two* does not presuppose that *innate* goodness and innocence are at the basis of human nature, over-laid by the corrupting influence of modern society. Rather, such virtues would only appear if the environment is arranged such as to permit them to do so. Sagal[44] writes:

Skinner is in many ways a man of the enlightenment – a throwback to that age dominated by faith in science and the perfectibility of man.

By the 1960s, interest in *Walden Two* had risen dramatically, as reflected in sales. In 1955, it sold only 250 copies but this escalated to 100,000 in 1971[45]. Why was this? It could be that the youth of the 1960s counter-culture were more enthusiastic towards this kind of radical change involving a rejection of consumerism, though the book was never exactly intended as a *Good Hippy Guide*. However, one critic wrote that *Walden Two* resembled[46]:

...a kind of dull, mid-western small town with a well-endowed arts centre.

A small number of communities sprang up inspired to lead a life modelled on *Walden Two*, by assimilating principles of ecological viability, positive reinforcement and avoidance of punitive control. One of these, *Los Horcones*, in Mexico, had success with reshaping disturbed children[47]. Skinner was commonly asked why he didn't go to live in one such community and replied that his contribution in life was as a scientist. The necessary intellectual stimulation was presumably more easily gained in Harvard (to which he was destined to return) than in *Walden Two*. Another good reason was that his wife, Eve, expressed a total opposition to any such move.

Back to Harvard

In 1948, twenty years after finishing his doctorate at Harvard University, destiny was to take him back there, this time as a full professor. There were some reservations felt by the Psychology department about the new appointment, of the kind, "Would he be so temperamental that he would be a nuisance to us?"[48]. Amongst other research projects, he investigated the use of reinforcement in helping psychotic patients to develop some engagement with the world[49]. At Harvard, Skinner continued to expound the behaviourist message and, in so doing, he suggested why psychology had hitherto not progressed[50]:

> We were looking in the wrong place for explanations of human behaviour – in mental or psychic states rather than in genetic and environmental histories.

While at Harvard, Skinner's philosophy of education developed in part from the observation of his children. He[51] recalls an experience in 1953 of visiting his daughter Debbie in school. Noting what he regarded as some fundamental errors in the method of teaching, he came to the realization that education needed to change. First, the pupils were not being told immediately whether their answers were right or wrong. Feedback, Skinner argued, needed to be immediate in order to serve as a reinforcer. Secondly, they were all being expected to move along at the same pace regardless of ability. This left some frustrated because of inability to keep up and others idle for having finished the tasks early. Thirdly, Skinner identified excessive amounts of punishment in the system. This did not necessarily take the form of corporal punishment but more subtle forms such as signs of displeasure or put-downs from teachers.

In his autobiographical writing, Skinner expressed some of the strongest emotion in the context of his children. One instance concerns when he was awarded an honorary degree by the University of Chicago. As he got up to receive the award, he spotted Julie in the audience, and asked rhetorically[52]:

> How in God's name could I keep from crying?...tears flowed as I passed Julie on the way out.

One of Skinner's pet interests developed at Harvard. He became convinced that mechanical teaching machines could be constructed such as to provide pacing for students. These machines would provide immediate and reinforcing feedback. Each student could advance at his or her own pace and would not suffer from being exposed to a competitive environment. Unfortunately, industry did not respond to the challenge of producing these machines in the way that Skinner hoped it would and the teaching establishment offered some resistance to their adoption. Later, Skinner came to appreciate that computers could act as very effective teaching machines[53].

With the invention of the Skinner box, large pharmaceutical companies saw this as a chance to test the effects of their drugs on non-human subjects. For example, it could be used to test new medicines that were designed to lower anxiety. Typically, a rat would be exposed to pairing of a tone and a mild shock to the feet. It would also be trained to press a lever in a Skinner box to earn food. Then the tone alone is sounded during the course of lever-pressing. Depending upon the level of fear the tone triggers, there is a suppression of responding, i.e. a lower rate of pressing immediately after the tone is sounded. If a drug that has been designed to lower anxiety is administered, the effect of the tone is reduced, i.e. less disruption of lever-pressing.

Skinner was a keen observer of everyday human behaviour and from this he was able to exemplify many of the basic principles of behavioural control, including the unintended effects of reinforcement. He writes[54]:

> When we were on the train from London to Exeter, two young girls, perhaps four and two, came into our compartment with their parents. For half an hour they were beautifully behaved. Then the younger tried to get a comic book away from her sister. They fought and the younger girl cried. The parents separated them and immediately got

out a bag of sweets. "To keep them quiet?" Possibly but in any case to reinforce fighting and crying.

Reinforcement does not have to be consciously perceived in order to be effective. Indeed, there are situations where, presumably, if the process of reinforcing were to be consciously detected, then it might be less effective. A good example to illustrate this, and incidentally an element of mischief in Skinner's behavioural repertoire, is provided by an encounter with the psychologist and philosopher Erich Fromm. Fromm was giving a lecture in which he argued that people are much more than wingless pigeons and his remarks were being addressed specifically to Skinner. So, Skinner decided to demonstrate a common feature between these two species. On a piece of paper, he wrote "Watch Fromm's left hand. I am going to shape a chopping motion", and he passed this across to a colleague. Fromm was heavily gesticulating, and whenever his left hand was raised, Skinner tried to reinforce this response with a direct gaze. When the hand was lowered, this was reinforced by a nod and smile from Skinner[55], who reported that:

Within five minutes he was chopping the air so vigorously that his wristwatch kept slipping out over his hand.

Colleagues passed the note back to Skinner with the addition:

Let's see you extinguish it.

Skinner diverted his gaze from Fromm. However, the chopping motion continued for a long time. Presumably, the lecture was finished before there was time to extinguish the response.

From this example, one should not infer that Skinnerian psychology is simply some devilishly cunning bag of tricks that can be applied to an unsuspecting population. Although reinforcement might well sometimes be unconscious to the recipients, defenders of Skinnerian principles argue that its best effects are obtained with their full knowledge and consent[56].

Skinner recognized that long-delayed aversive consequences are often ineffective as a control of behaviour. After all, threats of eternal damnation had established his own guilt but there is little evidence that they were a very effective control of his behaviour.

In 1960, Skinner attended a conference on smoking and young people, organized by the American Cancer Society[57] and pointed out the weakness of long-delayed aversive controls. Indeed, an emphasis upon aversive effects, he argued, might trigger anxiety and make matters worse. Rather, the immediate consequences of smoking needed to be changed. For example, the emphasis needs to be on finding alternative behaviours (e.g. what to do with the hands) and establishing immediate positive consequences of *not* smoking. Anticipating research to be reported some 39 years later[58], Skinner argued[59]:

> ...make clear that the supposed satisfaction and lift from smoking is merely a return to the normal state enjoyed by non-smokers.

Skinner's autobiography reflects on one particular very pleasant evening when he was about to go into his study for 2–3 hours of work accompanied by Wagner's music[60]:

> So my life is not only pleasant, it is earned or deserved. Yet – yet – I am unhappy.

He then pondered on why this should be and asked whether it could be guilt about the suffering of humankind, a vestige of his Puritan background. In conclusion, it was not only the suffering as such but rather that:

> ...so little is being done about it! We are trapped – in the love of a life like this, in false social science...Is it up to me? (A Wagnerian theme, if I ever saw one!).

One can only dread to imagine how Skinner would feel now if he were to witness climate change and the inadequate efforts being made to counter it. After spending an evening listening to an outdoor concert of *a capella* singing by university students, he silently reflected on[61]:

> ...the fact that this kind of harmless, beautiful, sensitive pleasure was probably nearing the end of its run.

However, he did not entirely lose faith in humankind and for this we need to be thankful for a chance encounter with the driver of a subway train. The driver got annoyed with Skinner for trying to force the door open. As Skinner took his seat in the carriage, so he fantasized revenge against the driver. Should he get the driver's number and report him for bad behaviour? How would you treat a person like this if he were in the Skinnerian Utopian community of *Walden Two*? This, of course, raises the possibility that such undesirable behaviour would not by then have been extinguished even there!

Then Skinner was led to reflect on the possible causes of the driver's behaviour. Could he have been tired? Could he have had a hard day? Might the passenger's own action have been misunderstood as aggressive? As Skinner was about to alight, the driver turned to him and apologized. Skinner records[62]:

> In a burst of warm feeling I said I had supposed he might have misunderstood, and could hardly blame him, having to drive such old equipment. We all but embraced in a spasm of good will. I walked home glowing in optimism for the human race.

Of course, such altercations are an everyday feature of life, alas not all of which end as happily as this one. However, there is a profound message contained in this tale. It is one that fits Skinner's environmentalist and ethical principles, though he did not develop the theme. In a microcosm, the incident reveals vividly the interdependence of humans and just how strong is the effect that a few words can have on the behaviour and emotional state of another. It illustrates the value of speculating on an individual's possible behavioural history and it reveals the power of conflict resolution.

Surely the driver could never have imagined that he was destined for immortality in the form of a place in the psychology literature. One can only hope that the experience of meeting Skinner was a positively reinforcing one for him, in that he would have tended to repeat such behaviour on future occasions, whilst extinguishing angry reactions (The possible basis of such reinforcement is something discussed at several points in the following chapters).

Skinner's notes, written in 1963, give insights into the complexity of his make-up. By now, he was something of a celebrity but fame was hard to take. He wrote that successes[63]:

> ...have plunged me into a sustained depression. Feelings I can vaguely describe as guilt and anxiety overwhelm me...

A particularly good example of Skinner's proneness to such emotions is provided by his reaction after speaking to the Royal Society in London, which he regarded as his most prestigious invitation. On reviewing his behaviour the following day, he felt that he had not acted appropriately (e.g. to accept only one glass of sherry!) and said the wrong thing several times (Any reader who also relentlessly ruminates over a past *faux pas* or misdemeanour, real or imagined, might take comfort in knowing that such tormenting emotions are shared with even the most prestigious amongst us). He wrote, with echoes of upbringing in small-town Susquehanna[64]:

> For months I felt a twinge of shame upon hearing any reference to London, seeing anything I had bought in London, seeing an English movie, hearing an English accent, or even seeing people sitting around a large table.

One can only speculate as to the emotions that were revived when he returned to the same London venue in 1984. In response to persuasion by the Open University Psychology Society's chair, Dr. Lilli Hvingtoft-Foster, he spoke to a packed and over-spilling audience of the society.

Skinner spent a considerable part of his senior years living under controlled conditions, somewhat of a monastic nature. In the mid-1980s he was given a box, known as a *beddoe,* by some Japanese friends. Equipped with cassettes of Richard Wagner, the beddoe was located in the basement of his home and he would climb into it to sleep. An alarm inside the box would wake him from his night's sleep at 5 am each day, not as a summons to prayer but to a secular equivalent: the start of the writing day. Later in the day, in keeping with ecological principles, he would walk the two miles from home to his office in Harvard and also return by foot.

Beyond freedom and dignity

Beyond Freedom and Dignity was published in 1971 and this sealed Skinner's fate and drew national attention to him like never before. It soon got to number 1 in the bestseller charts[65]. At this stage, some 82% of all American college students could correctly identify Skinner[66]. The book proclaimed that large urban centres could not survive (though doubtless these provided most of its sales) – the future lay in a series of *Walden Twos*. Lauren Slater, in her book *Opening Skinner's Box* writes of it[67]:

> Although it was written in 1971, I might as well be reading a speech by Al Gore, or a Green Party mission statement from 2003.

The book seemed to strike at the heart of how Americans of all persuasions and walks of life viewed themselves. The dramatic claim was that survival made the immediate application of the science of behaviour imperative, while the pursuit of freedom, as most understood the term, was a hindrance to what was needed for survival. Society required fundamental structuring such that desirable behaviours are reinforced and the emphasis moves away from punitive controls. Given the brazenness of its title, a misunderstanding of the book might even imply the author's wish to dethrone from their pedestals such national icons of freedom as Lincoln, Kennedy, Roosevelt and Luther King. In retrospect, it might have been better entitled as something like *Redefining Freedom and Dignity*. The timing of publication was significant. It[68]:

> ...appeared at a crucial moment in the nation's history, when Vietnam War protestors, African-Americans, feminists, and gay rights activists, as well as libertarians and humanists, were insisting that it was precisely *more* individual freedom and dignity that was needed to counter an insensitive government...

The term 'dignity' which Skinner urges us to move beyond is open to some misunderstanding since he employs it in a rather peculiar sense. He is not using it in the sense of the dignity that is owed but often denied to, say, the dying in hospital, senior citizens or ethnic minorities. Rather, it is the dignity that is earned from *achievement* that Skinner urges us to move beyond. The logic is clear. If we are not to blame people for their failures and misdeeds then, by the same token, we are not to praise them for their good deeds. We like to feel that good deeds spring spontaneously into action rather than being the product of genetics and environmental history but Skinner urges a rejection of this. In the spirit of Skinner, Nye[69] suggests that:

> ...if better environmental control resulted in more productive, happy, healthy, and creative people, wouldn't that *increase* our dignity or worth?

In writing *Beyond Freedom and Dignity* Skinner polarized opinion, like very few scientists before or since (a possible comparison is with Charles Darwin). On the same day that an audience of 6,000 students cheered Skinner at the University of Michigan, he was hanged in effigy at Indiana University[70]. Skinner was proclaimed 'Humanist of the Year' for 1972 by *The Humanist Society*. The book triggered the following comments in letters[71]:

> I have always considered you a fatuous, opinionated ass...Quite obviously you are an apologist for totalitarianism. You seek an

ant-heap culture, the abolition of all humanistic values, in a word, the destruction of the human spirit.

and in another:

> For one, I would rather go down in a nuclear holocaust as a free soul than live 1,000 years as a protected, living, statistical man under your evil scheme.

In a speech, US Vice-President Spiro Agnew stated[72]:

> To the behaviourist, man is not an individual; he is one of a herd, a particle in a mass of humanity who does not know what is good for him and who needs to be saved from himself by a superior elite using intellectual cattle prods.

In truth, cattle-prods, whether of the real or metaphorical variety, have never featured in Skinnerian psychology. A number of critics, who did not go so far as to evoke fascism, none-the-less suggested that life in a Skinnerian utopia would be, at best, somewhat sterile and soporific[73].

In the opinion of Jerome Kagan[74]:

> Unfortunately, the reactions to *Beyond Freedom and Dignity* were less the product of a dispassionate analysis of Skinner's ideas than a defensive reaction to the anxiety his theme created.

As a broad generalization, most of the public appears to find mentalism more palatable than behaviourism, the assumptions of the latter appearing not only frightening but as somewhat counter-intuitive. Many people find any comparisons of humans with rats and pigeons, however well qualified, to be threatening and hardly flattering. Appeals to cross-species similarities of the kidney and heart do little to placate. To many, the comparison of humans with machines is, if anything, even less flattering than is the rat image. At least rats are warm-blooded! The comparison with machines is especially alarming when humans even appear to come out of it unfavourably, as in the case of teaching machines[75]. To some, the 'meaning of life' is seriously challenged by all such approaches, the adoption of which would guarantee that life becomes devoid of meaning[76].

In his autobiography, Skinner occasionally drops his guard with respect to language, implying chains of causality, which on reflection he would doubtless deny. A good example of this concerns chest pains associated with the efforts of the promotion of *Beyond Freedom and Dignity*. He wrote[77]:

Will my sense of responsibility, my Protestant ethic, kill me?

The central paradox was that the author of *Beyond Freedom and Dignity* saw himself as a liberator. As Bjork[78] expresses it:

Indeed, his creations as a social inventor were meant to be liberating: The aircrib liberated the child from physical restraint and the mother from domestic drudgery; *Walden Two* liberated the modern individual from a wasteful, competitive, unrewarding world; and a technology of teaching liberated teachers from custodial and disciplinary roles in overfilled classrooms.

On reaching senior years, Skinner's celebrity spread still wider. After appearing on the front cover of *Time* magazine and on numerous TV chat shows, he became a household name and was often stopped by strangers. Amongst all scientists, Skinner earned the distinction of the one best-known to the public, uniquely achieving the kind of fame more usually associated with pop-stars and actors[79].

To put Skinner into context, it should be noted that there were other famous behaviourists, who carried on the movement of Watson, most notably Clark Hull. However, by the 1950s, their influence was in decline, relative to that of Skinner. Hull and his associates tried to develop comprehensive *theories* of behaviour based on internal events such as 'drive', whereas Skinner was not much interested in theories and urged broad *application* of behaviourist principles. Skinner became something of the flag-ship of the behaviourist way of doing psychology; he was the leader of a school of psychology and was massively influential. Skinner 'gave' psychology to the public like very few others. Reinforcement techniques and behaviourist methods came into wide use. However, some of those who employed Skinner boxes in their research had no commitment to the Skinnerian philosophy but simply found the piece of apparatus very valuable. Some pioneers of therapy[80] incorporated Skinnerian principles of reinforcement in their armoury, e.g. to reinforce successes along the way.

If we, like Skinner, had had a world-wide impact in classrooms, prisons, juvenile detention homes, the military, pharmaceutical testing, industrial training, experimental psychology laboratories and psychiatric hospitals[81], most of us might feel content with our contribution but Skinner did not. The ultimate prize still eluded him: radical overall change of society in such a way as to guarantee its survival.

Decline

In 1989, Skinner was admitted to hospital for examination and discovered to have leukaemia. It was estimated that he had six months to one year to live, news which Skinner took courageously. He worked right up to the day before he died, which came on August 18th 1990, when he was 86 years of age.

His daughter Julie recalls that, unlike many people of fame, her father answered every letter that he received[82]. Marc Richelle, a student of both Piaget and Skinner, recalls the latter with great affection, describing him as[83]:

...by far the least directive teacher I have ever had.

In an obituary for Skinner, in *Zygon*, the journal of science and religion, it was written[84]:

He was a person with great concern for all members of society, not merely for the "intellectual elite". He had a big heart and went much further than most people to help the handicapped and disadvantaged, which he could do by giving them the benefits and applications of his behaviourist philosophy and techniques (for instance, enabling handicapped readers to learn to read in a very short time). This facet of Skinner may not be widely appreciated, since he was a matter-of-fact person rather than a boaster. For all who knew him, he was a model for effective "do-good" behavior.

This completes the biographical sketch of Skinner, though his personality and life-history should be well evident 'between the lines' in the subsequent chapters. Next we turn to consider experimental findings, especially recently generated ones, which relate to Skinner.

3 Looking at the Evidence

This chapter will look broadly at some of the experimental evidence that relates to the perspective of Skinner. It will consider his argument that we can advance the understanding of behaviour by assuming a deterministic world and using behaviourist techniques, even without studying the phenomenon of consciousness as a topic in its own right. The chapter surveys the evidence that people can act without having conscious insight into the causes of their actions. It will then turn more specifically to the issue of reinforcement, noting some of the situations in which the notion has been applied and the insights found. Finally, we will consider the Skinnerian approach to the subject of mental images.

The role of consciousness

General principles

Can we, as Skinner suggested, be deluded as to the true determinants of our behaviour? There is accumulating evidence in favour of this, though not all of it relates directly to Skinner's principles of reinforcement. Mounting evidence favours an *adaptive unconscious*, rather than the Freudian notion of the unconscious mind being a cauldron of repressed sexual impulses. That is to say, unconscious activity by the brain plays a role in our adaptive coping with the environment, as in controlling movement and decision-making etc. Skinner would be comfortable with this notion.

Sophisticated experimental methods are providing accumulating evidence that the determinants of so much of our behaviour lie in the environment and outside of our conscious awareness. The reasons people give for their behaviour can sometimes be fallacious. Evidence points to our dependence upon the environment and thereby to the viability of environmental interventions to alter behaviour. It also points unambiguously to some serious undermining of the 'autonomous person', as one who behaves in ways known only to him/herself.

In one classical study, people were asked to choose a pair of stockings from a display[1]. Afterwards, they were asked why they chose that pair. In most cases, they gave reasons in terms of the particular qualities of the chosen pair. In reality, all of the stockings were identical and people chose predominantly those from the far right of the display, showing a simple position preference. So, a verbal report might give very little insight into the true cause of something.

It is not just in such relatively mundane things as choice of an item from a display that the control by the environment can be demonstrated experimentally. Rather, our attitudes and goals can be largely set automatically by factors outside our conscious control[2]. The expression 'autopilot' is sometimes employed here. If we pursue this analogy, not only does this particular autopilot tune the position of the aircraft's flaps and rudder, it even has a part in setting the flight's destination.

For example, subliminal prior presentation of an emotionally-coloured word such as 'good' or 'bad' can bias our assessment of a person. Subliminal priming of words related to aging (e.g. 'grey') can cause us to act in an older manner[3]. Our behaviour can even belie our conscious expressions of feelings. Someone might claim quite sincerely to feel no prejudice against a member of another ethnic group, whereas their behaviour reveals avoidance. Such evidence could be seen to support Skinner's wish to dethrone autonomous man from centre-stage. In a case such as this, if we were shocked to learn of our prejudice and wished to overcome it, we might be better advised to monitor our *behaviour* rather than the contents of our conscious mind and its assessment of ourselves[4].

As Wilson[5] notes, a person who is concerned about prejudiced behaviour might try to seize every opportunity to *behave* in a non-prejudiced way. In so doing, non-prejudiced behaviour might become automatic. In keeping with a Skinnerian approach, Wilson writes[6]:

> One of the most enduring lessons of social psychology is that
> behaviour change often precedes changes in attitudes and feelings.

And furthermore[7]:

> ...if we want to become a better person, we should follow a "do good,
> be good" strategy.

Conditioning and conscious insight

Conditioning might well occur sometimes with no conscious insight into what is going on. However, the human to be conditioned might have insight into the process. Let us take some examples of how this could arise. Consider some participants, whose reactions are followed by the verbal stimulus of "mmm-hmm" by the experimenter[8]. One could imagine this acting as reinforcement in an 'unconscious' way, i.e. a participant (A) does not have any conscious appreciation of the reinforcement process but still shows an increase in frequency of behaviour. One might also imagine another participant (B), who interprets the signal to mean 'well done' and makes a conscious effort to increase the frequency of responding. By Skinner's definition, the situations of both A and B amount to reinforcement. However, many would surely wish to distinguish them. Conversely, one might imagine another participant (C) who interprets the signal to indicate a mistake and hence decreases responding. This emphasizes that an interpretation of *meaning* can play a role in conditioning.

Chapter 2 described Skinner's conditioning of Erich Fromm's[9] arm-jerking reaction, something which exemplified to Skinner the quite automatic and unconscious nature of conditioning (This anecdote is amusing and possibly illuminating. However, in the absence of a formal controlled experiment, how much weight should be attached to it is quite another matter). Suppose, for instance, that Fromm had been warned in advance about Skinner's penchant for mischief and therefore of the need to be especially vigilant. One imagines that Fromm's behaviour might have changed as a result of the forewarning. He might have refused to play the game of being conditioned, though equally he might have missed the particular trick on this occasion.

When placed in an operant conditioning situation, adult humans typically behave rather differently from both young children and non-human species[10]. Both of the latter groups react in a similar way, evidence suggesting that control is based upon processes to which they do not have conscious access. Adults, by contrast, appear to be trying, with the help of language, to make sense out of the arrangement of behaviour and reward, as revealed by their somewhat idiosyncratic behaviour and subsequent verbal reports of trying to 'crack the code'.

Powers[11] suggests that, since humans can twig what is going on, this will tend to defeat even the best efforts of the Skinnerian operant conditioner. The human will refuse to 'play the game' of being conditioned.

This might sometimes occur but conditioning can perhaps best be performed with the consent and full insight of the person to be conditioned. Also relevant here is the technique of 'self-reinforcement', where people voluntarily agree to operant terms and reinforce themselves for desirable behaviour[12].

The argument on the role of conscious insight in conditioning has gone back and forth between extreme positions: the cognitive, claiming that insight is always needed for conditioning to occur[13], to the behaviourist position that insight is irrelevant. Perhaps the safest approach is to see conditioning tapping into different levels of control, though this is a form of theoretical speculation that Skinner would never have pursued. At a low level, conditioning might proceed in an automatic and unconscious way. This is a 'pure-Skinnerian' level, evident in non-humans and young children. In addition, in the case of adult humans, there is a conscious process. At this higher ('cognitive') level, a person gains conscious insight into what is going on, which might weaken or strengthen the conditioning that occurs. The theme of multiple levels of control is one to which the book will turn repeatedly.

The nature and effects of reinforcement

The technique of deliberately applying reinforcement is a powerful one. Skinner[14] made an interesting observation:

> ...rats and pigeons had, in fact, done things during the past thirty years which they had never done before in the history of the species, simply because the necessary contingencies had never before arisen.

So, let us now turn to the nature of reinforcers and relate this to Skinner's position. First, let's ask – what can serve as a positive reinforcer?

Social reinforcers

Platt[15] notes the dynamic interactions that inevitably arise from the mutual basis of reinforcement:

> ...all social interactions become chains and networks of mutual transactions that go on and on throughout life as we shape each other. We have always known this in a general way, but now we see

the detailed mechanisms of the transactions, and see how they can be improved.

Platt[16] compares the reciprocal nature of reinforcement between two individuals to the influence of gravity between two bodies. No physical body can exert a gravitational pull on another body without itself being pulled. By analogy, the shaper will be shaped in return.

Psychologists from a wide range of perspectives have found the notion of reinforcement valuable. For example, in trying to explain the camaraderie of soldiers in war, Patterson[17] invokes social reinforcement:

> The explanation for effectiveness in combat rests on the most basic of human experience: relationships with other human beings and positive reinforcement.

This probably involves a complex of factors including[18] "reinforcement by peers for combat effectiveness".

It is a little ironic that Skinner wished to abandon praise as a feature of our culture since it can be a particularly good (positive) social reinforcer. This was noted by the science fiction writer Isaac Asimov[19]:

> ...I respond favourably to praise. It has an extraordinary reinforcing effect on me. All my publishers and editors find this out at once... No one has ever handed out praise in larger servings than I can swallow.

In an influential book on self-help techniques, the broad theoretical conclusion drawn by Watson and Tharp[20] lends powerful support to the perspective of Skinner:

> Ten years ago, many writers seemed ready to put reinforcement out to pasture. More recently, however, there is a new consensus: Reinforcement is still the most reliable horse in the stable.
>
> Contingent rewards, when delivered by the social environment, will strengthen the behaviours they follow, and thus become reinforcers. Very little in psychology is more certain than that.

Sensory feedback and competence

Sensory feedback arising from environmental manipulation as such can serve as a positive reinforcer[21]. There need not be any other consequence than the feedback brought about by the environmental change[22]. A baby learning to shake a rattle exemplifies this[23]. Skinner suggested that there could be evolutionary value in a process in which reinforcement derives from manipulating the world: the young animal is encouraged to learn by doing. One manipulation that might be viewed in such terms is a social one: simply gaining the attention of another human, e.g. parent or teacher.

The reinforcement notion of Skinner's, along with the work of other psychologists, formed a foundation for the theory of 'competence'. White[24] suggested that animals, including humans, acquire a tendency for manipulation of the environment. Thereby, they develop competence in dealing with it. He assembled evidence in support of this hypothesis, including that animals will learn an operant task for no reward other than a change in the environment. Such experiments led Zimbardo and Miller[25] to suggest that the:

> ...opportunity to explore a 'novel' environment or to effect a stimulus change in the environment is the reinforcing agent.

Mastery of the environment, learning what leads to what, would have clear survival advantage for species that forage, hunt and avoid predation, which forms a particularly good fit with the argument of Skinner. White[26] describes:

> ...transactions between the child and his environment, the child having some influence upon the environment and the environment some influence on the child.

In Skinnerian terms, the influence on the child is one of reinforcing the action performed. In future, the child will come to search out the object that provided the reinforcement by its manipulation.

Drugs, reinforcers and the problem of addiction

Drugs are famous for their potency as controllers of behaviour; expressed in Skinnerian terms, drugs are very powerful positive reinforcers. The best-known addictions, such as to alcohol, nicotine and heroin, all involve a massive immediate reinforcement, often followed by aversive effects that are delayed after taking the drug.

Consider, for example, nicotine, which is strongly addictive as indexed by the tenacity of its pursuit and the difficulty in quitting in spite of harmful effects. Yet, surely few would describe nicotine's effects as hedonically mind-blowing. This illustrates the Skinnerian point that reinforcement does not necessarily equate to hedonism in any simple one-to-one way. Assuming ten puffs per cigarette, the average smoker using one pack per day will obtain 73,000 reinforcements of nicotine in a year[27]. Life can surely offer few comparable sources of such strong and regular reinforcement, which makes it all the more remarkable that anyone is ever able to quit. An analysis in reinforcement terms allows us to examine more closely what determines this potency. In fact, it is a *combination* of the arrival of nicotine in the body and the motor act of smoking[28]. In devising smoking cessation programmes, it is vital to understand this combined source of reinforcement.

The strength of a drug as a reinforcer is dependent not only on its chemical properties but also upon the environment in which it is taken[29]. Many US servicemen fighting in the Vietnam War had a serious drugs problem. On their return to the USA, whether they continued to use heroin depended upon their environmental context[30]. In reinforcement terms, those who continued their drug habit found themselves in a context impoverished in terms of reinforcers, whereas those who were able to give up had relatively many alternative sources of reinforcement. There is even a rat model of this: rats in a socially rich environment consume much less opiate drug than rats in a socially impoverished environment[31]. The message is clear and has a Skinnerian flavour: pay careful attention to all sources of reinforcement.

The term 'contingency trap' applies to drug use: the user is trapped by the contingency between use and the immediate consequence[32]. Drugs bring immediate positive reinforcement whereas the aversive effects, such as withdrawal, heart disease and cancer are long-delayed. Stated in terms of rule-governed behaviour, the rule 'abstain' must call upon hypothetical future events that might never even happen. Even a hangover is experienced several hours after the alcohol ingestion.

As a solution to a pressing personal problem, drug use brings an immediate change of mood and behaviour. By contrast, long-term resolution of the problem (e.g. change jobs, leave an abusive relationship) might bring an immediate *increase* in pain with only a distant prospect of improvement.

How does drug use get started in the first place? One imagines that some people experiment with drugs and discover for themselves a reinforcing effect. Of course, by exposure to the popular media, people will hardly be unaware of, for example, the supposed positive social consequences of drinking alcohol. Much drug-use occurs under peer pressure or at least encouragement and here it is possible to identify social reinforcers[33]. These could set the scene for chemically reinforcing effects of drug-taking. For example, in terms of negative reinforcement, a child might find that the social stigma of being a non-user is lifted by 'joining the club'. Subsequently, there could be possible positive social reinforcement, obtained from 'club membership' and status as a user. There is every reason to suppose that these types of social reinforcement will lock into complex interaction with the drug's intrinsic reinforcing potential.

Just as it appears that social reinforcement can play a crucial role in acquiring a drug habit, so can it also be involved in extinguishing this behaviour[34]. *Alcoholics Anonymous* places great weight upon the strength of community of those trying to quit and in large cities runs several meetings each day. New-found converts immediately find a network of telephone contacts and at meetings are warmly reinforced with approval for their resistance.

An approach to overcoming a drug habit, with a strong Skinnerian flavour, is to reward people for their abstinence. One can immediately hear the howls of protests – "I have never taken drugs but no one ever rewards me for this!" Two points can be made here. First, this approach might well prove less onerous on the pockets of taxpayers. Second, is it true that non-addicts have not been rewarded for their abstinence[35]? Surely every day brings innumerable rewards at work and in the family.

Of course, cultures develop ways of bringing immediate punishments to such habits as cigarette smoking and thereby oppose the susceptibility of individuals to the immediate reinforcing effects[36]. There might be some punishment in the protests of a wife or husband that the breath smells awful or that the family budget is suffering. However, we should not over-estimate the potency of such punishment.

People often apply rational reasoning to drugs and addiction – addicts must know it is harmful, so why do they keep on doing it? The phenomenon illustrates the severe limits of such rational reasoning and highlights the application of the principles of reinforcement, as developed by Skinner.

It is not only chemicals that can act as potent reinforcers of behaviour with a risk of addiction. Gambling yields rewards on a partial reinforcement schedule, which proves irresistible to some. Slow long-term financial loss is no match for the very occasional and sudden wins. Skinner demonstrated the particular potency of schedules in which reinforcement came only occasionally and at unpredictable times. This is the hallmark of the gambler's situation.

Even television can meet some criteria of addiction, as judged by the amount of time people spend looking at it and the wish to view much less[37]. Its immediate effect is to produce changes in the activity of the brain that serves to reinforce viewing. A walk in the park or reading a book cannot compete, even though people often admit that it would be more pleasurable and better for them (see also Chapters 4, 7 and 12).

Risk-taking and 'highs'

There is evidence that criminals often get a buzz from crime ('reinforcement'), comparable to an addiction[38]. The prospect of punishment is unlikely to counter such a buzz; indeed, it might even enhance the buzz. In order to understand why crime is committed, it is imperative to understand what could be reinforcing it, which appears to be sometimes a *combination* of factors:

* Gain of something such as money, property.
* Bonding with one's colleagues in crime.
* An intrinsic chemical change, giving the buzz, triggered by the risk.

Rational considerations suggest that the often low gain of crime and high probability of capture should make it unlikely to occur. This is to ignore the potential high reinforcement value of the buzz and the social network[39]. Illicit drug-taking might also owe some of its potency to the buzz of dealing with the illegal[40]. Crime is an example of where Skinnerian thinking has crossed discipline boundaries: some highly influential theories based upon sociological factors give a role of central importance to Skinner and the notion of reinforcement derived from social factors[41]. It is suggested that a factor leading to crime is the lack of mild 'punishment' (in the form simply of facial and spoken gestures of disapproval) during childhood. In parallel, bad behaviour is positively reinforced.

Broad effects of reinforcers

Events that are described as 'reinforcers' have certain effects in addition to those characterized as strictly 'response reinforcement' but which underline the power of reinforcers. For example, finding money might improve a person's mood, quite apart from increasing the frequency of our looking for further money. It would seem that the external event triggers a particular mood, which sensitizes a range of behaviours that are congruent with the mood. Skinner acknowledged such an effect. An emotional state can outlast its trigger and exert a bias on subsequent behaviour. For example, after a positive mood has been induced, the person is more likely to display altruistic behaviour[42].

It would appear that the most parsimonious explanatory language is in terms of emotions, motivation and cognition, in addition to that of reinforcement. So, although arguing against the value of involving hypothetical internal states in the explanation of behaviour, Skinner seems to rely on them implicitly as part of his account. He prefers to put such states in inverted commas, suggesting a mere short hand and the need to focus on the environmental determinants of these internal states. For example, Skinner[43] writes:

> We have noted the important case in which someone is "favourably inclined" toward a particular person or set of circumstances. Building morale is usually concerned with generating such a predisposition. The effect often follows from the same events which reinforce behaviour. Gratuities, for example, serve as a mode of control not only through reinforcement but by generating "favourable attitudes".

Some issues raised by the notion of reinforcement

A criticism is sometimes made that the notion of reinforcement is circular. Indeed, we cannot independently identify what is a reinforcer but only know that it is this by observing an increased frequency of behaviour. This need not be a devastating critique since it does not undermine the efficacy of the process. Furthermore, the same criticism could equally be made about the notion of *adaptation* in evolutionary biology: something is 'adaptive' if it increases the survival and reproductive chances of the animal. This consideration has not been allowed to halt the progress of biology. Also, of course, some things such as water, food and praise are universal human reinforcers.

Contrary to what some unkind critics assert, reinforcement principles apply not only to humans with learning difficulties and rats, though they certainly do apply there. The applications to humans span the whole range of human experience[44]. On this subject, Flora[45] perceptively notes:

> Reinforcement is a natural phenomenon just as natural selection or gravity are natural phenomena. Claiming that "reinforcement doesn't work" is as logical as claiming that "natural selection doesn't work" or that "gravity doesn't work".

Flora argues that, if we observe an aircraft to be flying rather than falling to the ground, this does not mean that gravity has been found not to work. Rather, it means that other factors in addition to gravity need to be taken into account. Reinforcement is just a fact of the natural world, presumably to be explained in terms of evolution and adaptation. It just *is* and it makes no sense to argue whether it is ethical or not. What might logically be argued is whether contrived reinforcers deliberately employed to achieve an end are ethical or not. Surely this depends upon the end in question, the nature of the reinforcer and any alternatives that might or might not be available.

Critics of behaviourism sometimes argue that reinforcement amounts to nothing more than bribery for getting someone to do something that they should do in any case[46]. Bribes can indeed act as positive reinforcers but the term 'bribe' only has relevance where the behaviour in question is illegal, immoral or against the wishes of the person being bribed. For example, it would be absurd to argue that, in accepting an agreed fare, a taxi driver is thereby taking bribes from passengers in return for driving them.

Flora[47] writes:

> If a behaviour occurs, it must occur for *some* reason. If reading and learning to read occur without obvious contrived reinforcers, such as pizza or money, learning to read still *must* have been reinforced, and reading must still be reinforced in some manner or else it wouldn't occur…*The ultimate reinforcement for learning to read is being able to read!*…

This might well be true but we cannot simply assume it to be true from the increased amount of time spent reading with increasing age. Although operant conditioning is important, other processes exist in parallel with it. We cannot rule out a role of intrinsic developmental changes within the brain unrelated to feedback from the environment. There could be intrinsically triggered growth of new connections between the neurons ('nerve cells') of the brain, a form of brain maturation.

Carpenter[48] questions the extent to which operant conditioning can account for a number of types of learning. For example, much learning appears to be incidental and it occurs on a single exposure, such as the learning of isolated facts or what someone said on a particular occasion. People tend to gather banks of trivia in their memories. It can only be highly speculative or tautological that reinforcement could be powerfully and selectively operating in all such instances.

Punitive controls

In an important sense, coercive methods do work[49]. Such things as threat of expulsion from the social group, physical pain or imprisonment do help to keep a number of people on the straight and narrow. The problem is two-fold: (1) these techniques do not work for everyone and (2) they create unwanted side effects such as resentment, hostility and aggression. Skinnerians acknowledge that coercion can work up to a point but oppose its use on pragmatic and ethical grounds.

In a variety of species, including humans, an aversive stimulus, of the kind that might be used to form punishment, triggers aggression[50]. If the presenter of aversive stimuli is still present they can be the target, if not an innocent third party will sometimes do just as well. This is another reason to try to avoid aversive control.

Private events

Finally, let us turn to the Skinnerian position on so-called private events. Skinner described mental events as 'internal behaviour'. The skin as a boundary in the physical world had no particular significance and processes on each side of it behave according to similar principles of organization.

Rachlin[51] defends the behaviourist position on mental images by asking his readers to imagine that they are standing in front of an elephant. They report "I see an elephant". The elephant starts to walk away into the distance and they report "I still see the elephant". The elephant gets further and further into the distance until the image on the retina is little more than a grey dot but still they report "I see the elephant". Rachlin notes that, in the far distance, the statement of seeing relates to very little of what is actually triggering the perceptual apparatus. Rather, most of the information relates to past experiences of seeing elephants. The person is undergoing 'seeing-type behaviour' in reporting the presence of the elephant. When it is completely out of sight, so that they are left to only imagine an elephant, the seeing-type behaviour is not supported by any corresponding retinal image.

The mentalist believes that in the absence of the real elephant, an inner representation of an elephant arises and occupies the contents of the conscious mind, whereas the behaviourist sees this as superfluous to the explanation. The behaviourist argues that any such inner image of the elephant would require an inner viewer of the image, an homunculus.

Similarly, and in the tradition of John Watson, Rachlin invites his readers to imagine speaking something out loud. This is clearly and unambiguously *behaviour*. Now try gradually reducing the intensity of the speech until you are speaking only to yourself. Rachlin claims that there is a continuum here rather than an abrupt transition, as we pass from speech that disturbs the air molecules around your mouth to total inner speech. Silent speech would appear to be derived from overt speech and to follow some similar patterns to it[52]. Skinner[53] observed that people often note that they are privately talking to themselves. The expression "I said to myself" is a common one, where Skinner argues, there are similarities in the controlling process to that expressed as "I said to her". Indeed, some argue that silent speech is important in controlling behaviour, as in exerting restraint on impulsive tendencies[54].

Practising an action in the imagination (e.g. a move in sport) can facilitate subsequent performance of the action in reality[55]. However, it remains speculation as to how far one can extend such examples.

So, it would seem that, in the light of recent evidence, much of the Skinnerian argument fares rather well. The next chapter addresses how the Skinnerian perspective fits within the broader context of psychology.

4 Linking Skinner to Other Perspectives on Behaviour

The Skinnerian perspective on psychology is a deterministic one, at centre stage of which sits the notion of reinforcement. How might Skinnerian psychology be related to other perspectives? Is conflict between schools inevitable or can points of agreement be reached? This chapter will look mainly at three other major perspectives within psychology (e.g. schools of psychology), with which Skinner is usually compared and contrasted: cognitive, psychoanalytic (Freudian) and humanistic. We shall see where their assumptions are compatible with, or at odds with, Skinnerian behaviourism and where possible bridges can be constructed.

In looking at links with other branches of psychology, Winter and Koger[1] make the interesting point that behaviourism might even "have been too successful for its own good". Their argument is that the measurement of behaviour is so much a feature of psychology that the historical roots of the approach tend to be taken for granted.

The cognitive perspective

Nature of the conflict

The cognitive perspective is usually seen as in direct conflict with Skinner's. It looks at mental processes and incorporates into its analysis the kind of terms that Skinner rejected. For example, 'attention', 'working memory', 'plans', 'intentions' and 'expectations' form an integral part of theories described as 'cognitive'. In recent years, the term 'consciousness' has also become a feature of cognitive theories.

Cognitive theorists, such as Skinner's contemporary Edward Tolman, describe what they term a 'goal-directed' or 'purposive' aspect of behaviour, suggesting that behaviour is controlled in part by comparisons between plans and what behaviour actually achieves[2]. Animals flexibly pursue goals[3]. All of this seems to be very far from the Skinnerian perspective, based upon reinforcement. So, do we have to decide which is right – to accept the one and reject the other? A compromise is possible here, along the following lines.

To understand the fine details of *how* an animal produces flexible behaviour, we need to assume such processes as cognition, intention and goal-direction. As a bonus, the cognitive perspective creates bridges with the study of the brain, in a way that the Skinnerian perspective, by its focus on the environment, misses. An analogy with technology could prove useful here and help us to affirm our scientific credentials. Inner representations need be no more mysterious and ghostly than the software of a computer. By analogy to how brains work, engineers have long been familiar with the design of systems that pursue goals, e.g. radar can be used to track an aircraft.

However, no one need reject the Skinnerian perspective entirely since, in a number of situations, these two perspectives refer to two different aspects of the same reality. Skinner was concerned with describing the events in the environment that change behaviour. His principles of reinforcement define well a whole class of determinants of behaviour when viewed from a perspective outside the animal. If we 'lift the lid on the box' and look inside, asking how reinforcers work and change the ways in which the animal controls its behaviour, then we are taking a cognitive perspective. Of course, Skinner would accuse us, at best, of time-wasting by opening the lid. However, we need not be tied to Skinnerian orthodoxy to acknowledge the power of reinforcers to change behaviour.

Non-human species and extrapolation to humans

One of the principal cognitive psychologists, Tolman, is often described as a 'cognitive behaviourist'. He was a behaviourist in the sense of wanting to explain the *behaviour* of rats but was prepared to adopt cognitive terms in doing so. Tolman spoke of rats forming 'expectancies' and 'cognitive maps' as they negotiated mazes. To him, behaviour was said to be 'purposive': for example, the rat was guided by a representation of the goal to which its behaviour was directed. The rat had an expectation (or, as it is sometimes described, 'expectancy') of what was in the goal box (e.g. size of pellet of food). Its subsequent behaviour could be understood as being influenced by whether this reward was better or worse than what was expected. Of course, such terms were anathema to Skinnerians, who suggested that they were explanatory fictions derived simply from watching the *behaviour* of the rat.

Consider that a rat learns to press a lever for the reward of food. This can be described in pure Skinnerian terms as the food being a reinforcer that increases the probability of lever-pressing. However, some psychologists prefer to use the language of cognition to account for this same observation. For reasons explained shortly, the rat could be described in cognitive and purposive terms as forming an *expectancy* that lowering the lever is followed by the appearance of food. Indeed, somewhat ironically, the Skinner box is a particularly good piece of apparatus for demonstrating the existence of expectancies in rats[4]! This is, of course, a measure of the importance of Skinner as an inventor.

Two examples can illustrate cognition, as follows. Suppose that a rat is trained to earn pellets of food of a particular flavour in a Skinner box[5]. The food is then devalued *outside* the box by means of an association with gastric upset. Finally, the rat is returned to the Skinner box *without the pellets being present*. An immediate reduction in lever-pressing activity is observed, as compared to the behaviour of a rat that did not have this paired exposure to food and illness. How is this to be explained? The cognitive theorist would argue that the rat has formed two cognitions:

1) Pressing this lever causes food to appear.
2) The food that is normally made available by lever-pressing is now less attractive.

When the rat puts these two cognitions together, this lowers its motivation to pursue the goal of gaining the food. Using cognitive language, it is evident that the rat's capacities exceed what can be accounted for in Skinnerian terms.

Another well-known study also leads to the notions of cognition and expectancy[6]. Rats were divided into three groups and trained to run in a maze to obtain food. One group received a small number of pellets in the goal-box (S), whereas another group received a large number of pellets (L). A third group obtained a medium number of pellets (M). Rats that obtained the larger reward ran faster than those running for the medium reward, which, in turn, ran faster than those obtaining the small reward. Crespi then tried giving both S and L groups a medium number of pellets (M). Rats trained on a large number of pellets and then suddenly finding a medium number (L → M) slowed up drastically. The group switched from a small number to a medium number of pellets (S → M) accelerated in their running.

How might we explain this? The medium number of pellets was reinforcing for the group obtaining them from the beginning but switching to this reward following experience of a larger reward (L → M) seemed to disrupt the behaviour of the rat. The cognitive theorist would claim that, when a large number of pellets were received, this created an *expectancy* of a large reward and when the pellets were fewer in number, the expectancy was violated. Conversely, when the pellet number was greater than expected, the rat was 'energized'.

The Skinnerian would simply wish to describe all this in terms only of the rewards but the cognitive account seems to bring some extra explanatory value. Skinner[7] felt that the notion of expectancy was not useful:

If you explain behaviour in terms of expectancy, then in turn you must explain the expectancy, and to do so you must turn to a history of reinforcement. I prefer to go straight to the history.

I prefer to look at both reinforcement and cognition in parallel but will leave it up to the reader to decide.

The cognitive principles that have been applied to instrumental conditioning can also be applied to classical conditioning. Early theorists suggested that the pairing of neutral stimulus and unconditional stimulus served to increase the strength of the conditional stimulus in its capacity to produce a response. Take Pavlov's experiment as an example. The bell had no capacity to trigger salivation at the start of the experiment but by pairing the bell with food the bell acquired such a capacity. It seemed that the bell acquired some of the power of the food and the term 'stimulus substitution' was used. However, later theorists showed that it could not be as simple as this. Rather, the bell acquired a signalling capacity[8]. The conditional response is not necessarily like the unconditional response. What the animal does in response to the conditional stimulus depends upon the situation in which it finds itself.

Skinner[9] described the process of classical conditioning as one of stimulus substitution. However, this soon gets him into trouble. As an example, he cites the following:

When the Jewish child first learns to read, he kisses a page upon which a drop of honey has been placed. The important thing is not that he will later salivate at the sight of a book, but that he will exhibit a predisposition "in favour of" books.

On the basis of strict stimulus substitution, one might indeed expect the child to salivate to the sight of the book. A contemporary understanding in terms of classical conditioning is that something of the goodness value of the honey gets transferred to the book.

Incentive-motivation theory

A theoretical perspective that has gained ground in recent years is within the study of motivation and is termed *incentive motivation theory*[10]. It fits rather well to a cognitive perspective. The basic assumption is that motivation is aroused by external incentives and internal representations of them. The animal moves towards incentives because of the pull that they exert. Stimuli associated with incentives, such as a bell that has been paired with food, are able to excite motivation, which keeps the animal going.

Arising within the incentive motivation tradition and the work of Kent Berridge and associates, considerable evidence suggests a distinction between wanting something and liking it. Let us commit the double Skinnerian heresy of attributing mental states to rats and lifting the lid on the brain. The rat that presses a lever in a Skinner box might be described as *wanting* to obtain the food. From its facial reactions to the food when it is in its mouth, the rat can be described as 'liking it'. The procedure of reinforcing lever-pressing with food sets up the state of wanting by the rat. Again, one does not need to choose between these languages since they both a have a role in the account: one has created a state of *wanting* by *reinforcing* responses that lead to reward.

Such an analysis suggests an important qualification to the claim of the behaviourist writer Howard Rachlin[11]:

It is not possible in behaviourist terms for Mike to watch television a lot, have other alternative behaviours available, but not like to watch television.

In fact it might be quite possible for Mike not to like television a great deal but still to spend hours watching it.

The study of goal-directed instrumental behaviour in humans

The behaviourist William Baum uses the following devil's advocacy[12]. Suppose that it is suggested to someone that she should obtain a copy of *Moby Dick*, since it makes an excellent read. She had never before searched for this book. The person is then observed to go from shop to shop until finally she manages to obtain a copy. Common sense would suggest that the person had a mental representation of the book and an expectancy of finding it. These cognitions guided her search until the point where reality (actually getting the book) matched the goal and the purchase was secured. This is surely indicative of purpose, since at this point the search is terminated.

Behaviourists such as Skinner and Baum object. The suggested representation of *Moby Dick* is described by them as "ghostly" and the rhetorical question is posed[13]:

How could an inner representation of *Moby Dick* cause you to hunt for it?

They would suggest instead that searching for a novel object could be explained by a history of reinforcement for other similar searches in the past. For example, the person recommending *Moby Dick* might always have made recommendations that had paid off in the past, so searching had been reinforced.

That finding *Moby Dick* causes the search to terminate might be felt to be problematic in a behaviouristic account. Why doesn't the reinforcement of finding it only serve to energize still more *Moby Dick* searching? By something of a sleight of hand, Baum[14] simply suggests that finding constitutes "the occasion for proceeding to other actions". Whether you find that any more convincing than the cognitive language, is perhaps largely a matter of taste.

Skinnerians sometimes go to inordinate lengths to avoid the language of purpose and in so doing end up boxed into a corner with statements that seem hardly less cognitive. For example, consider the remark "I want some ice cream". If we were good Skinnerians, we would presumably not be permitted to rephrase this as "I have an intention to get some ice cream" or "my move towards the stall is with the intention of buying some ice cream". This is excepting when we acknowledge that we are engaging in a non-scientific language and using metaphor. However, it seems that we are permitted under all conditions to state[15]:

> I would eat some ice cream if it were set in front of me, and I would go to some trouble (drive to the store, clean up my room) to have ice cream.

The logic of permitting these statements is that[16]:

> In other words, I am saying that right now ice cream would act as a reinforcer for my behaviour.

Baum[17] also suggests that:

> All intentional statements, including self-reports, although they appear to refer to the future, actually refer to the past.

It is argued that this is because of the similarity of the present context to other events experienced in the past. One might accept this up to a point. The statement "I intend to eat fish and chips for lunch today at Joe's café" might well be informed by the recollection that one has eaten this same dish every time on visiting Joe's café and the past therefore has predictive value. Empirical observation would point to the strongly reinforcing effect of Joe's fish and chips.

Can such logic be applied universally? It would appear that novel behaviour poses a profound challenge to this[18]. As Lacey and Schwartz[19] express it:

> But behaviour may occur in order to bring about a certain conse-quence without previous instances of the same kind of behaviour ever having been reinforced or even having occurred.

How about 'Tomorrow I intend to propose marriage to Jane'. One can only speculate – is this necessarily because of a history of making similar proposals?

Another example that springs to mind is a sudden suicide, which is hard to explain in reinforcement terms. The unexpected hero, who makes a dramatic gesture to save a person in distress, would appear to tell a similar story. Consider also a person with a history of anti-social behaviour, who then, say, in prison experiences extremes of guilt and remorse. It could be that they had earlier earned reinforcement for remorseful behaviour but have we the evidence to assert this dogmatically? Alternatively, one might suggest that painful ruminations altered cognitive processing such as to throw up states of guilt and remorse.

May[20] cites the case of Christopher Burney, a British secret service agent, who was captured in the Second World War and placed in solitary confinement for 18 months. Having no book or pencil or paper, Burney kept his sanity by reviewing in his mind the lessons that he had learned in school and later at college. Geometrical theorems alternated with the philosophy of Spinoza. A behaviourist might describe this as 'sub-vocal speech' and 'vision in the absence of visual stimulation' but the value of so doing, as compared to the more cognitive language, is not obvious.

To summarize the present argument:

- In a range of situations, reinforcement and goal-seeking refer to two different aspects of the same complex system and it is illogical to try to say which is the most accurate or useful. For example, the fact that a person has been reinforced in the past for following advice might serve to establish and maintain the kind of goals that lead to buying books.
- It is suggested that, whereas goal-seeking can very often be instigated and strongly influenced by the experience of reinforcers, it might prove impossible to find a history of reinforcement underlying every instance of what appears to be purposive behaviour. Novel behaviour exemplifies this.
- The behaviourist notion of 'functional equivalence' is compatible with an interpretation in terms of purpose. For example, the searcher for *Moby Dick* might fail to find it in a series of shops and then go home and turn to the internet. These are very different behaviours but are functionally equivalent in terms of end-point, getting the book.
- In a range of situations, whether one thinks that the behaviourist language of reinforcement or the cognitive language is the most useful can sometimes depend upon what one is trying to achieve.

Confronted by the need to improve education and change society by encouraging socially-desirable actions, the focus might be on the behaviourist language. If the wish is to understand underlying brain processes, then the cognitive language can be useful. Also, it is important to note that therapeutic techniques commonly involve both cognitive and behaviourist assumptions, and attach importance to reinforcement[21].

The work of John Bargh's group: a recent source of some reconciliation

In the last section, the possibility of reconciliation between cognitive and Skinnerian perspectives was mentioned, a theme continued here in the context of the work of John Bargh and his associates[22]. In recent years, they have articulated some similarities between a cognitive perspective and that of behaviourism, e.g. both subscribe to a deterministic ('cause and effect') philosophy. The terms used by cognitive psychologists, for instance 'attention' and 'working memory', might be anathema to Skinnerians but they were introduced in a way that supposed no mysterious elements such as free will. In principle, the kind of components and flows of information could be described mechanistically and modelled by computer programmes. Both behaviourism and cognitive psychology have gathered evidence that the determinants of behaviour can lie outside of conscious awareness and rational choice (see Chapter 3).

In the last 20 or so years, the social-cognitive perspective adopted by Bargh and associates has revealed the amazing extent to which behaviour is influenced by unconscious determinants. This applies to not only unsurprising examples, such as well-practised tasks, known to switch into an automatic mode with extensive experience, e.g. tying a shoe-lace. Rather, features that were considered to be quintessentially rational such as the setting of goals and the attitudes adopted towards others can be powerfully influenced by factors to which the person has no conscious insight[23] (see Chapter 3).

Somewhat paradoxically, Skinnerian behaviourism, by its denial of the value of studying intervening variables, particularly those of a cognitive flavour, would have missed much of the evidence potentially available to confirm behaviourism's own principal philosophical foundation: determinism. Bargh and Ferguson[24] note that:

…the deterministic philosophy that was developed and embraced by behaviourism nearly a hundred years ago is still guiding psychological research and theory today.

Bargh and Ferguson see the future in terms of a coming together of the deterministic stance of behaviourism and the study of those variables that mediate between environment and behaviour, as studied within cognitive psychology.

Bargh[25] wrote:

> ...by theoretically extending the reach of external stimuli to the internal representations of the environment that they automatically activate (e.g. types of behavior, goals, social groups, specific other people), much of what Skinner (1957) claimed in terms of direct environmental control over the higher mental processes has now been validated in contemporary research on priming effects across a variety of psychological phenomena...[26]

Now for something really controversial.

The study of language

The most famous critique of Skinner was by Noam Chomsky and it broadly fitted a cognitive perspective[27]. The critique took the form of a review of Skinner's book *Verbal Behaviour*. The review appears to enjoy the perhaps unique distinction of being as well-known and well-read as the book itself. Indeed, some critics consider this single blow to have slain the monster of behaviourism once and for all[28]. Space precludes all but a brief summary of some of its principal arguments.

Skinner had described the functional relations between environmental events and verbal behaviour. It might be noted here that parents appear to reinforce the first tentative utterances of their offspring by signs of approval. As children grow, so the parents then appear to shape successive utterances by a more demanding criterion of approximation to their own spoken language[29]. The Skinnerian approach also involves such notions as 'automatic self-reinforcement', as when people are said to speak to themselves because of the reinforcement that they derive from doing so.

Chomsky's critique of this had several prongs but, as a general feature, concerned the ease with which Skinner extrapolated from the principles of reinforcement in non-humans to the complexity of human language. The notion of reinforcement can sometimes be defined and tested objectively, e.g. as applied to rats in Skinner boxes. Here, the experimenter has control over the situation. It is difficult to extrapolate from this to the natural speech of humans and to assume the role of reinforcement. To do so, would seem to be a leap of faith rather than something that can be assessed scientifically. Chomsky was left to question a number of assumptions of the account based on reinforcement. To him, it appeared to be stating little more than the tautology 'what is being said now must be the product of earlier reinforcement, otherwise it could never be said'.

For example, how do children manage so rapidly to pick-up 'incidental' language information 'in the street', with little evidence of a history of reinforcement for their use of it? Chomsky suggested that slow and careful shaping appears not to be involved. To this a Skinnerian would respond that it does not need to. Rather, shaping can occur naturally and without intention, e.g. by social approval for imitation[30].

Chomsky also argued that, if complex language is based largely upon species-general processes of reinforcement, why does it appear to be specifically a human attribute? This is not necessarily a devastating critique of the role of reinforcement. Even though reinforcement might be involved as one component process, implicit in the advocacy of its role is the idea that other factors are also necessary. The notion that genetic differences between species might yield nervous systems with different properties does not in itself undermine an important role for reinforcement. By analogy, ethologists are familiar with species-specific behaviours that are only evident given an appropriate environmental trigger, such as the behaviour of young geese in following a suitable moving target.

Chomsky criticized the paucity of factors that Skinner employed. The review argued that, in addition to external factors, understanding of the internal structure of the brain's processing systems is essential in trying to explain language. For example, *maturation* of the nervous system doubtless plays some role in language's acquisition, under the control of a range of genetic and environmental factors. Given a linguistic environment, the nervous system matures in such a way as to virtually guarantee the emergence of the cognitive processing that lies at the basis of language.

The strong tendency of children to imitate the utterances of others is a vital component in language acquisition and simply to assert that it is reinforcing would, in Chomsky's eyes, appear to yield little explanatory value. Without the necessary supporting evidence, it might appear somewhat glib to claim that reinforcement underlies how imitation and repetition of sounds including self-monitoring via feedback ultimately yields an accomplished spoken language. Chomsky raises the possibility of an independent intrinsic component from within the child, a process that exhibits some autonomy from environmental feedback.

Reinforcement might sometimes play a role in certain bits of language acquisition. It would be surprising if this were not the case. However, to assert that *all* language acquisition is necessarily based upon reinforcement would be seen by Skinner's critics as a leap too far. Consider the performance of an accomplished speaker following the basic acquisition of language. Chomsky is similarly unconvinced that reinforcement principles are necessarily able to carry much explanatory weight here. For example, he is prepared to acknowledge that giving the answer 'Paris' to the question 'what is the capital of France?' might reflect a history of being reinforced for this response. However, a completely novel question of the kind 'Where is the seat of the French government?' might similarly evoke the reply 'Paris'. Quite how the necessary extrapolation from component bits of information is performed would seem to demand complex cognition hardly captured by the notion of reinforcement.

Chomsky asks – how can we understand novel utterances that seem to bear little resemblance to anything that we have been exposed to before? How do we recognize such novel utterances as being grammatically correct? Chomsky sees little reason to assume that we are simply generalizing on the basis of their similarity to expressions to which we have been exposed already. Rather, we are able to recognize a novel sentence as grammatically correct because it conforms to rules of grammar that have been encoded ('internalized') in our head. A related question is – how is the appropriate grammar brought to bear on the novel utterances that we make? It would seem unjustified to suppose that the novel ones are simply generalizations from familiar utterances. Rather, it appears that a set of abstract rules are extracted from the speech to which the child is exposed and then both heard and spoken expressions are compared with these abstract rules. Except in the case of very serious impairment, all children manage to internalize grammatical rules in an apparently similar way. This suggests to Chomsky[31] that "human beings are somehow specially designed to do this", presumably with genetics playing a specific role in the production of the encoding process.

Some compromise between Skinner and Chomsky might be possible along the following lines. Humans might well have a predisposition ('bias') to learn language and, if so, genetics doubtless plays a role in this. However, the linguistic environment surely plays a crucial role in shaping connections within the brain that underlie language processing.

Skinner and Freud

Surprising as it might seem, Skinner was influenced by his reading of Freud[32]. He warmed to the Freudian idea that introspection is an unreliable guide to the causes of behaviour. Both Freud and Skinner emphasized the role of history in determining current behaviour and neither placed any faith in statistical averages, preferring to consider individuals[33]. Skinner admired Freud's attempt to describe a lawfulness of behaviour, instead of seeing events as accidental. Both were keen to see their ideas applied to social, even global, problems. As Overskeid[34] notes, Freud and Skinner both professed an affinity to the principles of positivism, and they even:

…emphasized the same basic causes of the human predicament:
To a large extent, people are controlled by forces of which they are not conscious. Civilization creates conflicts between unconsciously controlled tendencies on the one hand and cultural rules and practices on the other.

However, none of this undermined Skinner's view that, by probing the inner workings of the mind rather than looking to environmental change, Freud had set the subject back by 50 years. According to Skinner, such things as complexes and defence mechanisms come to acquire a life of their own and detract from environmental determinants of mental disturbance[35]. Unlike Freud, Skinner attached no significance to the distinction between conscious and unconscious processing[36].

Skinner did not object to the Freudian idea that early life-time experiences can exert lasting and controlling effects on later behaviour. However, he argued that we should not put too much weight upon these events as opposed to later experiences[37]. In principle, early experiences might have played a sensitizing role but would not be of major importance were it not for the problems arising in the contemporary environment. There is the danger that inner states such as guilt and anxiety are allowed to 'steal the show'[38]. The Freudian emphasis upon tuning the mental apparatus could well mean missing the most important current environmental factors underlying the problem. It makes the implicit assumption that the patient can adjust to the world as it now is.

In a Skinnerian view, there is no way that an inner state can be directly targeted. If there is any improvement in the patient's mental state, it is because of a change in the environment[39]. Skinner[40] suggested that, where psychoanalysis works, it appears to do so because the therapist forms "a nonpunishing audience". The patient will have experienced typically a life-time of aversive and punishing events. Indeed, on first encounter, the psychoanalyst might well, by generalization, evoke negative reactions. However, given enough sessions within which the patient finds an empathetic and nonpunishing listener, aversion tends to be extinguished and replaced by something nearer warmth.

Taking a broad swipe at all psychotherapy, Skinner[41] argues that it is a fallacy (an "explanatory fiction") to look inside the person for the causes of mental distress, such as neuroses. As part of the fiction, these causes are then said to be removed, much as a surgeon might remove diseased tissue. According to the Skinnerian analysis, any improvement consists in changing maladaptive behaviour through changing the environment. Skinner[42] notes the 'sin' that behaviourist-orientated therapists are accused of: "treating the symptoms rather than the cause". He argues that this misses the point that the true cause rather than a fictional inner cause is being targeted. This is particularly well exemplified by treating stammering by means of exercises in vocal expression and faulty posture by means of shoulder braces.

Skinner and humanistic psychology

Skinner was particularly scathing in his attack on humanistic psychology, though he regarded Carl Rogers, one of its principal founders, as a personal friend. In his notebooks, Skinner[43] made the following entry under the heading 'Dangerous Nonsense':

"Announcing a special journal for –
...*those searching for new direction and deeper meaning, for personal growth and inner harmony, for greater understanding, for the realization of their real nature, of their deepest potential for emotional, mental and transpersonal unfoldment.*

New, deep, real, growth, harmony, understanding potential, unfoldment – an opiate soothing syrup for humanistic psychologists, hashish for the searchers for identity".

In his well-balanced analysis of Skinner, Carpenter[44] asserts:

What is called "self-actualization" cannot be produced through self-indulgence or by fad or technique that fails to shape mutually reinforcing behaviours and to strengthen them by intermittent schedules.

Indeed, the humanistic notion of *unconditional positive regard* could well be something of a mixed blessing. From a Skinnerian perspective, at some stage, such regard should be conditional on efforts by the client. On the principal of humanistic psychology that the notion of control is to be rejected, Skinner[45] suggests that this is "merely to leave control in other hands". Skinner reminds us of the Rogerian principle that each individual holds within him/herself the solution to their problems. Skinner then compares two individuals. First, there is one for whom there has been an adaptive history of reinforcement within education and family etc. Such a person might indeed be able to solve her problems with little intervention. Skinner asks us to contrast this with a second individual who has been subject to a damaging upbringing characterized by social deprivation and excessive punitive control. It is highly unlikely, he claims, that this individual has the resources "within himself" to find a solution.

According to a Skinnerian analysis, thinking, rather like behaviour, is under the control of the environment. Individuals growing up in different environments would be expected to have quite different patterns of thought[46]. Positive and negative events will each trigger their respective thought patterns.

Two recent developments

This section looks at two theoretical perspectives that build upon earlier work (e.g. cognitive and humanistic psychology) and it shows the links between them and the Skinnerian perspective.

The self-determination theory of behaviour

Working within a social-cognitive and humanistic framework, while using the notion of 'competence' developed by White (see Chapter 3), Ryan and Deci have promoted what they call a 'self-determination theory' of behaviour[47]. At first glance, this would appear to be diametrically opposite to Skinnerian behaviourism, where the external environment exerts control. Indeed, the authors contrast behaviour based upon self-determination and that described by Skinner, which they refer to as based upon 'extrinsic motivation'. However, some of the differences might be more apparent than real and there is room for cross-fertilization. The theory of Ryan and Deci is subtle and nuanced. We will look at parts of it, searching for possible common features and differences with Skinnerian principles of reinforcement.

The theory is designed in part to explain some of the variation between individuals, ranging from, at one pole, those exhibiting curiosity, persistence, vitality and self-motivation to, at the other, individuals characterized by apathy and alienation. Of course, a behaviourist would explain these differences in terms of different histories of reinforcement[48]. Ryan and Deci[49] exemplify apathetic individuals as:

...millions who, for hours a day, sit passively before their televisions, stare blankly from the back of their classrooms, or wait listlessly for the weekend as they go about their jobs.

Understanding the role of social environments in the development and maintenance of these individual differences in self-motivation clearly has enormous potential in improving the human condition. The theory rests upon the postulation of three human needs that must be met for self-motivation, optimal functioning and well-being, those for:

- competence
- relatedness
- autonomy

Ryan and Deci compare these needs with the physiological needs for nutrients and water. Of course, life itself depends upon nutrients and water, whereas we don't die through lack of autonomy. However, the analogy points to dependence of optimal functioning on meeting all such needs. Food and water are primary positive reinforcers and so the analogy raises the possibility that fulfilling the three 'psychological needs' identified by Ryan and Deci could also act in a reinforcement role.

The authors suggest that those environmental factors that hinder self-motivation have the common feature that they thwart these basic needs.

A foundation of the theory is the difference in the basis of motivation in different individuals[50]:

> People can be motivated because they value an activity or because there is strong external coercion. They can be urged into action by an abiding interest or by a bribe.

As Flora[51] explains, this is hardly damning evidence against the principle of reinforcement. People might be moved into action by a combination of external and intrinsic factors. It is misleading to equate positive reinforcement with bribery (Chapter 3).

In some ways the distinction drawn by Ryan and Deci, maps rather well onto a Skinnerian distinction between acting because of either (a) a history of positive reinforcement or (b) because of punishment and its threat and/or negative reinforcement.

According to Ryan and Deci, acting for an "abiding interest" is said to reveal "intrinsic motivation". This might be described in Skinnerian terms as finding sources of positive reinforcement inherent in the performance of an activity. Indeed, they[52] note:

> ...that social-contextual events (e.g. feedback, communications, rewards) that conduce toward feelings of competence during an action can enhance intrinsic motivation for that action.

Tim Kasser[53], in his book *The High Price of Materialism*, works within the framework developed by Ryan and Deci and takes what he terms a 'humanistic and existential' perspective. Kasser contrasts two people, both of whom go to church every Sunday but who reflect respectively intrinsic and extrinsic motivation[54]:

> One of these people might do so autonomously, because the people she communes with, the songs she sings, and the prayers she recites all provide her with a deep sense of satisfaction. She finds being at church stimulating, interesting, and enjoyable, and she is strongly committed to it. It feels to her like a full expression of her truest desires, interests, and needs. The other person feels controlled and alienated when going to church. Although he still shows up every Sunday, his motivation is primarily to look good in the community. Furthermore, he knows his wife and in-laws would give him a hard time if he were to sleep in on Sundays. Finally, he has a lingering

concern that God might punish him for his failures when he dies, so he hopes that attending church will provide a few points in his favour.

Again, this might be reconstructed in terms of the history of the people concerned. Let us call them Mary and Bill. Mary might derive intrinsic reinforcement value from church attendance, having had a history of experience of this. The activity is pleasurable to her. She derives social reinforcement from the contact with others and her prayers might also be described as reinforcing. Bill is also using church as an instrumental act, which is reinforced by social approval. In addition, Bill's history is one of escape from aversion by going to church – the aversion of a nagging wife, disapproving in-laws and the fear of damnation.

I am not saying that we need to abandon the humanistic style of language. However, insights can be derived from a Skinnerian analysis and we might try some kind of synthesis between the two perspectives.

Intrinsically-motivated people are associated with greater persistence, creativity, vitality and well-being. Indeed, Ryan and Deci argue[55]:

Perhaps no single phenomenon reflects the positive potential of human nature as much as intrinsic motivation, the inherent tendency to seek out novelty and challenges, to extend and exercise one's capacities, to explore, and to learn.

However, this does not argue against the notion of a history of reinforcement lying behind the state attained by such people. Indeed, there is considerable evidence that creativity does not just spring spontaneously from nowhere but is a culmination of a process that involved reinforcement along the way[56].

According to Ryan and Deci, for intrinsic motivation to be present, people need to experience not only competence at a task but also a sense of autonomy, i.e. that behaviour is self-determined rather than a response to demands from outside. This can also be reconciled with a Skinnerian perspective, which left a zone of indeterminacy on exactly when responses were emitted. That people can perceive themselves to be acting autonomously has been noticed already, even though some would argue that the autonomy is illusory. Illusory or not, the *feeling* of sometimes acting autonomously is beyond dispute. In fact, positive reinforcement for actions, rather than aversive control, generates feelings of autonomy in the recipient[57].

Ryan and Deci go on to ask why employees fail to show initiative, why children reject the values of their school. The theory argues that intrinsic motivation has been undermined and the causes they suggest are ones that fit well to a Skinnerian analysis. Thus, we need to turn first[58]:

> ...to individuals' immediate social contexts and then to their developmental environments to examine the degree to which their needs for competence, autonomy, and relatedness are being or have been thwarted.

Presumably, the opposite side of the same coin is that those people who display intrinsic motivation had a developmental history of reward for behaviour, which answered these needs.

Positive psychology

Consider the following quotation:

> Entering a new millennium, Americans face a historic choice. Left alone on the pinnacle of economic and political leadership, the United States can continue to increase its material wealth while ignoring the human needs of its people and those of the rest of the planet. Such a course is likely to lead to increasing selfishness, to alienation between the more and the less fortunate, and eventually to chaos and despair.

Doesn't that have such a very familiar ring to it? Surely, it just has to be Skinner but wait: it appeared in 2000, ten years after his passing. Is it wisdom transmitted from the afterlife? No. It is the proclamation of the new science of *positive psychology*[59], in which a plea is made for psychology to focus, not just on pathology, but on positive states such as happiness. It is surprising that the proclamation fails to cite Skinner, since he more than anyone was the prophet of the desirability of emphasizing positive events and avoiding aversive controls.

To conclude the chapter, a review of the principal theories of psychology reveals where reconciliation is possible (e.g. the difference between Skinnerian and cognitive perspectives would sometimes appear to be one in terms of different *aspects* of the whole animal-environment interaction). However, it also reveals points of fundamental disagreement. Examples include (i) the assumption of some autonomy within a humanistic perspective but its rejection within Skinnerian psychology and (ii) the value of probing the unconscious mind in Freudian psychology but the rejection of this approach within Skinnerian psychology. The chapter also reveals where there is scope for much more synthesis (e.g. in historically framing positive psychology).

So much for Skinner seen within the context of data and theories within psychology, the next Chapter considers him within the context of the biological sciences.

5 The Relationship with Biology

Skinner took what some might consider to be an odd perspective on biology. On the one hand, he claimed to be a dedicated Darwinian and saw the principles of evolution as providing the foundation on which to build a science of psychology. Indeed, such a science should be a part of biology[1]. On the other hand, he saw little or no value in trying to build bridges with those studying the brain. This chapter will in turn look at each of these aspects of the Skinnerian view.

The link with evolution

There is wide agreement that the evolutionary significance of learning in its various forms is that it allows an animal to adapt to its environment. Life-time experiences can be assimilated and used to guide behaviour flexibly. In this context as elsewhere, Skinner emphasized only one form of learning, albeit a crucially important one: operant conditioning.

Operant conditioning and evolution

Operant conditioning and evolution by natural selection exhibit several features that make it logical to consider them together. For a start, Skinner saw an analogy between the two. Each of them serves adaptation, to bring the animal into a better fit for coping with its environment. In the case of evolution, small inherited changes can give an animal an advantage over others of the same species and hence increase in frequency in the population. This is analogous to emitted behaviour leading to consequences that increase the survival chances of the animal and hence this behaviour increases in frequency.

Natural selection occurs only *between* generations but operant conditioning increases adaptation *within* the lifetime of an individual. A particular behaviour, for example, a new technique for gaining food is reinforced by the arrival of food. Hence, the animal shows this behaviour more frequently and is placed at an advantage. Natural selection is too slow to be of use when the environment is changing rapidly. It is then that conditioning solves the problem of adaptation. Conditioning provides a means for adapting each individual animal to the vagaries of its particular environment, within limits.

Darwin's theory of evolution provided Skinnerian behaviourism with an analogy showing that adaptation does not require purpose[2]. Species do not need foresight in order to adapt, since the invisible hand of natural selection does this. Similarly, behaviourists saw the blind hand of positive reinforcement by the environment at work unaided by cognitive anticipation. However, the analogy might be a mixed blessing in one regard: evidence (reviewed in Chapter 4) suggests that there is a form of purpose revealed in animal behaviour, whereas there appears to be no comparable purpose evident in evolution.

Many have speculated as to why it took so long for the principle of evolution by natural selection to be discovered. Surely the evidence was there for all to see. This aspect of the analogy is not lost on Skinnerians, who argue that we have still not come to terms with change by operant conditioning, an ongoing process in the natural world analogous to natural selection.

To pursue the analogy, there is a curious paradox within the life sciences, as follows. Evolution by natural selection forms an intellectual foundation of modern biology. A similar process has been described for the survival of individual neurons and the connections between them[3]. However, operant conditioning, which follows identical principles, is regarded by many even in psychology, with some suspicion.

As Platt[4] observes:

Learning by reinforcement may go back 500 million years or more, so it is primitive…Undoubtedly, some day we will discover far more sophisticated principles of higher brain response and capacity to put on top of this. But at this stage it is only clear that we all need positive reinforcement, like lower animals, for shaping our behaviour and happiness, just as surely as we need food. It is only surprising that the demonstration has taken so long and has been so resisted.

Processes in addition to operant conditioning

It appears that evolution has provided various processes that are involved in the control of behaviour, operant conditioning being only one of these.

For example, Comfort[5] argues:

> ...Skinner ignores the possibility of imprinting – special, high-speed learning at a particular point in development and facilitated by built-in arrangements...Had he worked initially with ducks rather than rats I think this element would have bulked larger in the Skinnerian view.

A conflict with classical ethology

An area of intellectual conflict has been that between Skinnerian psychology and an important faction within the discipline of ethology, which is a branch of zoology. Ethologists research a wide range of different species in their natural environment and emphasize differences between them as much as similarities. This academic school has also shown a particular interest in innate factors, whereas the emphasis of Skinnerian psychology is on learning. The most famous ethologist was Konrad Lorenz[6] and, in his writings, we see a profound difference with Skinnerian principles. The best-known difference concerns how to explain aggression, and it is hard to imagine a topic that has greater social implications. Lorenz described aggression as an instinctive drive and explained it in terms of a hydraulic analogy: the pressure to perform aggression increases for so long as there is no suitable target for the aggression.

The model of Lorenz paints a gloomy picture of human nature with its intrinsic and possibly inevitable tendency to revert to barbarism. It has been heavily criticized within ethology, anthropology and psychology[7]. These criticisms undermine the notion of 'intrinsic drive' and paint a picture of aggression that would bring considerable comfort to a Skinnerian, whether concerned primarily with explaining behaviour or with reforming society. Evidence used against Lorenz includes the observation that cultures differ widely in their tendencies to aggression, ranging from passivity to prolonged war-making[8]. Montagu[9] notes:

> Where aggressive behaviour is unrewarded and unrewarding, as among the Hopi and Zuñi Indians, it is minimally if at all evident.

There are few or no grounds for believing in a satiety effect as a result of 'releasing' aggression. On the contrary, in terms of functional equivalence of responses, as Berkowitz[10] notes:

> Rewarding a child for making aggressive remarks can increase the likelihood of other kinds of aggressive reactions.

What constitutes reward for aggressive behaviour? It would appear to be the perception of an effect on the target of the aggression, such as defeat, injury or humiliation. An increased likelihood of aggression following an initial act of aggression is what would be expected on the basis of reinforcement rather than energy discharge[11].

Aversive stimuli and frustration are widely regarded as powerful triggers to aggression but their source, of course, lies in the *environment* rather than in any intrinsic drive to aggression[12]. One can see the evolutionary value in the triggering of aggression by society's two historically principal modes of coercion: pain and threat of a loss of resources[13]. In a state of 'aggressive motivation', triggered by, say, pain or frustration, aggression could well be reinforcing in that an animal might learn an operant response for a suitable target to attack. However, reinforcement might only occur *in such an aversive state* and that is far from saying that there is an 'innate drive' to aggression that could be manifest even outside such an environmental context of aversion. Excessive competition is another powerful environmental trigger to aggression[14]. These are all triggers that are addressed in Skinner's writing and his attempts at social reform suggest ways of reducing their toxic influence. Indeed, in criticizing the idea that a pent-up drive underlies aggression, Skinner[15] would appear to be much nearer to the truth than Lorenz. Skinner's criticism was directed against claims of the following kind:

> ...competitive sports permit both the participant and the spectator to rid themselves of aggressive tendencies.

By contrast, Skinner suggests that competitive sports are more likely to *increase* tendencies to aggression rather than to lower them. However, we

also need to see sport in the broader context of giving young people something to occupy their time and which does not involve violence.

Evolutionary psychology

In recent years, a branch of psychology termed 'evolutionary psychology'
has assumed considerable importance[16]. It derives from biological principles and suggests that we understand behaviour by taking the perspective
of *design*. The term 'design' is used in a purely metaphorical sense, meaning
that animals, including humans, give the *appearance* of being designed to
fit their particular environment. For humans, this was the environment of
the hunter-gatherer, before the appearance of settled agriculture. The argument goes that, as the result of genes and early development, animals come
into the world with certain behaviours having a high probability of appearing. This is the case even in the face of a range of different environmental
pressures. In effect, prescriptions for what to do are encoded within the
developing nervous system. This sets severe limits on what the environment is able to achieve. For example, language shows an intrinsic organization that is not simply the result of reinforcement. Similarly, under very
widely different cultural contexts, children have a tendency to show signs
of attachment to a caregiver and distress when they are separated.

The counter position to this is sometimes summarized by the term 'the
blank slate', meaning that the infant is completely at the mercy of the environment. By analogy, one can write anything on a blank slate since nothing
is written already. Steven Pinker[17] in his book *The Blank Slate* presents a powerful argument in favour of evolutionary psychology and against the notion
of the blank slate. As a political dimension, he strongly criticizes utopian solutions to the world's problems since they seem to fly in the face of human
nature. When human nature fails to yield to the desired solution then coercive methods have been employed, as in the Communist 'utopias' of Eastern
Europe and Asia. By implication, the Skinnerian utopia of *Walden Two* also
runs the risk of turning totalitarian and Pinker uses the term 'Maoist' to
describe Skinner. As one example, Pinker notes Skinner's preference for communal dining halls and suggests that this runs counter to the natural tendency to dine in small family units. The critique and label are somewhat
unfair since Skinner went to such great lengths to avoid punitive controls.
Sadly, Skinner died before evolutionary psychology really came into prom-
inence so we shall never know what his reply to this would have been.

Skinner's objections to studying the brain

Skinner never argued that the brain is unimportant in the control of behaviour. Clearly, to do so would be absurd. Skinner had occasional kind words for those who attempted to straddle the disciplines of brain science and psychology. However, he argued that brain science is seductive – too seductive[18]. He saw dangers in psychologists migrating *en masse* to the study of the brain, in that this lured them from the study of the determinants of behaviour in the environment[19]. Psychologists could be deluded into thinking that the study of the nervous system was somehow more fundamental than the study of the environment. A science of psychology needed to be based upon environmental determinants, rather than psychologists knocking on the door of another discipline, biology and brain sciences, for their inspiration. Skinner considered that a prior understanding of behaviour *in its own right* was necessary before one could understand the brain.

Of course, in addition, the problems of the world require addressing at the level of the environment rather than by trying to fix the brains of people so as to adjust to the environment. None-the-less, Skinner's lack of attention to the brain might well surprise people, given his identity as the champion of a *materialist* approach to behaviour[20]. After all, what could more obviously constitute the 'material' part of the story than the neurons of the brain?

Layers of control by the brain

Theoretical models

A number of psychologists, myself included, do not resist the investigation of the brain, even though we are strongly drawn to much of the writing of Skinner. The remainder of this chapter will show where such an integrative approach can deliver useful insight.

A model within psychology, which commands broad approval and which appears to explain a considerable amount of behaviour is described as 'hierarchical'[21]. According to such a model, behaviour is under the control of two different kinds of process. The first of these is direct, reflex-like and automatic, whereas the second is indirect, cognitive and involves conscious deliberation. These two processes can act in collaboration in determining behaviour but they can also be in competition for control. A typical example of the latter is when we are consciously trying to overcome an habitual behavioural tendency or when we are offering resistance to temptation.

Could this model be fitted to Skinnerian principles? The process of reinforcement would appear to act simultaneously at the two levels of the hierarchy. At a low level, reinforcement would strengthen tendencies to behave in a fairly automatic fashion. At a high level, reinforcement would be a process that would teach certain cognitions about the world, e.g. what leads to what. At this point we are reminded that Skinner described 'contingency-governed behaviour' and 'rule-governed behaviour'. In hierarchical terms, contingency-governed behaviour would correspond to behaviour that is performed directly and automatically when in the presence of particular trigger stimuli. Rule-governed behaviour would be represented at a high level in the hierarchy, as when one is resisting temptation based upon having learned a rule. In fact, Skinner identified a particularly good example of such levels, which involves immediate positive reinforcement value but delayed aversive consequences. He[22] observed:

> Freud was unable to stop smoking cigars, up to 25 a day, though smoking must have been obviously related to the heavy "catarrh" he suffered from most of his life, as well as to the protracted cancer of the jaw in his last years. (*Did* he stop toward the end?) An astonishing lack of self-understanding or self-control. Was he not bothered by it, or did much of the theory spring from the need to acknowledge that the habit was "bigger than he was" – that contingency-shaped behaviour (the "unconscious") prevailed against rule-governed ("the rational conscious mind")?

Consider another example, which would also seem to lend itself to an interpretation in hierarchical terms but where Skinner misses the opportunity to forge integrative links. He describes an incident in which a man (presumably Charles Whitman) climbed to the tower of the University of Texas in Austin and fired at people on the campus below. The man was later found to have a brain tumour. Skinner notes that various explanations were offered for this behaviour but they all tended to downplay environmental history. He writes[23]:

> Whatever effect, if any, the tumour had, it did not cause the behaviour of taking an arsenal of guns and ammunition to a tower,

barricading the doors, and shooting innocent people. It could not even have interfered with "cortical inhibition normally suppressing such behaviour", or, if it did, we still have to explain the behaviour.

Skinner offers no reason why the tumour could not have interfered with cortical inhibition. In reality, a wealth of subsequent evidence points precisely to the possibility of such inhibition[24].

A possible basis to superstitious behaviour

Skinner described so-called 'superstitious behaviour', e.g. the behaviour shown by a pigeon in a Skinner box, where pellets are delivered automatically at intervals and without any effort by a pigeon. In such a situation, pigeons develop repetitive behaviours termed 'stereotypies', such as repetitive turning movements. It appears that the pigeon just happened to be doing this at the time the pellet arrived and hence was reinforced for doing so. Superstitious behaviour might be better understood by viewing the biological evidence in terms of a hierarchy of control. An animal with damage to the hippocampus is more prone to superstitious behaviour than one that has an intact hippocampus[25]. This can be interpreted in terms of the hippocampus serving to inhibit the effects of a reinforcement process.

The biological bases of learning and motivation

Much current research is devoted to trying to understand the biological bases of learning and motivation. This involves building and testing theories, something Skinner tried to avoid[26]. However, suppose that we defy Skinner's advice and we look inside the brain. What do we see in terms of processes that might form the biological bases of reinforcement? What sort of process does the behavioural evidence suggest underlies reinforcement?

Plasticity of the brain

In looking at the biology of reinforcement, our attention is drawn to the notion of plasticity of connections between the cells of the brain. A learning animal, human or otherwise, is a changing animal in that there are assumed to be changes in the brain corresponding to changes in behaviour. As a very general principle that cuts across situations and species, the connections between neurons that are formed at synapses are known to be able to change their strength corresponding to learning. For example, the acquisition of the skill of lever-pressing for food would be associated with an increased strength of the links between certain neurons. It is assumed that, for the hungry animal, the arrival of food triggers changes in the connections between particular neurons in the brain. These changes encode, as a memory, the experience of learning that lever-pressing leads to food. If the food is now removed from the box and lever-pressing undergoes extinction, it is assumed that either these connections are weakened or their influence is overridden by other neural connections.

The biological bases of reinforcement

Imagine a rat or human to be in a situation that a Skinnerian would describe as 'reinforcing', e.g. receiving food for an operant action when hungry. In humans, brain-imaging techniques enable researchers to look at the activity of different brain regions when reinforcement occurs. A number of regions are shown to be particularly activated under these conditions, including the nucleus accumbens and the orbitofrontal cortex[27]. Equipped with this tool, researchers are in a position to ask which events appear to be positively reinforcing and some very valuable data is now appearing. Indeed, if Skinner were still with us he might find it entirely compatible with the viability of constructing a more humane or even utopian society (see Chapter 11).

As one example, researchers have found what they claim is "a neural basis for social cooperation"[28] and candidate genes have been identified[29]. People were given a task that invited cooperation in its solution. The areas associated with reward tended to be activated in a situation of mutual cooperation, which was felt as subjectively pleasing to the participants. The authors[30] suggest that activation of these brain regions is associated with feelings of trust which serve to "reinforce the cooperative act" and that this occurs before any conscious calculation of reciprocal benefit. It seems reasonable to suppose that the processes underlying trusting interaction with others are derived from those involved in infant attachment[31].

What kind of neurochemical and hormonal change underlies cooperation and altruism? Evidence suggests that changes in activity of the hormone oxytocin play a central role in both the motivational and rewarding ('reinforcing') aspects of altruistic behaviour, as well as its long-term health benefits[32].

As noted already, it is often assumed that positive reinforcement equates to pleasure ('hedonism') and indeed most often the action of positive reinforcement is perceived subjectively as pleasure. It would be a cruel world indeed if things were otherwise! However, as noted earlier, Skinner avoided any simple assumption of a one-to-one equivalence between the two. Rather, positive reinforcement was defined in terms of what increases the frequency of behaviour.

In a classical study of biological psychology, Olds and Milner[33] found that rats would press for long periods for electrical stimulation of the brain. This was intuitively taken to mean that a pleasure centre in the brain was being stimulated. Others were more cautious and suggested that such rats did not look as if they were basking in a glow of pleasure[34]. Rather, it was suggested that a process something like wanting was being triggered.

Work within biological psychology has provided further evidence to justify Skinner's caution that positive reinforcement does not necessarily equate to pleasure. Chapter 4 described the distinction between *wanting* and *liking*, which was first articulated by the team of Kent Berridge and associates at the University of Michigan, Ann Arbor. In terms of the underlying brain mechanisms, these researchers have gathered a range of evidence to point to the involvement of dopamine in the *wanting* component, whereas *liking* is mediated by opioids[35].

There are some powerful implications of this distinction. Under certain conditions, wanting and liking can be dissociated. For example, repeated taking of drugs can sensitize the wanting system but without correspondingly increasing liking of the drug. As a case in point, nicotine is highly addictive by the criterion of wanting and the difficulty associated with quitting. People addicted to hard drugs and trying to quit have reported that they would find it harder to quit nicotine than the drug that was being targeted in the therapy[36]. Nicotine is a potent *reinforcer* by the criterion of the frequency with which smokers engage in this behaviour. However, few would say that nicotine brings high degrees of euphoria, comparable to hard drugs or sex.

Evidence is emerging on the biological basis of the reinforcing effect of smoking[37]. It appears that nicotine has the effect of strongly activating certain pathways of neurons in the brain, which in part employ dopamine.

These neural pathways are responsible for forming strong associations with the act of smoking.

Chapter 1 noted that users of hard-drug could learn an operant response for drug delivery even though the drug's arrival could not be detected[38]. The drug was reinforcing in terms of increased lever-pressing even though it was not consciously detectable. These researchers also point out that, for many people trying hard drugs, the initial effects are not necessarily pleasurable. Indeed, on some occasions, they might trigger strong displeasure and yet still the potential addict repeats the experience. Of course, in some cases there is social reinforcement for drug use (Chapter 3). However, we need to entertain the idea that, by virtue of their intrinsic chemical properties, drugs can be positively reinforcing even in the absence of a positive hedonic effect. Further evidence points even more dramatically to a fracture between reinforcement and conscious pleasure. Consider the paradox[39]:

A puzzling, yet central, question in the study of amphetamine psychosis is why individuals who are experiencing acute terror and other unpleasant effects continue to use amphetamines in large doses.

To summarize, Skinner sits in an ambivalent position with regard to a biological perspective on psychology. On the one hand, it would seem to make very good sense to place operant conditioning within a broad Darwinian framework of adaptation. Looking at the reinforcement process from a biological perspective, gives valuable insights and shows where caution is in order in defining reinforcement. On the other hand, Skinner's reluctance to engage more broadly with researchers into the biology of reinforcement is to be regretted.

This completes the principal account of Skinner seen from the perspectives of psychology and biology. The next chapter will look more closely at the assumption of determinism with Skinnerian psychology and its broader implications.

6 Determinism, Freedom and Autonomy

Earlier chapters looked at some of the psychological and biological evidence that relates to Skinner's perspective. Chapter 6 puts Skinner under the microscope concerning the deep foundations of his approach, i.e. its theoretical basis. Some of the fundamental assumptions of Skinnerian psychology can be logically separated and we shall look at the following:

(a) The assumption of determinism: behaviour is the product of genes and environment.
(b) Psychology can be most usefully studied in relation to the external environment, avoiding internal cognitive terms.
(c) The notion of free will is not a useful one and is indeed a hindrance to the progress of behavioural science.

Accepting one or more of these assertions does not necessarily involve accepting all three. For example, as we saw in Chapter 4, some cognitive theorists would accept (c) but would, of course, reject (b)! We shall look at each of these three assumptions.

Environment and genes – an analogy

Starting with assumption (a), that behaviour is the product of genes and environment, on reflection at one level this is doubtless true. However, it might be true only in a trivial and axiomatic sense, in that it could not possibly be false. The assertion raises the issue: at one level of analysis, what could there be *other than* genes and environment? Of course, some people might wish to assert that there are supernatural influences at work but, if they were to be identified, presumably they would be defined as 'environmental'!

For possible insight, let us make a comparison with understanding our physical body. The constituents of the body and hence its structures arise because either they were in the original fertilized egg cell that was the start of us, or they were taken into the developing body subsequently in the form of the blood supply from the mother, or later as food ingested or oxygen breathed etc. However, the biological and medical sciences would hardly have made much progress based simply upon this assertion and the related assumption that one need only study the inputs from the environment in order to understand the performance ('behaviour') of the body. Although such things as stressors and water and food taken from the environment are clearly of fundamental importance in understanding the workings of the body, assembling a complex documentation of such information would not be enough for effective biological and medical sciences. Rather, we need a theory of how the internal organs develop, what they do and how they interact etc. In order to understand how abnormalities arise, we need insights into the differences between people, e.g. deficiencies in the production of hormones or weakness of the heart in particular individuals. By analogy, cognitive and biological theorists within psychology would argue for the necessity to study cognitive processes and associated underlying biology (e.g. attention, working memory) in order to understand behaviour and mind.

Skinner argues that we can afford simply to focus upon genes and environment (with an emphasis upon the latter) as sources of information in accounting for behaviour. A comparison with biology suggests that such an approach might miss some crucial sources of insight.

Concerning assertion (c) above, even if one accepts as axiomatic that everything depends upon genes and environment, this might not necessarily rule out a notion of free will. Just as the heart takes on so-called 'emergent properties' by virtue of its structure (e.g. it beats regularly), so, in principle, might the brain take on a property captured by the term 'free will' (discussed next). At this point, the analogy outlives its usefulness in that we can understand how the spontaneous property of the heart-beat arises. By contrast, we have little or no idea of what would constitute free will, let alone how it might arise.

Skinnerian determinism or free will

Understanding the issue

At risk of offending philosophers, I will try to express several centuries of their subject in one paragraph. In its basic terms, the issue of free will and determinism can be framed as follows. Suppose that the behaviour of an individual can be *uniquely defined* in terms of the genes and all that happens to that individual, such that, at a point in time, only one outcome is totally predictable and inevitable. This fits the criteria of determinism. By contrast, the criteria of free will are met, if, given this same history, *more than one outcome is possible* under the control of the individual in question.

Skinner was unwavering in his assumption that scientific progress will inevitably push free will further and further into retreat and will advance the cause of determinism. This might be true but it remains an act of faith. Further scientific insight might even support a notion of some autonomy and undermine determinism[1]. If physics is a role model for psychology, then it is worth noting that the 20th century saw a mind-boggling array of quirky phenomena and concepts emerge, which served to undermine all-embracing principles of determinism.

It is important to distinguish between determinism and fatalism[2]. Fatalism suggests that outcomes will be met in spite of our efforts and seems to imply a kind of purposive but bizarre form of supernatural intelligence. It is exemplified by the fear of some soldiers expressed as "if it has your number on it, it will get you". Determinism presupposes no such process and includes the outcomes of our efforts in the deterministic sequences of events.

A clear polarity is usually expressed in the terms of free will *versus* determinism. Skinner and Freud are well-known exponent of the latter position. Skinner offered us a stark and uncompromising choice: *either* subscribe to a scientifically-rooted determinism *or* attach your colours to a pre-scientific view. But is this the only choice available to us? As we shall discuss in a moment, some would reject Skinner's clear dichotomy and would not equate a scientific understanding with strict determinism.

In defense of determinism, Skinner[3] comments on the fact that, at present, it is difficult to predict the flight path of even a fly, let alone the behaviour of a human. He argues that difficulty of prediction "does not prove capriciousness" and goes on to note that the weather has proven very difficult to predict. However, given time, even apparently hopeless cases become manageable (thanks to computers and satellites, the weather is much more predictable now than it was when Skinner drew this analogy). Current lack of predictability of behaviour does not undermine determinism.

In his book entitled *Psychology and the Human Dilemma*, Rollo May defines freedom not as the opposite of determinism but rather as[4]:

> ...the individual's capacity to know that he is the determined one, to pause between stimulus and response....

May defines mental health in terms of:

> ...the capacity to be aware of the gap between stimulus and response, together with the capacity to use this gap constructively.

He goes on to suggest that[5]:

> The progress of therapy can be measured in terms of the progress of "consciousness of freedom".

People tend to admire others for the good deeds that they appear to perform voluntarily and we allocate blame for bad deeds. It seems logical then that people feel good about themselves for their own voluntarily-enacted good deeds. Harcum[6] suggests that to remove such a notion of voluntary choice could undermine a person's self-esteem.

It is interesting to observe the kinds of circumstances under which people are or are not held responsible for their actions. Skinner comments on this[7]:

> "We do not hold people responsible for their reflexes – for example, coughing in church. We hold them responsible for their operant behaviour – for example, for whispering in church or remaining in church while coughing".

Skinnerian determinism given a cognitive flavour

Skinner was, of course, not the first to defend a fully deterministic position and neither has he been the last. Recently, defense of this philosophical position has come with a cognitive flavour and it fits rather well to Skinner's assumptions, as does some of the related material described in Chapters 3 and 4.

Wegner[8] distinguishes between two meanings of the term 'conscious will'. It is sometimes used in the sense of an experience that we have when we engage in so-called voluntary action, which might be called 'phenomenal will'. We feel that we were the instigator of a piece of voluntary behaviour and the term describes such a feeling. This feeling is surely an integral part of what it is 'to be human'.

The other sense of the term 'conscious will' is to describe a *process* that underlies the control of behaviour. In this sense the voluntary will is said to cause our behaviour to occur, e.g. I consciously will an action to occur and shortly afterwards it happens. Based on the kind of evidence given in Chapter 3, Wegner rejects the notion of free will as used in the latter sense. This is implied by the title of his book *The Illusion of Conscious Will*. Rather, and in keeping with Skinnerian assumptions, Wegner argues that our behaviour is caused to occur by a range of inscrutable factors that lie outside our conscious insight. It is important to get straight exactly what is claimed to be illusory: not the feeling, which we all seem to experience vividly, but rather the idea that the will is a process in the causation of behaviour. We have the conscious feeling of willing an action and the action usually follows this very shortly afterwards. According to Wegner, this regular close correlation in time leads us to the illusion that the will was the causal factor underlying behaviour. For an analogy, if one church clock chimes the hour a few seconds before another, someone might think that the first chime causes the second but this would be illusory.

So, suppose that we have a brain that creates a mere illusion of free will. Why, one might ask, has evolution provided this peculiar illusory process? If it is not part of the causation of behaviour, what kind of functional advantage could this feeling serve? Wegner suggests that it has the property of an emotion and thereby serves to tag actions as being those that are the product of our own nervous system. That is to say, it identifies authorship of such actions. This might then serve, for example, to assist a process that monitors the result of our actions and stores this in memory.

As an exercise in devil's advocacy, Wegner asks us to suppose for just a moment that the term 'free will' *does* refer to a process (the 'free willer') underlying the control of behaviour. What properties does the process exhibit? It might introduce some randomness into behaviour by acting as a kind of neural coin-flipper. This would serve to give behaviour some unpredictability and capriciousness, which might thereby thwart the best efforts of, not only predators, but also those psychologists intent upon predicting behaviour. However, if people were suddenly to find themselves acting randomly, it would be a strange kind of free will. A neural coin-flipper between input and output hardly meets the design criteria set by an advocate of free will.

Why, it might be protested, if free will and personal agency are a myth, has the belief in their controlling influence been so persuasive for so many people and for such a long time[9]? Why, to ask a closely-related question, did Skinner arouse such disbelief and anger? First, as noted already, we all have the strong feelings of instigating action and this so often appears in our conscious minds just prior to the corresponding action. Hence, it is logical that we should infer a causal link from mental state to behaviour, whereas really there might only be a correlation (see Chapter 3). Second, as a mirror image of the same issue, the determinants of behaviour in the environment can often occur at a time that is remote from the actual behaviour. For example, a slowly accumulating history of deriving reinforcement for angry outbursts would be remote from the expression of this history in the form of a particular physical assault.

Wegner makes a powerful case for the position that much of our free will is illusory. However, some argue that he does not entirely destroy the notion[10].

A compromise position

Since it would seem that very few indeed would totally reject determinism, maybe a compromise is possible. A number of commentators fully accept the powerful role of genes and environment but argue that something is missing from Skinner's analysis. The historian, Arnold Toynbee, uses the example of exceptional humans to make this point[11]:

> I do not think that either heredity or environment, or these two forces together, fully account for the behaviour of Hosea, Zarathustra, Jeremiah, the Buddha, Socrates, Jesus, Muhammad, and Saint Francis of Assisi. I believe that these "great souls" did have the freedom to take spiritual action that has no traceable source. I also believe that there is a spark of this creative spiritual power in every human being.

Some[12] defend a compromise position, acknowledging that the philosophical debate invariably leads to stalemate. Which side of the choice between free will and determinism is favoured can be an issue of simple pragmatics. In deciding social policy, it would sometimes seem to be naïve and unproductive to assume free will, especially, for example, in the case of people growing up in a ghetto and turning to drug addiction and crime[13]. Surely, no one would voluntarily opt for such a life and it might be cruel to assume that they did make this free choice.

One of Harcum's[14] starting points is to look more critically at that half of the dichotomy termed 'free will'. He suggests that this term contains a semantic trap: there must be rather few who actually believe that the will is absolutely free. If the will were literally free, it is difficult to imagine how any science, or even university discipline, of psychology could have arisen. Presumably, the only quality of human behaviour to be studied by such a discipline would be its total capriciousness and inscrutability. Any science must necessarily presuppose some lawfulness of its subject matter[15].

In Harcum's terms of compromise, the will is influenced by external factors such as life-time history but it is not *entirely* determined by them. The will has some capacity to spring idiosyncratic surprises. Harcum[16] continues:

> To say that personal choice is possible is not, however, to say that it is easy or even likely to be achieved in every situation.

Harcum[17] relates these considerations to the position of Skinner, who:

> ...is correct in denying the existence of a literally "autonomous man", which means a person who responds entirely independently of environmental influences. But he is not correct in denying the existence of semiautonomous human beings who are not totally controlled by the environment.

Given the current state of our science, we cannot prove that there exists such an element of even limited autonomy but neither can we prove that there is not. The issue is one of metaphysics[18]. We might want to locate our perspective at some place on a sliding scale between the poles of absolute free will and absolute determinism. To account for a given instance of behaviour, where we put the pointer on such a scale could depend upon a range of factors, such as the mental health of the person concerned and the nature of the 'choices' that confront them. The case of a martyr is perhaps the most extreme example of where someone appears to be exerting autonomy in the face of counteracting environmental determinants[19].

A pragmatic solution might well be optimal for dealing with the events of life[20]:

> The idea that we shift frequently from a deterministic mental set to a freedom set and *vice versa* is fundamental to the main theme of this book, because it suggests that neither Skinner nor the most radical

believers in freedom can be accepted as *generally* correct. The most defensible position is that determinism and freedom are working assumptions that we employ to fit specific experiences.

An analogy that springs to mind is that of wave-particle duality in physics. Sometimes a fundamental unit in physics can be best understood as a particle and at other times as a wave. In these terms, we might take a subjective view on an action and feel ourselves to be free in taking it. However, looking at the same action from the outside, we might describe it in terms of its environmental determinants.

So what does the notion of a limited autonomy imply concerning the control of behaviour? In principle, it is not hard to see how deterministic processes within the brain might act to steer a choice mechanism based upon, amongst other things, histories of reinforcement. The crucial question that perplexes all of us is how even a limited autonomy might arise and be able also to influence these same brain processes. For whether a behavioural decision is determined or semi-autonomous, it can only be put into action with the help of brains and muscles.

Creativity

Creativity poses problems for an absolute determinist position[21]. For example, consider the cognitive workings of Newton or Einstein, as they discovered the principles of physics. Doubtless, much routine work was needed to set the scene for this creativity[22] but there was also the abstract manipulation of symbols. The products of this labour were hardly chance events and yet they seem to defy any account simply in terms of predictability and routine. Almost by definition, such creative ideas fly in the face of habit and convention.

So, can such creativity be explained deterministically and what would have been the role of operant conditioning? Any assertions would appear to be acts of faith. As Carpenter notes, it would seem premature and going beyond the evidence to rule out some autonomy of cognition and behaviour.

Chess makes a similar point. Each player is presented with an almost infinite number of choices. His or her external environment indeed changes as the opponent makes a move. However, can a history of acting within such an environment (based largely upon operant conditioning) take the dominant role in explaining the subsequent choice that is made? For a given external environment (e.g. places on the board), lengthy cognitive rumination can precede any move. Again, explanatory assertions exceed the evidence and reflect faith rather than science.

Skinner's distancing from a stimulus-response approach

Operant behaviour comes close to what is normally termed 'voluntary behaviour' and, to many, is thereby deserving of praise or blame. However, Skinner suggests that this is just because of our ignorance of the more elusive causal factors underlying so-called voluntary behaviour.

As was noted in Chapter 2, Skinner did not belong to the stimulus-response (S-R) school of behaviourism, though some of his critics would like to force him into that position. Clearly, an S-R formulation lends itself rather well to a deterministic ('mechanistic') interpretation – the animal is passive unless a stimulus triggers it into activity[23]. However, Skinner did not claim to know exactly what triggers each response of the kind that he studied. It is just a fact of nature and so there is an element of doubt in the formulation. Of course, once a response occurs, its future frequency comes under the deterministic control of reinforcement contingencies. The Skinnerian term 'emitted' draws a distinction with the 'elicited' responses of S-R psychology. So, if we try to speculate on what causes an animal to start to *emit* responses, we are free to suggest that there could be an element of indeterminacy, possibly limited autonomy, built into the system.

Do beliefs make a difference?

General issues

It remains a metaphysical question as to whether determinism is true or not and no experiment can (at least, as yet!) provide the answer. However, there is a related question which is, at least in principle, open to experimental investigation: does it make any difference whether people *believe* that Skinner is right or wrong on the issue of free will? After all, it might be argued, no matter what Skinner writes, he can hardly abolish free will if it really exists. Neither can his critics create it if it does not. But, of course, such discussion can affect whether people *believe* that free will and autonomy exist or are merely remnants of pre-scientific thinking. This could make a real difference to how they lead their lives. For example, it appears that people who believe in free will are more likely to support punitive measures in the treatment of offenders than are those who believe in deterministic principles[24].

In a book entitled *Precision Nirvana*, which attempts to reconcile Buddhist teaching and behaviourism, Deane Shapiro argues that knowledge of our conditioning can be empowering to us. It is an ingredient in the achievement of self-awareness. Shapiro also tries to reconcile both of these with some principles of humanistic psychology, arriving at the interesting argument[25]:

> ...the first step in behavioural self-management involves learning to see *the ways we are determined by the environment.* The second step involves believing "as if" we have free will and *can take responsibility for our own actions.* The third step is to *use certain techniques,* such as environmental planning and behavioural programming, *to increase our freedom.*

As described earlier, Wegner noted that people believe that they have freedom of will and indeed a belief in its possession could be used as a sign of good adaptation and mental health[26].

People exhibit a strange ambivalence in their belief systems. Skinner[27] discusses a paradox in the history of the study of humans: although cultures believe passionately in the notion of free will, none-the-less they have always been at great pains to find 'deterministic causes' for behaviour. Astrology is one ancient method for trying to establish causality and millions of people turn to such methods. Some are paid money for what are claimed to be their psychic abilities of prediction. Inheritance has also been examined as a causal factor, as has the location of contours on the head. Examination of facial features has been made with the aim of the prediction of behaviour. It is not just in past centuries that people exhibit such an ambivalent attitude to this issue. Bethlehem[28] notes the paradox:

> ...that as a scientist one accepts the working hypothesis that all behaviour is determined, but as a person one stands outside the determined system.

On the role of a belief in autonomy, Carpenter[29] suggests that:

> Self-autonomy or free will is needed as a working assumption to protect one from complete passivity, a dysfunctional state that

accompanies such mental diseases as catatonia...On the other hand, psychological health also requires awareness of conditions beyond one's personal control.

There are a multitude of such conditions that one is powerless to control, most obviously these include the rotation of the earth and the weather. To believe in agency over such things is to suggest mental instability. The development of a human so as to achieve mental health requires a delicate balancing act between[30] "...two logically incompatible beliefs: self-autonomy and environmental determinism".

Carpenter suggests that even if free will is a fiction, as argued by Skinner, it is a fiction that makes a difference. Presumably, in Skinnerian terms, a belief in free will is merely a bit of verbal (or sub-vocal) behaviour that has been reinforced by the verbal community of our culture. Therefore, it is an aspect of behaviour and we are free to speculate whether it makes a difference for good or bad. The argument is somewhat like that on religion. No one can prove the existence or otherwise of God but whether one believes in it must surely have a great impact.

An experimental test

One could imagine taking two groups of people and subjecting them to different conditions. One group would be saturated with Skinnerian philosophy, whereas the other group would be taught the validity of agency, free will and choice. Investigators could then compare the performance of the two groups when it came to decision-making, the motivation to take action in the world and the person's reaction to the good deeds, sins and foibles of others.

The experiment would present difficult practical and ethical issues. In the absence of knowing its result, we can only speculate. However, an experiment suggestive that one's beliefs concerning free will and determinism make a real difference was done by Kathleen Vohs and Jonathan Schooler[31]. Experimental participants were asked to read either material supportive of absolute determinism or neutral with regard to this issue. They were then given tasks that allowed for the possibility of cheating. Those exposed to the material arguing for determinism were more likely to cheat than the control participants. Vohs and Schooler speculated on how the material on determinism could have exerted this role: such exposure might induce a "why bother" mind-set or the denial of free will might give a perfect excuse to do as one wishes.

A practical application

Harcum[32] asks us to consider a young man, Charlie, a drop-out from society. Charlie had a troubled upbringing and is now described as "a one-person model of our failing society – unhappy, irresponsible, ill-equipped psychologically". Charlie, seeing himself as a victim, blamed society for all of his failings and saw no reason to seek remedial help.

Harcum expressed sympathy for Charlie and his view that he was a victim of society. However, he added that Charlie's behaviour[33]:

> ...may be understandable, but it is not excusable – because human beings make choices.

In fact, Charlie did get to see a professional counsellor but not as a means of achieving change. Rather, Charlie saw this merely as a means of gaining a sympathetic audience, to whom he could complain about the injustice that society had inflicted on him. When the counsellor realized Charlie's intentions, he suspended the sessions until such time as Charlie might seek change. Otherwise, Harcum suggests, the counsellor would have run the risk of rewarding Charlie's victim stance by lending it a sympathetic ear. Harcum cautions[34]:

> If the Charlies of this world do not see the need to participate in their own change of behaviors, they will simply march themselves
> off in pursuit of some person or agency who will buy into their dependence.

Charlie and his counsellor had different world views. Charlie was a hard determinist, though maybe he would not have used exactly that term. His counsellor believed in a degree of autonomy and agency.

Harcum suggests that, much as he was denying the fact, Charlie was exerting considerable control over his life. However, this was in a destructive way through the manipulation of those around him. As Nye[35] argues, it is true indeed that Skinner provides no new excuse for delinquents. However, his message might add moral support to the existing excuses. It is also true that the present system of allocating personal responsibility has not been notably successful at dealing with such problems.

The freedom to change society

Skinner was concerned with changing the world into a better place, a form of radical political action. Putting Skinner under the microscope in this context throws up a further set of philosophical dilemmas (the more practical aspects of social change are addressed in Chapter 8). Fontana reminds us of this[36]:

> ...if all learnt behaviour is indeed determined by conditioning, then which arguments appear to the individual as valid and which appear to him as fallacies are also thus determined. In consequence any preference he may have for the behaviourist argument is of no value in demonstrating whether this argument is correct or not.

Toynbee[37] makes a related point in the context of implementing Skinner's social programme:

> But if human freedom is truly an illusion, no human being would be free to plan and carry out the requisite biological and social "engineering".

Similarly, Neal[38] suggests that Skinner:

> ...makes an impressive case against the concept of the autonomous man. But does he really dispose of it? For example, if man can consciously alter his environment in desired ways, is this not an example of autonomousness?

However, as Fontana[39] argues, such arguments are problematic only if we assume that a Skinnerian process of conditioning is the *sole* one at work. If we suggest the existence of additional processes, these could be used to reflect upon the role and importance of conditioning. One possible way of viewing this is in terms of a hierarchy of control (Chapters 3, 4 and 5), with a higher layer having something of autonomy about it and able to override a more automatic and low-level reinforcement process.

The Skinnerian message has some rather obvious links with social history and politics. Pirages[40] writes:

> Industrial society has become technologically overdeveloped while remaining socially underdeveloped. The same society that uses applied science to orbit Mars and put a man on the moon seems

incapable of maintaining a stable social order and promoting a more satisfactory life for all citizens.

Skinner repeatedly pointed out the contrast between technological sophistication and the poverty of our understanding of human behaviour.

Neil[41] draws a comparison between Skinner and Karl Marx. Both devised radical analyses of the sources of the problems of humankind and how they might be solved. Both saw the controlling environment as being the target for intervention. However, where Marx saw the Capitalist system as the root of all evil ('aversive contingencies') and hence in need of change, Skinner left somewhat vague just how, at the level of the organization of society, utopian conditions might be brought about. Neil argues[42]:

> Because the objective is, more specifically, "human betterment", is there not a gap between Skinner's claim that his concept is broadly applicable to society and his failure to deal with the question of how a society operates *qua* society.

Neil suggests that, if a society were to start to change in a direction suggested by Skinner, there might be unforeseen consequences. The new society could take on properties that were not anticipated by those who initiated the change. Of course, by definition, we might never know in advance whether this would be the case but the possibility needs to be considered.

Amongst the other sins said to be committed by Skinner is that of 'reductionism' and this comes into particular focus when the issue is one of social change. In Skinnerian terms, human activities can be *reduced* to a series of component parts, the principal class of component being that of emitted behaviour.

Wheeler[43] comments on Skinner's reductionism:

> When he looks at society, he does not see structural forces, such as capitalism, or spiritual forces, such as the Protestant ethic; he sees individual behaviour. Skinner believes that all social problems can be reduced to individual problems.

As a very crude approximation, if we can draw a distinction between 'pure' and 'applied', this chapter completes the more 'pure' academic account of Skinner, as studied within psychology, biology and philosophy. The remainder of the book is concerned with the application of Skinnerian ideas to solving the problems of life, in such areas as education, criminology, mental health, interpersonal relations and climate change.

7 Skinnerian Advice for Living Life

Skinner was greatly concerned that psychology should be used to improve the human condition. This was at all levels, from the global right down to the behaviour that involves just a single individual. This chapter considers a Skinnerian perspective and its implications, at the level of individuals and their interactions with others. That is to say – how can we each use Skinnerian methods to improve our lives?

An important Skinnerian message was introduced in Chapter 1: we need to be more like scientists in our everyday lives. We should perform careful observations of any interventions we make in our own or others lives. Check the results against the intentions.

Antecedents, behaviour and consequences

An influential book entitled *Self-Directed Behavior: Self-Modification for Personal Adjustment* is now in its 9th edition[1]. It describes how individuals can use the techniques of psychology to change their lives for the better, e.g. to stop excessive drinking, end annoying habits, develop self-confidence in social relationships and study harder. It uses a hybrid of different psychological perspectives and the importance of goal-setting is emphasized. So, it is not a pure Skinnerian manifesto but this perspective permeates all of its pages. For instance, the crucial importance of observing and making a record of one's actual behaviour is stated throughout. The approach emphasizes the importance of taking note not only of what we should be doing (e.g. studying) but also what we are doing instead but would rather that we were not doing (e.g. chatting).

We are encouraged to think in terms of the behaviourist motto of A → B → C, that is antecedents → behaviour → consequences. When we want to change behaviour (B), we need to look carefully at the antecedents, i.e. the setting in which it occurs (A), as well as the consequences that follow the behaviour (C). These consequences might take the form of reinforcement, in which case the arrow not only points to the right but equally points back in the form of behaviour → consequences. By carefully observing A, B and C, suggestions can arise as to how to manipulate A and C, such as to alter B. The notion of goals comes in here, the goal being to change a particular behaviour (B), from where it presently is to where we would like it to be. So, the method is something of a marriage of cognitive and behaviourist approaches.

Concerning primarily the individual

General principles

When it comes to organizing one's own life it can make a difference whether we accept principles of determinism or not. According to some therapists, acceptance does not mean that we lose the motivation for action[2]. Rather, we might paradoxically even see our freedom increased since, armed with such insight, we can more effectively negotiate our social worlds.

Skinner[3] suggests that verbal stimuli given to ourselves might sometimes be effective triggers for behaviour. For example, on a cold morning, while having difficulty getting out of bed, repetition of the command 'get up' can help to trigger the behaviour.

The need to be more specific

A consideration of a history of reinforcement can give insight into how personality develops. Rather than using labels to describe intrinsic properties of a person, they serve better as a description of the person in *interaction* with his or her environment. For example, Winter and Koger[4] consider someone who is labelled as 'shy', because of their failure to exhibit smiling and eye contact. Of course, since these behaviours are not shown, they can hardly be reinforced by others. Reciprocally, attempts at smiling and eye contact by others are not reinforced and tend to extinguish.

Watson and Tharp[5] start by questioning the circular logic that is also a favourite target of behaviourists, e.g. "I cannot do it because I lack will-power". In the style of Skinner, they argue that will-power is not some intrinsic property like height that one carries around. The label 'low will-power' could exert a negative effect in persuading us not even to try to meet challenges. Careful observation of *behaviour* reveals that people's strengths and weaknesses can depend upon the context in which they find themselves. Once the specific contexts of our weaknesses are revealed, we can do something to target the particular behaviours. When we identify our strengths, this can help to undermine the toxic effects of thinking in terms of low will-power.

Similarly, a person might complain "I feel low" but this offers little or no help in what to do about it. Careful observation might reveal that the person feels low in a specific setting, which offers the chance of changing the setting. For another example, a person might report being unhappy because he is too self-centered but this is not specific enough. So, he is encouraged to observe behaviour compatible with this self-image such as "in company, I extol my own virtues too much" and to target this.

Strategies for resisting temptation

Using family and friends as dispensers of reinforcement can be an effective means of behaviour change. For two examples of this, a partner can agree to administer a powerful reinforcer in return for each two hours spent in not smoking or, over long time periods, in losing weight[6].

Finding an activity that is incompatible with an undesired activity has considerable application. For example, joining a gym and taking regular exercise will compete with overeating and smoking. Advance commitment in the form of a one-off joining fee might help. Also, the person can arrange rewards for himself in such a situation for good behaviour, such as buying a desired object after attending the gym for so many sessions. A con-federate might be recruited to oversee the reinforcement process. In all such situations an appropriate behaviourist-inspired motto would be: "Stop blaming yourself and start changing your environment"[7]. Of course, a simple adaptation of the same motto would apply to another person "Stop blaming the other and help her to change her environment".

The expression 'self-control' features in behaviourist writing and refers to a process that can act in opposition to the tendency to seek instant gratification of a kind that comes at the price of a long-term regret[8]. Self-control has been defined as[9]:

> ...when an organism produces a change in the environment which in turn alters the frequency of some performances in its own repertoire.

An example is when someone places tempting food in an inaccessible location in the home. For another example, a slice of cream-cake brings instant reinforcement but at the price of an increment in the waist-line. So how does one resist the cream-cake and what distinguishes those that resist from those that give in to temptation? To say that the latter are lacking in self-control might present a reasonable description of the phenomenon but it does nothing to explain it[10]. Neither does it help the person trying to resist. According to a behaviourist approach, behaviours incompatible with eating need to be reinforced and the person needs to be congratulated on any weight loss that they do achieve.

Another technique is termed 'augmenting feedback'[11]. For example, keep a record of the number of calories ingested and update it with each new item. Similarly, carefully monitor and record the number of glasses of wine drunk. Of course, the process of noting these measures would hardly grace a romantic dinner engagement but it could be applied under a number of other circumstances.

Unfortunately, the good behaviour of reducing food intake takes a long time before it is reflected in weight loss (i.e. as 'feedback'), so it is difficult for weight loss to serve as a reward. Hence, the reward needs to derive from a measure of calories ingested in each meal and the perception that this has been reduced[12].

Long-term habits might need to be overcome in changing behaviour. For instance, for the best possible reasons, some people are greatly upset at wasting food. They are in the habit of 'cleaning the plate' at each meal. To lose weight, a person might need to change this to a strategy of terminating feeding as soon as signs of satiety are perceived, even at the price of throwing away some food[13]. The ecologically conscientious might try acquiring some chickens to eat any leftovers!

A large number of people report wishing to spend less time sitting and watching television[14]. Based upon techniques of behavioural intervention, there are a number of things that can be tried to reduce the watching hours[15]. First, try to keep a record of hours watched, which, in itself, might help to reduce them. Change the context. It is easier to be captured by a behaviour once one is in the context in which that behaviour has been performed in the past. Try moving the television to a different room. Have readily available alternative rewards, such as a good book to read. Try to set realistic goals – if a person is watching television for three hours a day, attempt to bring this down to two-and-a-half hours at first. When this is achieved, try to bring it to two hours, and so on.

If there is an undesired activity that a person seeks to eliminate, a good technique is to avoid totally the context in which the activity occurs (assuming, of course, that this is possible). This might seem like too obvious to need stating. However, there is a subtle aspect to it, which involves environmental manipulation. Even if a person will invariably give in to temptation in the physical presence of a tempting situation, they might be able to exert some control prior to getting to that situation. Suppose that the canteen at work serves a particularly tempting but highly fattening dish on each Friday. When the person is anywhere near the restaurant, the temptation is normally irresistible. However, it might be possible to commit to resistance when at a distance by making low-fat sandwiches on the Friday morning and taking them to work. This is known as 'advance commitment'.

Advance commitment also applies to the temptation to sleep: placing an alarm-clock at the far side of the bedroom is an example of taking action at a time when you are able to make a rational decision.

Dealing with relationships between people

General principles

In dealing with others, it is worth remembering that the principle of positive reinforcement is a very simple one. Indeed, it might be too simple, such that we fail even to appreciate its potency and thereby fail to exploit it to the full[16]. It might well be that misinterpretations of the principle and unwarranted associations with 'control', 'big brother' and 'bribery' make people resistant to looking closely at the issue. Nye makes the valuable point[17]:

We frequently don't provide reinforcement when we should.
Many times we "expect" individuals to behave well and

therefore fail to positively reinforce their good behaviours when they occur.

The ubiquity of positive and negative reinforcement, as well as punishment, in social interactions is often unrecognized even though all of us have some hand in the relevant contingencies[18]. We are often quite unaware of what is going on and the effects that we are having. For example, a remark that one person makes to another following their behaviour might unwittingly punish or reward this behaviour. Correspondingly, each of us can push the other into despair or elation. One can only hope that a greater awareness of the role of reinforcement will be to the general good.

Controlling diet or television viewing need involve only one person but the complications of behavioural control increase sharply in the case of relationships between two or more people. How often have you heard the protest – 'I don't like people trying to control or manipulate me'? Such protest needs some qualification since everyone both controls and is controlled by those with whom they come into contact[19]. Only a hermit is not controlled by others. A more reasonable protest might be that 'I don't like aversive or coercive control' or 'I resent being controlled by him 24 hours a day'.

It seems that we expect good behaviour to arise instinctively and persist naturally without any environmental supports but this could be profoundly misguided. In trying to reinforce the behaviour of others, it is of course vital to select what are actual reinforcers to that individual[20]. This might seem obvious but it is very often overlooked. As a general piece of advice and a broad moral principle, it is surely good to do unto others as we would wish to be done to us. However, when we focus on the details of implementing the advice, some qualification is needed.

We are much more likely to acknowledge the good deeds of strangers than those performed by the people nearest to us, which are often taken for granted. This can lead to a weakening of formerly close relationships. The notion that love is blind, i.e. unaware of the other's failings, might sustain a relationship in the initial phase but could prove to be misguided in the longer term.

Wherever people interact, in a workplace, sincere praise works wonders both for the praised and the one giving the praise. By contrast, criticism breeds resentment and negative emotion throughout.

Blame is a form of aversive control, which might sometimes work but has potential dangers[21]. The blamed person might change their ways for the better but they might also attempt to reduce the aversive condition by means quite undesired by the giver of blame, such as total withdrawal from the situation. They might change their ways for the better only when in the presence of the blamer.

Self-blame is another form that blame can take and appears to be no more successful than blaming others. We tend to entertain this feeling in response to our misguided, stupid or morally unacceptable actions, e.g. in relationships. Endless rumination and introspection often appear to solve nothing and detract from more useful solutions. The answer could lie in reviewing the circumstances that led to the behaviour in question and trying to alter them such that it does not reappear. Merely gaining insight into the external causes of behaviour can sometimes have a beneficial effect.

Applying reinforcement principles – general issues

Watson and Tharp[22] give the example of Mary, who is upset at the amount of time that she spends in gossip. It emerged that it was more specifically the amount of time spent in malicious gossip that was troubling her. This translated into the *concrete goal* of reducing this particular activity. First, Mary kept records of her malicious gossiping, noting the times and the context in which it took place. It was mainly when she was with her sister or cousin and when she was feeling depressed. When again in this context, she was particularly vigilant. Presumably, the gossip had the immediate ('reinforcing') consequence of making her feel better but at the long-term price of making her very unhappy. Mary's solution was to try to substitute a new response for the old, in this case to replace put-down remarks with positive remarks. She monitored the frequency of positive remarks and gave herself rewards for achieving a good score.

Careful attention to our behaviour can make reinforcement effects or their absence explicit to us, in a way that was not previously exposed to scrutiny. For example, we might receive no reinforcement for the occasional performance of desirable behaviour and yet be obtaining regular reinforcement for doing that which we would rather not do. Consider a student, who reported[23]:

> I would like to be nicer to my roommate and be able to solve our little difficulties in a friendly way. But I usually fly off the handle and shout at him. The terrible thing is that I get reinforced for that. He gives in!

How then do you select appropriate reinforcers? Consider a student, Ramon, who wished to increase the time that he spent in the library studying[24]. He recorded the time spent there and the way that this was divided between activities. Careful observation revealed that only some 20% of time was devoted to study, the remaining 80% was spent in conversation with friends. It would appear that conversation was a more potent reinforcer than study. Hence, a plan was devised such that Ramon would spend 60 minutes or more in study in his room and then reinforce this with a trip to the library, where he would derive social reinforcement from conversation with his friends. Ramon's example can be generalized to other situations, where reinforcement is made contingent upon desired behaviour.

We can make use of what is termed the 'Premack principle', named after David Premack who first discovered it. Given that you have a free choice over certain activities that you perform, a high frequency activity can serve to reinforce a low frequency activity. So, suppose that, as in Ramon's case, you spend hours in conversation with friends (the 'high frequency activity') and little time in study (the 'low frequency activity'). Conversation can be made to reinforce study, provided that the contingency is arranged such that conversation is contingent upon prior study.

Sometimes identification of the reinforcer is not as easy as in Ramon's case and a factor that can make things more difficult is partial reinforcement (Chapter 2). Based upon evidence obtained by Skinner, we know that a reinforcer need not be present every time in order to be effective. Behaviour reinforced only occasionally can be very strong and persistent, with little sign of extinction.

Intimate relationships

Relationships, such as those in marriage, are crucially dependent upon the nature of reinforcement exchanged between the parties[25]. Irrespective of the amount of love that is professed, the ratio of positive to aversive interactions is a reliable predictor of whether a marriage will survive. Relationships that exceed the ratio of 5:1 positive: negative interactions (e.g. praise as compared to criticism) have a high probability of survival, whereas when the ratio is lower than this, the marriage tends to end[26]. From a behaviourist perspective, within a marriage or other intimate relationship, sexual behaviour should be based upon mutual positive reinforcement. It could not be a stable solution if, for example, the husband derived positive reinforcement from sexual behaviour, whereas the wife engaged in it merely as a result of negative reinforcement, e.g. as a means of escaping criticism or the risk of marital breakdown.

Consider what happens when an intimate relationship starts to turn sour[27]. Blame might be attributed to the other person. This is usually the trigger to nagging and criticism, which only serves to make matters worse. Self-doubts commonly appear, accompanied by anxiety, guilt and depression etc. Self-blame appears, often with endless rumination along the lines of – where did I go wrong? People sometimes assume that such introspection and self-blaming will ultimately yield the truth and thereby solutions will emerge. A Skinnerian approach would instead focus on behaviour and its consequences, seeing how these can take a maladaptive form. A careful and dispassionate analysis of how each person's behaviour influences the other and a comparison of actual outcomes with desired outcomes could be much more fruitful. Each partner might contribute a list of desired and actual outcomes of the other's behaviour. A partner might assess the extent to which he or she is reinforcing those behaviours that are desirable.

When things start to go wrong in a relationship it is not uncommon for one or both parties to revert to threats of punishment in order to bring them back to normal. The forms are very well known in marriage:

If you don't find me attractive any more, I can always look elsewhere.
If you don't want more sex, I might be forced to leave you.

These strategies are surely doomed to failure and endless bickering, whereas a careful consideration of mutual positive reinforcers could rescue the situation.

Consider the following as an example of where attention to antecedents can also yield subtle clues that might only have been processed at an unconscious level before. A married couple have drifted from resolution of disagreements by means of constructive discussion to a situation where the husband would frequently 'fly off the handle' and resort to abuse. Careful self-observation by the husband revealed that one particular antecedent set the scene for this[28]:

> It's a particular expression on her face. I think of it as her holier-than-thou expression...

In such a case, the wife might be asked to monitor and try to change her facial expression. The husband might be taught a technique such as the following. Each time he sees the expression and before doing anything overt, count in his head and give self-instructions of restraint.

Dealing with children

As with marriage partners, there is a similar armoury of punishers and negative reinforcers available for dealing with errant children, probably with equally undesirable consequences:

> If you don't keep your room tidy and eat sensibly, you will not be allowed out this weekend.
> You really must try harder at school otherwise your father will be very disappointed in you.

And with parents:

> I will run away if you won't let me do it.

From a Skinnerian angle we need to distinguish rewards and positive reinforcement. Lavish rewards that are unearned are likely to be counterproductive and could even reinforce those behaviours we wish to extinguish. A reward to keep a child quiet who is displaying temper tantrums might fall into this category. A Skinnerian approach would emphasize the undesirability of unearned rewards. As Carpenter[29] notes:

> "Operant behaviourism sees parents as indulgent if they reward their children too frequently and under conditions that require little productive effort on the part of the child. By doing so, such parents fail to condition perseverance and tend to produce such features in

their children as impatience, lack of industriousness, giving up too easily under challenging conditions, impulsiveness, and low frustration tolerance.

Carpenter suggests that modern technology conspires with the parents in providing immediate reward for very little effort, and lists television, cars and coke machines as examples. Since 1974, when Carpenter was writing, the advent of the internet has made available a range of ready rewards about which he could surely not even have dreamed.

Coming from a very different perspective, Kasser[30] arrives at a conclusion that is entirely congruent with a Skinnerian approach:

Many parents I speak with feel guilty about the long hours they work and the impact this has on their children. Unfortunately, the way that they sometimes compensate only adds fuel to the materialistic fire: they express their love and assuage their guilt by buying gifts for their kids. Video games and stylish sneakers can never replace hugs and time spent together, however. What's more, such purchases have the added effects of allowing material goods to infiltrate the relationships with children and of reinforcing the consumer message that love is truest when money is spent.

Rachlin[31] offers the following advice to parents:

...allow your child to manipulate your own behaviour and make your relationship one of exchange rather than one-way control. If an infant girl makes you happy by smiling, do not be ashamed to do what you can to get her to smile more. The more enjoyment you get the more she is controlling your behaviour by making you do what makes her smile. You are not spoiling your daughter. On the contrary, you are teaching her control of her environment.

It can sometimes be worth being aware of what Skinner[32] terms 'differential reinforcement'. For example, take the case of parents who complain of the 'whining and crying for attention' of their three-year-old child. It could be that only at a high intensity of the child's protest has the behaviour been reinforced with attention, while lower intensity actions were ignored. It might be that only after introducing whining into the sound is attention triggered and thereby behaviour reinforced.

Parents who are exasperated with a child's behaviour can try the technique of 'timeout from positive reinforcement'[33]. For example, suppose a child engages in thumb sucking and the parents decide to try to correct this. First, a desirable activity is found, such as the parents reading to the child at bed-time. Then, if the child starts to suck his or her thumb, the reading is halted until the child stops.

In the workplace

Relationships at work are also sensitive to positive reinforcement and lack of it. Nye[34] recounts an incident from when he was working in a factory. A new employee arrived and proved to be "fairly effective". Unfortunately, the supervisor completely ignored him. The man's performance deteriorated to a low level at which point the supervisor did take notice in the form of making threats to have the employee removed. This appeared to have the desired effect in that performance improved. Alas, it also had a number of undesirable effects: the employee became ill, he complained bitterly to his co-workers about the supervisor and finally quit. As Nye looks back on this case and reflects, he is led to conclude[35]:

A little positive reinforcement would have gone a long way.

The power of social reinforcement ('affiliation') has long been recognized implicitly by Japanese management as it divides work forces into small units[36]. The isolation of the assembly line is inferior to "quality circles", small units of production who see a product through assembly from start to finish.

Consideration of the workplace leads logically to the next chapter, which is concerned with the use of Skinnerian ideas in devising social policy.

8 Social Policy

This chapter considers the relevance of Skinner's perspective to how societies are organized locally, nationally and internationally. Skinner[1] complained that reviewers of *Beyond Freedom and Dignity* had failed to understand the core message of the book:

> They do not get the point of what will eventually lead to better cultural design, asking instead, "Who is to control?" They all miss the nature of control by the environment.

Skinner often faced the question – who selects the controllers? In response, he would note that we are already controlled but largely by punitive means. However, in spite of differences between Skinner and his critics, there is broad consensus on what is desirable in society[2]. Most people would want to eliminate poverty, famine, war and crime. Few would question the desirability of better education and health. The difference concerns the *means* chosen to achieve these desirable ends. Furthermore, Skinnerian change could be introduced piecemeal and initial results assessed before moving further.

To obtain Skinnerian social stability, the maximum number of interactions needs to be based upon mutual positive reinforcement. For example, the student is positively reinforced by the teacher in the form of approval and, reciprocally, the student's reaction is positively reinforcing to the teacher. The teaching should not be such that the student derives reinforcement by means of escape from expulsion, guilt, censure, embarrassment or disapproval.

How did things go wrong? Basic issues and the Skinnerian solution

In solving global problems, Richelle[3] identifies where a Skinnerian would see us going wrong:

> …we keep appealing to good will and to changes in mentality, as if these are the prerequisites for the solutions to be reached. We are

blind to the fact that such an appeal to "change of mind" has been the traditional strategy, but that it has widely failed. And it has failed because behaviours are not the by-products of human will or mind: they are the results of humans' interaction with their environment.

As Pirages[4] notes:

We can really no longer pretend that we don't know how to modify human behaviour. Private interests working for private gain make full use of the available psychological knowledge. The airwaves are saturated with television commercials designed to instil a desire to consume. Hardly an hour of television time passes without at least one sultry blond using the oldest conditioning device in the world to sell men's deodorants and after-shave lotions.

Skinnerian solutions to social problems are profoundly radical and are based on the desirability of a more egalitarian society.

Concerning *Walden Two*, Skinner[5] argued that it is "an early feminist tract". This is because it sought to establish a society in which there was greater gender equality. Lauren Slater, in *Opening Skinner's Box* pursues this theme, in noting the powerful message of interdependence of humans that runs through Skinner's work[6]:

...maybe he was the first feminist psychologist, or maybe feminist psychologists are secret Skinnerians. Either way we have viewed the man too simply.

Concerning the book *Beyond Freedom and Dignity*, Platt[7] observes:

It has been roundly condemned, as all his earlier books have been, by humanist critics who at other times call for improved human interactions.

However, to achieve a better society we cannot avoid making the issue of behaviour modification more explicit. It is not clear why this Skinnerian assertion raises such opposition. As Wheeler[8] notes:

...behaviour modification did not start with modern behavioural psychology. Plato stated this as his leading goal in writing *The Republic*. Our educational practices are devoted to behaviour modification. Each time we draft a new law we have in mind the modification of behaviour to conform with the provisions of the law.

Consumer society

Consumer society tends to act in a way that is counter to the long-term survival interests of humankind. We are encouraged to consume more and more, whereas restraint and conservation are needed for survival. How do we persuade today's generation not to bequeath its problems to future generations? Behavioural psychology can clearly articulate the problem but finding solutions is more difficult[9].

It has been argued that the solution to society's problems[10]:

...calls for a different distribution of the reinforcers, as well as changes in our verbal behaviour. If society's verbal behaviour places value on wealth and status, it reinforces behaviour aimed at *acquiring* wealth and status.

In the present case, the act of purchasing is, of course, rapidly followed by obtaining the item. A consumer society exploits this to the full in getting us to buy more and more. Purchasing can be intrinsically reinforcing, as evident by the number of unworn clothes, un-played discs and unopened boxes in the average home, as well as the amount of food thrown in the garbage can. Garbage is usually rapidly disposed of by a communal collection service rather than hanging around the house with punishing consequences, hence further reinforcing a throw-away culture.

If we actually get around to using the items that we purchase, this often guarantees further instantaneous reinforcement. It is not hard to find examples. New clothes have a novelty effect, which dissipates over time of wearing them. Popular music tends to sound less attractive with repetition. A journey by car, often equipped with music, heater or cooler, is available at the turn of a key, as opposed to public transport, which usually involves a walk in all weathers and a wait. At the squeeze of a button, an electric lawnmower offers a comforting sound and the sight of a sample of instantly-clipped grass. Manual lawnmowers require punishing effort and yield slow returns, while goats, Skinner's preferred option, are not instantly reinforcing.

In a number of respects, contemporary consumer society represents a Skinnerian nightmare (described in more detail in Chapter 12). Not only are we consuming far too much in the way of energy and other resources but we are doing so in ways that reduce or eliminate valuable social reinforcers. Internet shopping and out-of-town hypermarkets cannot have the social cohesion of old-fashioned local shops, involving reinforcement for socially-desirable behaviours such as merely exchanging greetings. Loss of public transport and the move away from the use of legs as a way of getting around means that neighbours often barely get to see each other, let alone reinforce each other's social gestures.

Addictions (Chapter 3) tell a similar tale to consumerism; indeed some would see consumerism as a form of socially-acceptable addiction.

Employment policy

Short-term solutions are sometimes also favoured against long-term interests when it concerns employment policy. Skinner[11] observed three men who were doing digging work in the gardens of Green Park, London and reasoned that the job could have been done with a machine, a rototiller, and only one man. However, further reasoning led him to suggest that this would not have been a good solution. First, the machine would have contributed to the pollution of London. Secondly, what would become of the other two men? He continued[12]:

> By "saving labour" the rototiller would dispense with these
> labourers. Would they then go on relief, in which case should we
> include the cost of the relief in the charge for the tiller?
>
> And how would the men on relief fare? They would be less strong,
> probably less healthy, and more likely to cause trouble.
>
> When is labour really saved?

Punishment, prisons and penal policy

Where interactions involve unilateral positive reinforcement there is the danger of social instability. For example, catching a criminal might well be positively reinforcing for a police officer but presumably not so for the criminal. This points to the need to address the causes of crime as a long-term solution.

If punishment is as ineffective as Skinner argues, why has it been so universally applied for so long? The Skinnerian answer is simple: it is reinforcing to the punisher. Suppose that a child is behaving badly, punishment is applied and the bad behaviour ceases. From the perspective of the punisher, the bad behaviour of the child is an aversive event and the act of punishment stopped the aversion, i.e. negative reinforcement. That is to say, the punisher is reinforced in making an act of punishment. It might be that the punishment has no long-term effect and the bad behaviour reappears. However, the immediate effect is what reinforces and long-term effects might do little to counter this.

Skinner[13] argues for the importance of contingencies in the treatment of prisoners.

> When you simply give people things that they have the time, skill, and energy to get by themselves, you allow their behaviour to atrophy. You make it less easy for them to "kill time", and stultified boredom or escape from boredom to violence follows.

Skinner returns to this theme in the third volume of his autobiography[14]. In one study, young offenders had been subject to daily exposure to reinforcement designed to teach them useful skills. As a result of reduced re-offending, the programme more than paid for itself financially, quite apart from its inestimable social value. A sceptical colleague at Harvard said that he was yet to see a rehabilitated prisoner, to which Skinner responded that he knew of several. A prisoner wrote from Philadelphia, informing Skinner that he was teaching behaviourist techniques of self-management to fellow prisoners. Skinner got a request for one of his books from a prisoner on Death Row in San Quentin, who organized discussions among fellow inmates. This prisoner even wrote a paper on the subject, which Skinner described as[15]:

> ...a beautiful summary of my position – almost uncanny in its anticipation of *Beyond Freedom and Dignity*.

The prisoner escaped execution, was released, and later went on to work as a volunteer for the editor of a behaviourist journal.

Platt sees close similarities between the perspective of Skinner and that taken within contemporary social work and criminology, where they consider[16]:

> ...most, if not all, of delinquency and crime as being due to genetics, brain damage, sickness, or a poor environment, for which the delinquent was not responsible.

The danger with prison is that, without serious attention to principles of behavioural control, attempts at reform can be countered by the influence of other inmates[17]. It is often remarked that prison serves as a university for crime. There are pressures to conform to the inmates' culture, which offers negative reinforcement for the aversive aspects of standing apart, e.g. escape from harassment and bullying. The act of 'joining the club' could make available positive reinforcers such as social acceptance and cigarettes. However, well planned behavioural interventions to reform criminals by reinforcing desirable behaviours can be highly effective[18].

International relations

Let us now turn to the international stage. Concerning the Vietnam war, Skinner[19] wrote that the US is:

> ...pouring enormous quantities of positive and negative reinforcers into Vietnam, [but] no one has really identified the behavior on the part of both North and South Vietnamese that we want to change. Certainly the contingencies are about as bad as they could be.

According to the theologian J.P. Moreland, an advisor to the US President blamed Skinner for the fact that the United States lost the Vietnam War[20]. It is true that Skinner opposed the war and, along with many other American intellectuals, paid for an announcement of opposition in the national press but that is surely far from causing single-handedly the loss of the war. The argument goes that the Pentagon strategy was strongly influenced by Skinner's writing. Hence the bombing was based on the assumption that it just had to change behaviour – bomb enough and the enemy will freeze or change course. The theologian suggested that the Vietnamese[21]:

> ...have souls, desires, feelings, and beliefs, and they could make free choices to suffer and stand firm in their convictions despite our attempt to condition them by our bombing.

It is a sad irony that, at a high level of government, Skinner, the disciple of non-aversive controls should have been misinterpreted as being an advocate of the efficacy of these methods.

War is itself open to understanding in terms of reinforcement: aggression has functional consequences such as acquisition of resources[22].

In terms of international relations, small steps can be tried in order to break a deadlock. The step can then be reinforced by a similar gesture from another power. Nevin[23] cites the example of East-West relations in the cold war. President Kennedy announced in 1963 that the US would exercise a unilateral moratorium on further atmospheric testing of nuclear weapons. Reciprocally, Soviet leader, Nikita Khrushchev, announced a cessation of the production of a type of strategic bomber. Further reciprocal gestures were agreed such as the sale of American wheat to the Soviet Union. It would appear that each side positively reinforced the gestures of the other.

It seems easier to mobilize public opinion and change behaviour when confronted with the threat of an enemy nation or a terrorist group, than is the case for climate change[24]. It could be that there is an evolutionary explanation for this. Sadly, human enemies have featured regularly in the history of the species, whereas climate change (discussed in Chapter 12) has not.

The chapter points to the crucial importance of a Skinnerian perspective on how we organize societies, locally, nationally and internationally. The next chapter continues this theme in the specific context of child development and education.

⑨ Development and Education

This chapter considers the related issues of child development and education, pointing to the relevance of Skinner's ideas and, again, looking for the possibility of some integration across different perspectives. Not surprisingly Skinner emphasized the role of reinforcement in child development and education. Again it is possible to set the role of the process of reinforcement into a wider context, which is an aim of the chapter.

Link to theories and ideas within the study of development

Bowlby

As one of the best-known names in this area, Bowlby[1] argued that a prime ('innate') motivator for the developing infant is a need for social contact. This emphasis upon the innate factor appears to conflict with the behaviourist assumptions that the mother becomes attractive by the child learning that she is a source of reinforcement. In behaviourist terms, the mother provides the primary reinforcement of food, and she then acquires secondary reinforcement value (Chapter 2) by association with milk delivery. Skinner[2] suggested that the basis of the emotion of love is the following:

...Love, etc. conditioned to person who feeds, bathes, clothes, etc. the child.

The evidence favours Bowlby, in that learning cannot carry the whole weight here. For example, given a choice of a wire dummy providing food or a cloth covered dummy providing no food, monkeys prefer to spend time on the latter[3]. The argument goes that the cloth-covered dummy offers an attraction which is similar to the texture of another monkey. To risk using the highly problematic word 'innate', the monkey has an *innate* preference for physical contact with a monkey-like texture.

Similarly, Skinner[4] appeared to see adult affection as something that acquired its value as a reinforcer only by virtue of its association with other reinforcers such as sex. He[5] suggested that

...love might be analyzed as the mutual tendency of two individuals to reinforce each other.

It is unlikely that an account couched in such Skinnerian terms would offer much competition to the creators of easy-listening music or great romantic literature. Moreover, it is doubtful that this can be the whole story, though it could well play a part. Early development along the lines described by Bowlby seems to mould later romantic attachments. Although some such preference appears to be 'innate', all is not lost for the Skinnerian cause; it seems that there is also an important element of learning in how attachment is manifest. Infants learn that the mother is rewarding of their approach behaviour or dismissive of it. In humans, this might establish a kind of template that plays a role in adult attachments, as in romantic relationships[6].

Bowlby[7] is famous for his ideas concerning the role of an 'internal working model', which is acquired by the developing infant. This model represents the parental figure, most usually the mother, and is used to make predictions based upon her behaviour. These include her availability at times of distress and the ability of the child to trigger reactions in the mother. This is a cognitive perspective but the same data might also be framed in reinforcement terms. Such reinforcement could be seen as refining the contents of the internal model in the light of the child's experience. As Baum[8] notes, certain stimuli provided by a baby are powerful positive and negative reinforcers. The smile positively reinforces parental attention, whereas the cry, which is a potent aversive stimulus, can serve as a negative reinforcer for the same behaviour.

Piaget

The theorist Piaget[9], in his emphasis upon inevitable stages of development governed by intrinsic factors, was in a very different tradition from the environmentalism of Skinner. However, some limited reconciliation is possible. Piaget noted that development is associated with a move from stimulus-based controls to more flexible controls that have some independence from triggering by external stimuli. Similarly, some evidence from within behaviourism suggests that development consists in part of a transition of controls from stimulus-based to operant control[10]. For example, the crying of human infants starts out under the control of such triggers as food deprivation and loud sounds. However, because of the effect of crying on the infant's social environment in the form of attention from parents, some autonomy from direct stimulus control is introduced. At times, a given instance of crying might well be explained in terms of both (i) trigger stimuli such as food deprivation and (ii) the history of reinforcement within a particular context (proximity of mother)[11]. Ultimately, a range of contexts might set the scene for crying somewhat independent of the original trigger stimuli.

The optimal use of reinforcement

Working in a behaviourist tradition Fordyce[12] asked: to what extent do parents reinforce infant signs of pain or distress? That is to say, is the future frequency of behaviour characterized as 'distress' and 'pain' increased as a result of such intervention? This raises the issue of what is the optimal level of intervention by parents (see Chapter 7 for a related discussion). One could imagine two extremes, each of which could be harmful to the psychological well-being of the infant: (i) an excessive level of attention and sympathy and (ii) lack of concern. It could be that parents only give attention when the signs of distress are intense. This might reduce the chances of mild displays of protest and specifically reinforce intense displays.

Learning about outcomes

In emphasizing the crucial importance of contingencies in healthy child development, theorists in a Skinnerian tradition[13] converge with those adopting a more cognitive language[14]. The healthy contingency can be summed up as (action) → (positive outcome), which the child learns. The term 'learned optimism' describes a state that arises from learning that actions bring positive consequences, e.g. smiling triggers smiling in mother. By contrast, the term 'learned helplessness' describes a situation in which the expectation is one of (action) → (no outcome). Having learned that behaviour fails to deliver a positive outcome in one situation, the child might then generalize this to other outcomes. Conversely, a state of learned optimism can help to immunize against learned helplessness.

Education in the home

Healthy development

Flora[15] examines the role of social class in the development of children's literary skills, noting that there tend to be more reinforcers for reading in a typical middle-class home relative to a disadvantaged family. The middle-class family might not set out to apply Skinnerian principles to their children's reading. Rather, the prompts, triggers, scene-setters and reinforcers for reading are more likely to be available naturally. This is no guarantee that reading will flourish, as indeed Flora exemplifies[16]:

> Although I came from a middle-class family and my father is an English professor, for some reason, the natural prompts and consequences for prereading behaviours and reading were not sufficient for me to learn how to read. Reading did not come "naturally". Therefore my father and various tutors used contrived reinforcers (Ping-Pong, comic books, and money) for reading to reinforce reading. Now I read for many reasons including pleasure. I hardly feel that I was "bribed" to read as a child. I was provided with special programmes and consequences for reading because I needed special help. Unfortunately, many who need special help do not get it, and calling reinforcement "bribery" makes effective help less likely.

Flora argues that, far from being unethical to employ such contrived reinforcers, it was the most ethical thing to do. To do nothing could be felt to be unethical. Once reading starts to 'lift-off', the contrived reinforcers can be removed, and the behaviour can be self-sustaining, with its own intrinsic reinforcement.

In the upbringing of children, a Skinnerian approach would not be one of *laissez-faire*, unrestricted permissiveness[17]. That would be seen as a cop-out, creation of a vacuum, which would inevitably leave control to chance factors or to the peer group. Control might be seized by aversive factors. Permissiveness would mean an absence of structure, in particular a lack of reinforcement for desirable behaviours. Based on the principle of contingency, children should make a valuable contribution to performing the chores of the home. They would feel needed, which would be ego building. Carpenter[18] argues that:

> The psychological robustness of the old rural family was rooted in the fact that it had an integrated reinforcement system.

The formal education process

General principles

The formal education process is a particularly good area in which to exemplify Skinnerian philosophy in terms of the wish to move from aversive forms of control to positive forms. Skinner[19] emphasized the historical and undesirable role of negative reinforcement in the education process (and also, in the quote below, refers to 'programming' by teaching machines, described shortly):

> Throughout history, students had studied to avoid the consequences of not studying, and in spite of a recent move towards permissiveness they were still doing so. That was why they worked hardest just before an examination: the subject had not suddenly become interesting; the threat of failure was then greatest. And that was why they drank coffee and took amphetamines when cramming and tranquilizers during the examinations. (Some teachers objected to programming just because it made subjects too easy. They were using a threat of failure for disciplinary purposes and lost control when their students were almost always right).

With its emphasis upon behavioural change, a Skinnerian approach to teaching and learning has an interesting implication[20]:

> But just as good teachers never have a "bad student", effective teachers *never* have students who "can't learn". If there has been no learning, there has been no teaching. It is as simple as that. A teacher cannot claim to have taught if there are no measurable changes in the students' academic behaviours. To say "I taught the material, but the students didn't learn it", is a contradiction of terms, an oxymoron.

Sometimes within an educational context the term 'bribery' is employed in situations where a behavioural psychologist would use 'positive reinforcement'. For example, Baum[21] describes the TV talk show hosted by Oprah

Winfrey, one episode of which concerned a programme designed to counter high rates of pregnancy amongst teenage girls. It aimed to encourage girls to finish high school by paying them a small sum each week for their attendance. A number of members of the audience voiced strong protests that it is wrong to pay someone to do what they should do without payment. The irony was that the programme was saving the US taxpayer large sums of money, which would otherwise need to have been spent on welfare payments to the mother of the child. In Britain, one frequently sees 'rediscovery of the wheel' in the form of rewards for school attendance, each such announcement suggesting that there is something very new about it.

In 1968, Skinner described the ultimate irony for a behaviourist: up to this point in New York City schools, extra homework was being given as a punishment for bad behaviour! Excusal from school work was being offered as a reward for good behaviour[22]. Surely, few could disagree when Skinner observed that this is simply "the wrong way around".

In case anyone gets the image only of a failing school to exemplify Skinner's critique of education, it should be recorded that the utterances that he made were equally scathing about Harvard, his own university and the cream of America's intellectual elite. It is not difficult to see why Skinner won enemies as well as friends. A memo, written by him in 1955, argued[23]:

> We do not teach; we merely create a situation in which the student must learn or be damned.

Application of principles of positive reinforcement

A book published in 2008 by Susan Hallam and Lynne Rogers from the influential Institute of Education of the University of London is warm towards Skinnerian methods[24]. The book is entitled *Improving Behaviour and Attendance at School* and it suggested solutions to problems of discipline and truancy. Far from Skinnerian ideas being passé, the book argues that

> The principles of behaviourism are particularly relevant in school settings.

The scale of the problem is given in the statistic that somewhere between 10,000 and 100,000 pupils appear to be missing from UK schools on any given day. Clearly, there is room for a more optimal use of positive reinforcement.

An obvious classroom application of Skinnerian methods is that of praise and attention given to appropriate behaviours, while inappropriate behaviour is ignored. That is to say, in the absence of reinforcement, unwanted behaviour should extinguish. In many cases, teachers are not aware of the extent to which they are attending to undesired behaviour and failing to reinforce desired behaviours[25]:

> It is, for example, easier and more natural to say to one pupil "Just stop that walking around when you should be reading", than it is to say to another: "It is good to see you reading".

A brief intervention to increase the ratio of desired to undesired behaviour acknowledged by the teacher (involving use of a training package) can have considerable effect in increasing the occurrence of desired behaviour. Listed under "Four essential steps to managing classroom behaviour" were the following:

> *Remember to look for the behaviour you want rather than the behaviour you do not want.* Whenever a direction or instruction is given, look for pupil(s) complying and either praise or inform them that they are doing what is required[26].

> ...do not draw attention to pupils who are off-task, praise/acknowledge on-task pupils next to or near such pupils[27].

School can provide examples of where something that appears to be punishment might in reality serve as positive reinforcement of attention seeking[28]. Expressing disapproval of undesired behaviour can actually have the effect of increasing its frequency[29]. Hence both parents and teachers can be unwittingly maintaining those behaviours that they seek to eliminate. Of course, there are degrees of undesired behaviour and no one suggests that serious violence should be ignored. However, much behaviour that is a candidate for being ignored is of a relatively trivial kind such as standing up when everyone else is sitting[30]. In a report published in 1984, it was noted that in British schools, rather few teachers are aware of the advantages that can derive from a behavioural approach[31].

The British educational psychologist David Fontana hits the nail right on the head in a statement that directly echoes Skinnerian philosophy[32]:

> A frequent error apparent in the behaviour of teachers (and one might perhaps say in the behaviour of all those in authority) is to act

as if behaviour problems in dependent others are for the most part initiated by these others, instead of recognizing that frequently they are a direct response to, or are sustained by, stimuli provided by those in authority themselves.

A consideration of this interdependence can lead the figures in authority to carefully examine and, if necessary, modify their own reinforcer allocation.

Teaching machines and computers

The ratio of students to teacher is normally such that there is little opportunity for appropriate 'active behaviour' by the student such that feedback can be provided[33]. For whatever reasons, some students find it impossible to exhibit any activity in such a situation. As a believer in the individual, Skinner was shocked by the averaging that he observed in face-to-face teaching. This is where his invention of *teaching machines* proves its value. Teaching machines can deliver programmed teaching in very small increments of increased difficulty, progression being conditional upon mastering the earlier material.

The teaching machine was never intended as a replacement for teachers, rather it would redefine the teacher's role. By removing the drudgery of teaching and learning, it would free teacher and pupil for the more creative aspects of teaching, such as exploring the natural world and developing the skills of social interaction and discussion. By increasing levels of competence of pupils, it would present the teacher with a more highly motivated class.

Each student progresses at a pace appropriate for him or her. Feedback is immediate and, if programming is appropriate, it is almost invariably such as to please the pupil.

Ironically, rejection of Skinnerian teaching machines by many teachers was followed in a few years by the emergence of small personal computers. These did not trigger the same objections that they dehumanized the student, even though they operate along very similar lines to that advanced by Skinner. The possibility of sophisticated individualized teaching machines took a giant step forward with the introduction of microcomputers on a large scale in the 1980s[34]. Rarely, if ever, is acknowledgement given to Skinner's pioneering work[35]. An exception to this is in a survey of the roles of computers in the classroom presented in 1997, by the British educational psychologist, Paul Light. In this, he makes an implicit acknowledgement of the influence of Skinner[36]:

> The psychological tradition which has had the longest and strongest influence in the development of "computers for learning" is associationist learning theory.

Light's account echoes Skinner in noting that the teacher cannot pace 30 pupils simultaneously and that the computer can act as a teacher. However, it is a teacher with the ability to give sustained and dedicated 'attention' to each pupil. Mercer and Littleton[37] write:

> Unlike real people, computers have the capacity to appear infinitely patient.

The kind of task for which the computer is particularly suited is the acquiring of skills, as in basic mathematics. In Skinnerian terms, reinforcement typically consists of a message of congratulation. Although Skinner urged reinforcement for correct responses and the ignoring of incorrect responses, modern computer-based systems are likely to give feedback pointing out where an answer is wrong.

Developments in software and the use of the computer include more open-ended tasks than those envisaged by Skinner[38]. For example, simulations allow children to 'explore' foreign countries or outer space. They can change such things as physical parameters of the universe to see what would be the anticipated effects. In addition, Skinner saw the teaching machine as applying to the individual, whereas some educational psychologists emphasize the *social* nature of learning. Computers can be used by pairs or larger groups of pupils and some researchers have suggested that computers can be very useful for group learning[39], suggesting an element of social reinforcement.

Creativity

It is sometimes felt that a behaviourist approach to learning is antithetical to creativity (see also Chapter 6). Simple behaviour can be reinforced by repetition but that is as far as it goes, since it is sometimes claimed that great creative leaps spring spontaneously from the minds of such individuals as Einstein, Picasso and Mozart. It might be that there is something inscrutable about the nature of the creative process. However, theorists working in the Skinnerian tradition argue that creativity owes much to reinforcement[40]. Original creative genius, whether in science or the arts, is preceded by a background history of steady dogged plodding in which the basics are first mastered. For example, Picasso needed to master conventional painting before being able to produce his unique style. It is hard to rule out reinforcement at these stages, e.g. parental approval for effort. Indeed, creative individuals such as mathematicians and concert pianists owe a great deal to parental encouragement. Later, as it starts to 'lift off', the creative person might be compared to the compulsive gambler who endlessly persists, with only the very occasional reinforcement for the long hours of investment. Creativity can occasionally be reinforced with peer approval, the sale of a work or performance of a concert, or just the intrinsic satisfaction from seeing or hearing the creative product. Children who are reinforced for originality go on to produce more original products as compared to those who were not reinforced[41].

How things can go wrong

Behavioural disturbance and teaching

The educational process brings the issue of behavioural disturbance into focus. At one time, disturbed behaviour was viewed as primarily a reflection of biological abnormality. Taking a behavioural perspective would shift the focus to the role of learning and the use of learning to modify behaviour[42]. One technique that has been used successfully in treating children with behavioural disturbances is that of the 'token economy'. Its use derives from Skinnerian principles and involves the earning of tokens as reward for desirable behaviours. These tokens can be collected and exchanged for desirable items[43]. It is necessary to monitor how the token economy is going, to record progress and identify any difficulties.

Roots of violence in childhood

Patterson[44] theorizes on the causes of violence and suggests that, for those prone to it, violence is 'functional', in that it serves useful ends (This fits the discussion of violence in Chapter 5). For such individuals, he refers to a 'developmental trajectory' of violence, starting early in life. Expressed in other words, violence arises and is maintained since it is reinforced. An analysis of anti-social behaviour in boys[45], places behavioural methods at centre-stage in devising programmes of intervention. True to Skinnerian philosophy, emphasis is upon the observation of the contingencies of reinforcement that are found in the homes of disturbed boys. Herein, researchers soon made an important discovery: there was little correlation between what parents said that they were doing and what, on close observation, they were actually doing. Equally suspect were reports of their children's behaviour, which seemed to reflect more accurately what the parents felt rather than what the child was actually doing.

There is a consistent observation of a relationship between anti-social behaviour and inappropriate use of reinforcers and punishers by parents[46]. In many cases there is an excessively high frequency of the use of physical punishment. It seems that such parental violence could act as a role model for the children's anti-social behaviour. In other cases, under pressure, parents had given up on the use of any type of intervention, termed 'rejection'. They fail to find anything worthy of an intervention that would constitute 'positive reinforcement', even for behaviour that would be classified as desirable in non-disturbed families.

Patterson *et al.*[47] concluded that children destined to become anti-social have been trained to be so by virtue of the dynamics of reinforcement existing between family members. Such children also fail to develop pro-social skills, within the family and outside. Any rare emission of pro-social behaviour remains non-reinforced[48]. The child often learns a pattern of showing such behaviour as temper tantrums and hitting, since only these are effective at gaining desired outcomes (e.g. to terminate a scolding that was triggered by homework not done). That is to say, other family members inadvertently reinforce aggressive behaviour. The aversive behaviour of other family members is terminated by the child's own aversive behaviour, i.e. negative reinforcement. Some extremely coercive children manage to bully the family into giving 'street time' at night, with the risk of an escalation of anti-social activities. Rejected by non-deviant peers, anti-social children naturally gravitate to deviant peers, who positively reinforce anti-social activity (e.g. by giving approval). The 'antisocial trait'[49]:

...consists in part of *a stable disposition to use aversive behaviours contingently*...to shape and manipulate their social environment.

By 'contingently', is meant in response to the behaviour of others. In addition, the trait is characterized by a vulnerability to certain positive reinforcers and:

...consists of behaviours that signify a tendency to avoid responsibility (e.g. chores and school work) and to maximize immediate self-gratification (e.g. stealing and using drugs).

10 Helping to Ease Human Suffering

This chapter looks at where the techniques of behaviourism can be used as therapy to improve the health of sufferers from psychological disorders and other conditions that have a psychological dimension. First, it will consider the origins of mental distress according to a Skinnerian interpretation.

Background assumptions

A Skinnerian approach might start with the assumption that, in many cases, mental illness and maladaptive behaviours can be viewed as the outcome of adaptive processes that have got out of alignment[1]. For example, fears, when in moderation and appropriate to the circumstances, are perfectly adaptive and serve to keep us out of harm. However, when they become out of proportion, the same fear is classed as maladaptive, e.g. a phobia. As already discussed (Chapter 3), evidence suggests that drug addiction is often a means of escape from insufferable conditions. Thereby, it involves a form of negative reinforcement[2]. Depression can be interpreted in terms of 'learned helplessness', as a reaction to an absence of positive reinforcement for contingent behaviours[3], whereas 'learned optimism' describes a pattern of learning that actions bring favourable consequences. Logically, such an analysis would lead to a focus on the environment as a site for intervention and upon prevention rather than cure.

According to a behaviourist perspective on disturbance, it is the behaviour itself that is aberrant and needs changing. This involves a move of attention away from inner causes of distress.

In the words of Richelle[4], Skinner highlighted:

> ...the hopelessness of increasing medical and psychological care for increasing numbers of patients if we know, from a behavioural

analysis, that the source of their disorder is mainly in their social environment.

However, it might be a mistake to dichotomize too sharply here. Consider by analogy a medical condition, such as blocked arteries. Clearly, prevention, in the form of a healthy diet, weight control and regular exercise is most desirable but this does not necessarily rule out, as a second best, interventions that target the internal pathology, such as drugs to lower cholesterol levels.

The position at which Skinner arrived was not far from that of the anti-psychiatry movement of the 1960s and 1970s, although it had a very different starting point[5]. Anti-psychiatrists took the position that psychiatry was applying labels to those deviants who could not cope with insufferable social conditions.

Changing behaviour

General principles

The expression 'behaviour modification' is sometimes employed interchangeably with 'behaviour therapy'[6]. The techniques of behaviour modification/therapy have several different sources of input, one of which is classical conditioning and another is Skinnerian operant technology. As with a broad spectrum of psychologists adopting a behaviour therapy perspective[7], a Skinnerian would see behaviour *per se* as a viable target for intervention in its own right. Such approaches stand in contrast to the psychoanalytic perspective, which sees behaviour as a mere symptom of conflict within the internal dynamics of the mind. However, most behaviour therapists would tend to draw on a broad range of processes, acknowledging that there is often a mediating role for cognition in the causation of psychological distress.

The emphasis of a behavioural perspective is upon active *doing* by the patient and the current state of behaviour, rather than historical determinants of behaviour and talking by the therapist/patient. Changes in overt behaviour are seen as the measure of success. As such, behaviour therapy was seen as a radical challenge to both psychoanalysis and to the use of chemical therapies.

In a Skinnerian analysis, maladaptive behaviour would need to be extinguished, while being replaced by desirable ('adaptive') behaviour[8].

The notion of rule-governed behaviour is appropriate here. The therapist might give advice to the client regarding some 'do's and don'ts', and the patient then attempts to implement them in his or her daily life. The hope is that the environment then reinforces the new behaviour patterns. Suppose a person is having marital problems and complains of feelings of guilt, anxiety and depression. Whereas some therapists would see these inner states as a prime target for intervention, a behavioural approach would see them as the product of maladaptive social relationships. The inner states would be expected to ease with resolution of the behavioural problem. Of course, the problems might be of a kind where resolution is difficult, if not impossible, e.g. debt or being trapped in a loveless marriage. However, it is possible that some, even small, intervention would be appropriate.

According to a behavioural analysis, any success achieved by client-centred therapists owes much to subtle forms of behavioural control[9]. That is to say, certain utterances and postures are being reinforced by the therapist's signs of approval. A transcript of a case of successful so-called 'non-directive therapy' performed by Carl Rogers was analysed[10]. It was found that the therapist was rewarding particular verbal behaviour. The reward took the form of empathy and warmth and was associated with an increase in frequency of the desired verbal behaviour by the patient.

Skinner[11] suggests that, in cases of occupational therapy, the therapist is providing reinforcement for the actions of the patient. He suggests:

> In re-educating the patient in the use of a partially paralyzed limb, it may help to amplify the feed-back from slight movements, either with instruments or through the report of an instructor.

Psychotherapy sometimes consists in supplying reinforcement for behaviour that has undergone extinction.

Time-out

In a moving account, Stephen Flora[12] recalls his experiences of dealing with clients suffering from life-threatening self-injurious behaviour. As an example, a boy named 'Carl' suffered from permanent disfigurement to his face as a result of self-inflicted damage. To protect him from himself, Carl needed to wear a helmet of the kind normally worn by goal-keepers and padded arm restraints, such that his arms would not bend at the elbows. He screamed and cried all the time. The initial step was to require Carl to eat a meal without the helmet in place but without inflicting injury on himself. If Carl attempted self-injury, the helmet was put back on and the meal was taken away temporarily, a procedure termed 'time-out from positive reinforcement'. Appropriate behaviour by Carl was reinforced. Times were tough at first but after some days Carl was able to eat without the helmet and arm restraints. Finally, it was reported that Carl largely stopped screaming, self-injuring and crying, often smiled and laughed and was able to work at various vocational skills. Taking food away might sound barbaric to some people but what was the alternative?

When the famous non-behaviourist psychologist, Philip Zimbardo[13], reflected on what contribution psychology had played in improving the lot of humankind, he was generous in highlighting the switch from punitive control to positive reinforcement. Specifically, he gave time-outs for undesirable behaviour as "remarkably effective" and the most popular means of managing the behaviour of children in the United States. Zimbardo argued that[14]:

> Skinner and his behaviourist colleagues deserve the credit for this transformation in how we think about and go about changing behaviour by means of response-contingent reinforcement.

Zimbardo also notes the importance of the behaviourist contribution in bringing to public awareness the fact that violence is in large part an example of learned behaviour (Chapters 5 and 9). Parents have been made aware that they serve as role models for violent or non-violent behaviours.

Pain

It might surprise some to learn that pain can be a target for behavioural intervention. Traditionally, pain was thought to be the inevitable response to tissue damage, with the intensity of the pain being proportional to the damage. If no damage could be identified, the assumption was often made that the patient was either a malingerer or a candidate for psychiatric intervention. Starting with the ground-breaking work of Melzack and Wall[15], there is now a fundamental reorientation in the way that pain is understood. Of course, tissue damage often underlies pain but this is sometimes neither necessary nor sufficient for pain to be felt. Pain is often not proportional to actual tissue damage. In such cases, a component amongst the causes of pain can sometimes be described as 'psychological' or 'psychogenic'[16]. This aspect is made up from such things as any associated negative emotions such as fear or depression and how the patient interprets the information arising from tissue damage. If a catastrophic interpretation is placed on pain, this can make it worse. Pain appears to fuse with other aspects of distress such as hypochondriasis, depression, anger and anxiety. Pain is made no less real or debilitating as a result of acknowledging a possible psychogenic component. Teaching of coping skills can sometimes go some way towards the alleviation of pain, hence the relevance of *psychological* interventions, e.g. cognitive-behavioural techniques, for pain. So where do behavioural interventions fit the picture?

A pioneering book on a behavioural approach to pain was presented by Wilbert Fordyce[17]. A patient typically exhibits pain-related *behaviours*, such as groaning or grimacing, as well as verbalizing their pain, altering posture and movement. Following the onset of pain, the behaviour repertoire changes; things done before are no longer done, whereas new behaviours, such as extensive rest, reclining or limping, emerge. The argument is a modest one that does not undermine other approaches to pain: some pain-related behaviour might have been reinforced by others and is a possible candidate for control via its consequences. It might sound callous and hard-hearted to claim that pain-related behaviour could be reinforced by the attention of carers and family members. However, this question needs to be posed and investigated. Attention, sympathy and taking over chores previously performed by the sufferer could increase the frequency of pain and the associated behaviour reappearing in the future.

The nature of the reinforcement has two aspects: removal of reinforcement of pain-related behaviour and introduction of reinforcement for 'well-behaviour' (e.g. use of an inactive limb, standing). Take the case of a carer who is over-solicitous towards a spouse in pain. The spouse makes an effort to be active but the carer insists that the spouse goes back to bed and rests. Immediate reinforcement is given to both parties. For the patient, there is the social reward of the pain-related behaviour of retiring, i.e. sympathy is earned and the pain is reduced. For the carer, their behaviour is reinforced by the spouse's gratitude and removal of expressions of pain. The 'well-behaviour' of being active was not reinforced, rather it might well have been punished by increased pain and signs of disapproval by the spouse.

Suffering and its alleviation raise, of course, ethical issues to which the next chapter is addressed.

11 Ethics, Religion and the Skinnerian Good Life

Skinner wrote a great deal about reinforcement and quite a lot about evolution. In addition, he earned fame as a prophet of how we should reform society and, thereby, how a 'good life' can be achieved. The Skinnerian 'good life' is both socially useful and ethically good. Skinner based the notion of the 'goodness of a society' upon the criteria of its survival in an evolutionary sense, its use of positive reinforcement and its avoidance of aversive controls. This chapter will try to find logically-coherent links between these aspects of his argument: society, reinforcement, evolution and ethics.

In addition, Skinner wrote occasionally about religion and so the chapter will explore the interface here. Although he found little or no use for the notion of 'motivation', in order to integrate his ideas into mainstream psychology it is necessary to see some links with this concept. The chapter will address these closely interdependent factors in the Skinnerian message.

Skinnerian ethics

Given that evolution forms a basis of the Skinnerian ethical code, what kind of ethics might arise from this? Skinner made little attempt to rationalize the basis of his belief that 'good' can be assessed by that which is in the best interests of human survival. He considered that the holding of this ethic is just another fact to be explained, if at all, in terms of its selection in evolution.

Skinner's advocacy of social change was mainly at a time when the threat to species' survival came from a possible nuclear war between East and West and his argument was coloured by this consideration. These days, the threat is probably greatest from ecological disaster but the same principle holds: we can think in terms of survival for all the species and how best to attain it.

As with the whole of human-kind, if we examine individual societies, we can consider both evolution and the Skinnerian notion of reward and aversion in deciding what is ethically good. For example, one society might prosper by employing slaves captured elsewhere but this would, of course, violate the Skinnerian ethic of avoiding aversive controls. Conversely, a traditional culture might live much in accordance with the basic ideals of *Walden Two* but would crumble in the face of competition from outside.

In terms of Skinnerian ethics, we would not permit one culture to exert an aversive and exploitative influence over another. So, it is ethically good in a Skinnerian world, for example, to try to eliminate poverty, prejudice and conflict, since they act counter to overall human survival. It is ethically justified to design a *Walden Two* and to try to promote the adoption of a science of human behaviour, since these actions are in the overall interests of survival.

Is Skinnerian philosophy utopian in the sense, unintended by Skinner, of being unattainable? Is there anything in our biological and psychological make-up that would encourage us to believe that a society, in which individuals overwhelmingly show cooperation in the collective good, is viable and durable? Is there anything that would encourage us in trying to devise such a utopian solution or will 'human nature' always thwart our best efforts? Since Skinner placed so much emphasis upon evolution and reinforcement, let us see whether a closer examination of these phenomena lends any comfort to those who would like to reform society along Skinnerian lines.

Basics of the link with evolution

We start by briefly looking at some details of evolution and later try to link this to the control of action by reinforcement. Going far into the details of current evolution theory is way beyond the brief of the present study but it will be necessary and insightful to keep certain basic evolutionary considerations in mind, as follows.

Whether in *Walden Two* or in an entire country that has moved in a Skinnerian fashion to 'beyond freedom and dignity', survival of all its inhabitants would seem to be best guaranteed by extensive cooperation. This is in contrast to the exclusive pursuit of self-interest by each. However, we need to consider the possibility that evolution might inevitably tend to act counter to cooperation and to favour only self-interest. In this case, the fact that people often cooperate might be inexplicable in evolutionary terms. Rather, it might only be explicable because societies impose laws for the collective good (something like Skinnerian rule-governed behaviour) and cultures develop customs of cooperation. We might need to stand 'outside evolution' and impose a different ('cultural') layer of explanation of why people so often cooperate and show altruism.

At first glance, the principles of Darwinian evolution might appear to be good at explaining human selfishness[1]. The opposite of selfishness is usually seen as altruism, which can be defined as acting with the motivation of helping another, even at some cost to one's self[2].

There are theoretical developments which suggest that, under certain conditions, altruism even to certain non-relatives could have acted to favour the genes underlying it and therefore Darwinian principles can be applied. Consider small groups of individuals engaged in collective endeavours such as hunting and compare two groups, one made up of altruists and the other of non-altruists[3]. The group of altruists can be shown to outperform the non-altruists, which benefits the propagation of the genes of the altruists. Even though altruists lose out when in the midst of non-altruists, a whole group of altruists will tend to prosper. One could imagine *Walden Two* to be of a size for it to thrive based upon mutual altruism.

In summary, a consideration of evolution and genes suggests the possibility of a genetic contribution to the potential for altruism and cooperation, as well as to selfishness. If this is indeed so, these possibilities must be manifest in terms of processes of brain and behaviour, possibly expressed in Skinnerian terms as 'reinforcement processes'. Which of the two tendencies dominates would be expected to depend on immediate circumstances and might well reflect in part a life-time history of social reinforcement.

So, this leads to a search for the nature of the underlying process of reinforcement.

The link with reinforcement

Basic principles

Human genes code for a nervous system that shows a great deal of flexibility in behaviour, and so cultures are able to exert a range of different influences on behaviour[4]. It does indeed appear that the relative weight given to altruistic and competitive interactions with others depends upon a history of the individual's social interactions, possibly starting when very young[5]. One could express this in terms of the relative weight of reinforcement for these strategies.

Surely, with no controversy, obtaining adequate food, water and shelter serve survival. Therefore, it is in the interests of society and, in a Skinnerian world, ethically good to help people to obtain them. The gaining of these clearly acts at the level of individual survival and there exist finely-tuned positive and negative reinforcement processes that guide the production of the corresponding adaptive behaviour. Sexual behaviour is more problematic; it is obviously a means of the survival of genes with associated powerful positive reinforcement value but complex ethical issues surround it. Clearly, some individuals derive reinforcement from non-consensual sexual behaviour. It was suggested in Chapter 5 that aggression can be reinforcing, depending upon such things as the current emotional state. A glance at the national news will reveal depressingly many instances of where individuals need to be restrained from acting against the collective good, otherwise they would presumably derive reinforcement from such things as robbery, assault and rape.

So, how do we explain altruism in terms of the controls of behaviour? An optimistic vision was briefly introduced in Chapter 3: the suggestion that reinforcement principles might even extend to altruistic acts. It was noted that brain regions of reward were activated at times of altruistic exchange. So, we might be led to ask how society can be organized to maximize the possibility of reinforcement for ethically good behaviour. Skinner himself suggests the viability of such an idea[6]:

> It would be a world in which people treated each other well, not because of sanctions imposed by governments or religions but because of immediate, face-to-face consequences.

The nature of altruistic reinforcement

There is good reason to believe that most humans can suffer psychological distress by observing the suffering of some, if not all, of their fellow humans[7]. Therefore, at times, acts of altruism might be motivated by distress and strengthened by negative reinforcement: a reduction in one's own psychological pain. Evidence suggests that those regions of the brain that underlie the processing of the pain that is triggered by physical stimuli are also activated by the sight of a loved one in pain[8], and presumably any action that alleviates the pain of the loved one also alleviates one's own distress.

There is much evidence to suggest that altruistic giving is good for the health of the altruist, which points to the triggering of positive emotions. For example, people who volunteer their services to help others tend to enjoy better health as a result of doing so[9]. This suggests the viability ('survival value') of a society in which altruism dominates, which would surely warm Skinner's heart if he were here to learn of it. There is some evidence that people actually enjoy showing altruistic behaviour, e.g. volunteering, which is compatible with the existence of a positive reinforcement process[10] (Chapter 3). There are surely different components to what constitutes the reinforcement from helping. Amongst other factors, volunteering exemplifies being able to exert agency over the altruist's social environment (i.e. 'self-efficacy' and 'competence') and appears to counter undesirable emotions such as depression and hostility[11]. For some people, it acts to counter the harmful effects of social isolation[12].

How can goodness prevail?

Alas, as Chapter 5 mentioned, there are also behavioural processes that motivate, organize and reinforce hostility and aggression towards others. This again raises the crucial issue of which system dominates and the factors that bias towards domination by one or other. Here we need to consider developmental factors such as early exposure to role models and reinforcement for either altruistic or selfish behaviour[13]. The kind of society in which individuals are placed and the temptations and threats posed within it also represent factors that surely play a profound role[14]. We can ask how, given a Skinnerian society, we could bias the controls to favour reinforcement of altruism rather than hostility.

It appears that cooperation and altruism will not inevitably dominate over the forces of darkness. However, there is some comfort for any aspiring young Skinnerian social reformer: a society which practices cooperative behaviour might be expected to show greater stability and success than one that does not. Indeed, within Europe, societies (e.g. Denmark) which show relatively high levels of welfare and concern for all have a relatively high happiness and success level.

Evolution is on the side of the Skinnerian in that altruistic societies tend to be more successful than competitive ones. Reinforcement principles are on the same side: altruistic exchanges can be positively reinforcing for both parties, whereas exchanges based on aversion might be positively reinforcing for the punisher but are decidedly not so for the recipient. Positive emotions tend to foster positive actions, with the possibility of stable virtuous circles. According to the present interpretation, the survival of a society can be best guaranteed by the promotion of measures that both prescribe altruism at the level of rule-governed behaviour and permit the individual processes of reinforcement for altruistic acts to prosper.

Religion

Link with altruism

Religion is a good medium for the valuing and promotion of altruism[15]. Churches, synagogues, temples and mosques are principal centres for the organization of altruistic activities, while people of religious orientation tend to be particularly attracted to volunteering help for unrelated others[16]. Of course, the notions of reward and punishment have always been evident in Christian teaching: good deeds done on this earth will ultimately be rewarded with salvation, whereas bad deeds will be punished[17]. Similarly, Buddhist principles also involve notions of reward and punishment: the principle of Karma suggests that actions, good or bad, tend to work themselves out over successive lives. So, where and how does religion fit into the Skinnerian perspective?

Religious practices

Skinnerian principles appear to be applicable to a number of features of religious behaviour. It is easy to make reasonable suggestions as to a possible positive reinforcement value derived from attendance at church or other forms of collective worship. There is also the potential for positive reinforcement in social approval, fellowship with others and community solidarity. In parallel, negative reinforcement could arise from some lifting of loneliness and the distress caused by the existentialist dilemma over the meaning of life. Seeking forgiveness, as in making confessions to a priest, could be interpreted as negatively reinforcing in the lowering of guilt. The argument is frequently made that the prospect of some kind of reward or punishment in an after-life and reunion with loved ones might underlie reinforcing actions of religious observance in the here and now, e.g. to lower fear levels.

Principles of reinforcement appear to have more trouble explaining some other features of religious behaviour, such as living a life of abstinence, flagellation (self- and other-performed), voluntary crucifixion as in the Philippines, apparent extreme physical discomfort experienced by Hindu and other mystics or showing martyrdom. With the obvious exception of martyrdom, even in such cases there can be a strong element of positive reinforcement derived from approval by relatives and friends of the performance of a sacrifice[18]. Skinner[19] suggests that such acts can be understood as providing a means of escape from a condition that is even more aversive than the acts themselves: guilt. It would be difficult to test this under controlled conditions and so it remains interesting speculation.

For religious behaviour, as for other aspects of behaviour (described in Chapters 3–6), it could be safest to assume that reinforcement plays a role in association with other processes, such as those characterized as purposive and goal-directed.

Getting the right balance and resisting temptation

Behavioural science of a Skinnerian kind appears highly relevant to the issue of competition for the control of behaviour, e.g. in resisting temptation. For example, the book of Genesis describes an internal conflict, which in Skinnerian terms, seems to pit reinforcement-controlled behaviour against rule-governed behaviour. Eve was commanded by God that she could eat from any tree in the Garden of Eden, except that which was known as the 'Tree of knowledge'. Eve disobeyed God's command and, as the saying goes, 'the rest is history'.

One would have to be hard-hearted not to sympathize with Eve's plight. She presumably had a history of deriving reinforcement from eating fruit. The fruit was physically present and was doubtless exciting her dopaminergic wanting system (Chapters 4 and 5). Even more so, the fruit of the forbidden tree was, by definition, novel and so this would have contributed to a particularly strong incentive value. The serpent was egging her on. Against this, inhibition ('rule-governed behaviour') consisted at best of a verbal command of restraint held in her memory and it proved no match for the pull of the incentive. Interestingly, on feeling God's disapproval, the reaction of Adam and Eve was little different from that of present-day psychology students and their instructors after failing to shape a rat in a Skinner box (Chapter 1). Adam blamed Eve and Eve blamed the serpent.

Subsequently, notable figures in the Judeo-Christian tradition recorded a similar dilemma of behavioural controls. For example, Saint Paul recorded just such a phenomenon:

> I do not understand my own actions. For I do not do what I want, but I do the very thing I hate (Romans 5:17).

As, it might appear, did St. Augustine (*Confessions*):

> Grant me chastity and continence but not yet.

Much religious practice might be understood in terms of forgoing immediate reinforcement in the interests of long-term reward, as mediated by a rule-governing process. Engaging in activities in the here-and-now might bring immediate joy but at the price of long-term suffering. However, there is more to it than that. Religious practices have their own immediate rewards, such as that derived from companionship and compassion for others[20]. In Buddhist philosophy, attaining non-attachment to worldly desires brings its own rewards associated with peace and tranquillity of mind. Baum[21] suggests that:

> In behavioural terms, advocating spiritual freedom can be seen not as arguing for freedom from all positive reinforcers, but rather as arguing for one set of positive reinforcers against another.

Religions are then seen more accurately as promoting a balance between positive reinforcers, taking the time scale of their consequences into account. Control by rule-governing processes is emphasized. The behaviourist theorist Baum[22] arrives at a conclusion with which surely few of religious belief would object:

> When a society arranges positive reinforcement for desirable behaviour and supports long-term contingencies, its citizens are productive and happy.

Carpenter[23] argues that religion provides a particularly good potential means of behavioural control by emphasizing rights and wrongs. This is irrespective of any metaphysical claims that religion makes. In practical terms, any religion has a set of practices that require conformity and a set of unacceptable behaviours. Difficulty with compliance has always been a major problem[24].

As with Adam and Eve, much deviation from desired ethical codes surely amounts to giving in to the pull of low-level controls ('reinforcement') in the face of the opposing influence of rule-governed behaviour. Skinner and his followers suggested ways in which self-control could be improved (see Chapter 7), and hence provide some common ground with religious practices.

Religion in the life of Skinner

Although brought up in a religious family, Skinner rebelled against religion at school and college[25] and later frequently took swipes at it, particularly its organized forms[26]. Blows were struck uncompromisingly at the heart of some cherished religious beliefs. As noted in Chapter 2, Skinner found it hard to come to terms with the notion of eternal damnation as either ethically justified or as a means to obtain desirable earthly behaviour.

Unlike the religious perspective, Skinner's understanding of the world is a self-proclaimed materialist one, in which he appeared to reject any notions of the divine and transcendent. However, in the other sense of 'materialist', i.e. meaning to value the acquisition of material goods, Skinner was firmly with the great religions, as an equally eloquent and persuasive critic of all that the word represents. This split according to word meaning surely appears paradoxical to some of his readers.

Skinner's challenge to organized religion was often profound and well-articulated. It was deserving of a response of equal measure. For example, Skinner[27] got to see a pastoral letter written by Cardinal Cushing, in which the Cardinal asserted:

> The world is immoral, and our salvation lies in a return to Christian morals.

Skinner's comment on this made an important point for believer and non-believer alike:

> One may agree that a world which abided by a Christian code
> would be a better place, but the test of a code is not the behavior

it would produce if followed but whether it is followed. Why have Christian principles not done a better job?

Of course, it is not difficult to guess as to what lies implicitly behind this rhetorical question: those living in Christian cultures have been insufficiently reinforced for their good behaviour and have been maladaptively punished for their bad.

In spite of his opposition to organized religion, Skinner occasionally made conciliatory noises towards it. Seen out of context, some of Skinner's words might even appear Biblical in their tone and content. This is exemplified by the following[28]:

> We are alive only to the extent that we affect others. We are dead as soon as we live for ourselves.

Perhaps also surprising to some, for a self-proclaimed materialist and devoted Darwinian, Skinner recorded moments of almost mystical wonder. For example, he describes[29] the experience of admiring a dragonfly:

> The beautiful design, the far more beautiful microstructure of its nervous system if it could be seen – is all that a by-product, a casual throwaway of an evolutionary process? It is hard to believe. I can understand those who are sceptical of *accidental* mutations.

Pattison[30] reminds us of Skinner's upbringing in a religious family in the early part of the 20th century and speculates on this influence:

> At that point, American Methodism was the centre point of the development of the "social gospel". Such Methodist theology, in American context, eschewed traditional transcendental theology. Rather, it was devoted to "reforming society", to "improving society", to "redressing social ills and evils".

A study of the historical background to Skinner and behaviourism reveals something of a contradiction in terms of the role of society. Individualism and self-determinism are at the essence of American culture, as exemplified in the notion that any child can grow up to be President. However, it can be argued that this represents[31]:

> ...a fantasised self-omnipotence that flies in the face of the fact that we are *not* born with equal opportunity or equal potential.

On the other hand:

> Although religious freedom was a rallying cry, in fact, Puritan New
> England was an experiment in social engineering to create the perfect
> society here on earth. Puritan child-rearing practices were manifest
> exercises in conditioning of mind and behaviour, to fulfil the
> mandate of the book of Proverbs to "train up a child in the way he
> should walk, and when he is old, he will not depart therefrom".

There has always been a succession of utopian visions within the religious
movements of America. These have been experiments in how to religiously
programme a society. This notion is exemplified by the Mennonites, Amish
and the Shakers. Indeed, Skinner himself in the last few pages of the final
volume of his autobiography recorded[32]:

> ...I see that the point of [*Beyond Freedom and Dignity*] could be
> summarized as a scientific defense of the radical dissenting
> Protestantism of early 19th century England.

Novak goes so far as to imagine Skinner as a "latter-day Thomas Aquinas"
and, concerning the credit for Skinner's creative works, puts the following
words into his mouth[33]:

> It was not owing to anything in me; everything was a gift. Yes, I set hand
> to paper, but only through God's grace sweetly disposing all things... .

Novak continues:

> In a powerful way, the wisdom of the Benedictines – who have
> successfully been building and multiplying utopian communities
> since the sixth century – is a sort of Skinnerism in advance.

Skinner's advocacy of *natural* contingencies of reinforcement converges
with Christian morality and culture, with an emphasis upon the ethical
value of work. For example[34], he records an experience in an airport restaurant when two young people came in and were obviously so delighted
with each other's company that they were somewhat unaware of the rest
of the world:

> I felt very warm towards them. They had achieved a kind of
> happiness that seemed an end in itself.
>   Then it occurred to me that they were high. Had they smoked a bit
> of pot before coming in? Was it, after all, a synthetic happiness?

Suddenly they lost all their charm. Why? What is wrong with pot-induced happiness?

In this case I think I knew. I had admired their happiness as a sign that they had hit upon a satisfying way of life. If it was due to pot, I could infer nothing".

Another instance of the desirability of natural and earned rewards relates to gambling. Skinner[35] raises the question "Puritan?":

Am I being a nineteenth-century prude in objecting to gambling? After all, isn't a national lottery a good way to make dull lives interesting? ...In the contrived contingencies of a gambling enterprise, winning is not contingent on useful, let alone ultimately useful behaviour. Gambling is wrong not because it ruins some people or is tabooed by a church, but because it commits a person to repetitious, stultifying behaviour.

Skinner, religious principles and metaphysical issues

It is not difficult to see where Skinnerian and religious metaphysics clash. Skinner unambiguously denied any special nature of humankind that arises by virtue of a unique capacity for forming conscious intentions (e.g. in the present context, to try to act in the image of God, to have a relationship with God) and he argued against a purposive creation. Rather, in his eyes, we are the result of an accidental sequence of evolutionary steps accompanied by the vagaries of equally unplanned schedules of reinforcement. Actions are to be judged good or bad merely by their contribution to the survival of the species rather than by their conformity to any moral code that has its basis outside of humankind. In such terms, religious belief and practices should be viewed simply as the expression of a history of living within a particular religious culture[36]. Given this stance, it remains a moot point as to quite how one is to interpret Skinner's[37] observation that the psychology course he taught at Harvard provided more students for the Divinity school than did any other taught course!

Religious belief usually entails the assumption of responsible choice in that, in a given situation, a person could have acted otherwise[38]. In such terms, freedom of choice, i.e. that a person can be the ultimate source of action, is seen as being of the essence of the human condition – a God-given attribute.

Furthermore, those of religious faith believe that the notions of intentionality, free choice, personally-felt guilt and remorse, accompanied by responsibility for wrongdoing, are essential to the formation of a morally good person. Taking this line of logic to its conclusion, the theologically-inclined might believe that the human soul will one day be judged for its earthly sins by a creator. In such terms, the defence plea of a history of maladaptive reinforcement might carry little or no weight. In this case, one is likely to reject much of Skinner's metaphysical message. As Harcum[39] argues:

We need a conception of free will in order to develop a social conscience and to promote social justice.

This is a point of fundamental divergence from Skinner's position.

To religious thinkers, it is by the realization and acknowledgement of sin, accompanied by the request for forgiveness, that we are drawn closer to God. Indeed, some theologians would argue that the existence of freedom is so fundamental to the human condition that we must pay the enormous price of the possibility that evil can arise. To have created humankind without this possibility would have amounted to the creation of robots[40].

The Christian perspective on sin involves the holistic notion of an agent, a *person* who is the sinner[41]. To gain forgiveness, this whole person must become consciously aware of the sin and seek forgiveness for it. This stands in stark contrast to the Skinnerian notion that it is sufficient for an 'outside-agent' to extinguish maladaptive ('sinful') *behaviour* by means of, say, the omission of the associated reinforcement.

A theologian might argue that a culture that tries to write the psychological states of remorse and guilt out of the script as being undesirable would be likely to have undesired and unforeseen consequences. Some secular thinkers might well agree. One could suggest that a fundamental psychological process of asking for forgiveness and pardoning from the offended party has value to society[42]. Triggering of the emotion of guilt tends to be followed by the performance of altruistic acts[43], possibly as a means of lowering the guilt. Indeed, a theologian might argue that lowering guilt is an effective negative reinforcer for the behaviour of seeking forgiveness. Suppose that people have the good fortune to be born in a Skinnerian utopia. From a Christian theological perspective, people are saddled with a dose of original sin 'encoded in the genes', so at least one person is surely bound to transgress sooner or later.

Attitude of religious people to Skinner

It is indeed the case that religious people often take strong exception to Skinner and would normally reject Skinnerian metaphysics. However, it might surprise you that some theologians have actually voiced approval of Skinner[44]. There are a number of reasons for this. First, many people of religious faith are explicitly pro-science; they welcome careful scientific observation and discovery as a revelation of truth and suggest that faith has nothing to fear from science[45]. Therefore, they are happy to accept the principles of behaviourism in so far as they describe scientifically-based observations on the lawfulness of nature, while rejecting its more metaphysical extrapolations.

Secondly, all great religions teach responsibility for how we treat our fellow humans and Skinnerian behaviourism is also very strong on this. Skinner and religions converge on the imperative of helping the poor, alienated and needy, while rejecting the excesses of materialism. The Skinnerian message of social reform has met with approval in certain theological quarters. In line with theological teaching across faiths, Skinner emphasized the importance of community and the interdependence of humans, while rejecting rugged individualism. The message from religion and Skinner is clear: live a simple life in harmony with one's fellow humans and avoid conflict. Skinner preached the message of the need to be good custodians of the environment (Chapter 12), which surely must ring true in theological quarters.

Clement[46] sees theology and behavioural psychology as orthogonal and, thereby, they are potentially able to coexist peacefully:

> Defining observable behaviour and environmental events as the data of an empirical/experimental psychology helped to make a science of human behaviour possible, but creation of a science of human behaviour did not speak to the meaning of life.
>
> Unfortunately, many persons who actively used a spiritual perspective to interpret part of their observations rejected behavioural methods in the process of rejecting the philosophical premises of the developers of those methods. The misperception that behavioural methodology and spiritual concepts are incompatible has led to

underutilization of behavioural psychology by religious persons and institutions.

When we consider the issue of wrong-doing from the point of view of the *transgressed*, a dimension of possible reconciliation between Skinnerian and religious ethics is evident. Forgiveness appears to be a form of altruism[47] and, as such, could be reinforcing and bring health benefits to the forgiver. Some feel that it is easier to forgive if the action of the transgressor is seen as the result of genes and events in his or her environmental history, as opposed to the product of free choice[48]. Suppose that the transgressor is thought to have a particularly heavy load of past or currently-present external determining factors that override any efforts of the semi-autonomous will to act better. This might similarly make forgiveness easier.

Skinner might be thought to be saying in his own idiosyncratic terms "hate the sin but love the sinner". To show tolerance and understanding in the face of hurt and injustice to oneself surely demands the patience of Job. A desire for retribution, which Skinner abhors, is similarly a cardinal failing from a Christian perspective. Indeed, forgiveness for past injustice as a part of an understanding of how the injustice might have arisen can be a powerful tool in therapy[49]. The Skinnerian supporter, John Platt goes so far as to see some of Skinner's message as a[50]:

...formulation of the principle of Jesus: Love your enemies, and do good to those who despitefully use you. It is the fastest and surest way of changing or converting the behaviour of enemies or masters, far more effective than hostility, which only reinforces their old behaviour.

In a reconciliatory spirit, the eminent neuroscientist and Christian theologian, Donald MacKay[51], draws a distinction between what he terms 'positive behaviourism' and 'negative behaviourism'. By 'positive behaviourism', he means simply the assertion that it is possible to define certain relationships between events in the environment and subsequent changes in behaviour. In these terms, MacKay argues, positive behaviourism is concerned only with documenting empirical observations and is thereby theologically neutral. Indeed, MacKay hopes that such observations might yield further revelations on human nature and presents some logic that is deeply insightful from a Skinnerian perspective[52]:

> Behavioural shaping is what we are doing to one another, willy nilly, all the time. The only choice is between doing it knowingly and doing it unknowingly. Because our nervous system is to some extent 'plastic', especially in early life, such mutual shaping is actually a necessity if we are to develop and maintain a normal healthy human personality.

MacKay notes that it would be a neglect of ethics to ignore the powerful role of social input in the formation of the developing nervous system of a young child. In the absence of appropriate shaping, the child would be expected to grow up deficient in the capacity to communicate. He argues that it would be an absence of compassion to deny the child this input. MacKay notes the paradox that, so long as we do such shaping unintentionally and in the absence of a scientific rationale, we tend to feel comfortable about it. Mention of a scientific rationale tends to make people critical of their role in shaping and hence they tend to deliberately avoid exerting such influence. Though noting that behavioural control can go too far, he argues that it is a mistake to deny the fundamental role of shaping and to try to avoid it.

From a Christian perspective, MacKay goes on to consider the ethics of Skinnerian behaviourism in so far as changing the behaviour of others is concerned. He uses the example of a teacher setting out to shape the behaviour of young children. This is clearly a case of an asymmetrical power relationship. However, a creative leap of the imagination allows the teacher to conform to a criterion of answerability. The teacher needs to imagine when the children are adult and in a position to ask what was done to them. Placed in this imaginary time-warp, the teacher should welcome questions as to the rationale of the shaping process and its desired ends.

By contrast to these warm words, MacKay strongly disapproves of *negative* behaviourism, which is defined in terms of what behaviourism rejects. It is, to him, most decidedly not theologically neutral. MacKay takes exception to the rejection of the notions of freedom, personal responsibility and dignity. Indeed, he develops a sophisticated argument as to why a rigorous scientific study in the spirit of positive behaviourism, which allows the prediction of behaviour, does not rule out the validity of these notions.

From a delightful anecdote recalled by Skinner's colleague, Robert Epstein[53], we know that at least one rabbi was favourably disposed to Skinnerian psychology. Epstein, who was well-versed in Jewish culture and faith, had taken his child for the ceremony of circumcision, at which Skinner was present. Alas, when it got to the surgical act itself, Skinner fainted and had to be seated on a sofa to recover. In a heavy Yiddish accent, the Rabbi then surprised everyone by explaining how the parents were advised to raise the child "in programmed steps using positive reinforcement". According to Epstein's account, Skinner, still weak but sufficiently conscious to nod in agreement, was "undoubtedly thinking he has died and gone to Heaven". The Rabbi had read Skinner's work while at rabbinical college and had meant to use programmed instruction to teach the Talmud but had somehow not found the time to do so. On asking who the elderly man was and assuming that he was the child's grandfather, the Rabbi was shocked to discover that it was none other than Skinner himself.

In 1954, Skinner participated in a conference entitled 'Religion in the age of Science', which brought together scientists and theologians. Skinner emphasized the power of rewards over punishments. The report noted that in response to this, some participants[54]:

"...felt that this implied psychological substantiation for the religious insistence on tolerance and love in dealing with other men rather than the aversive methods of punishment or war".

On the negative side, a number of participants found the argument:

That human life should be completely bound up in a chain of mechanical cause-and-effect...

...to be abhorrent. However, a complication emerged here, in which even Skinnerian metaphysics appeared not necessarily to clash with all theology. The conference report continued:

Skinner, when questioned about free will, referred to the doctrines of John Calvin – with the implication that a strict determinism was neither new nor antagonistic to a vital religious doctrine.

The kind of ethical issues raised in this chapter are clearly of relevance to the way in which we treat and maltreat our environment, a topic of great concern to Skinner and one that is examined in the next chapter.

12 The Environment and a Sustainable Future

As previous chapters have noted, the environment was at centre-stage of Skinner's perspective. This was both in the sense of the ('micro') environment as the immediate source of reinforcement and that of the ('macro') environment that might be designed optimally to maximize human satisfaction and survival chances. These senses are interdependent and the present chapter is devoted to considering this, with an emphasis upon the environment in the 'macro sense'.

What has gone wrong?

Winter and Koger point out that it is intrinsic to a Skinnerian behaviourist approach that there is reciprocity between people and their environment[1]:

> Much of our present difficulty stems from our having considered ourselves separate from, or even above, our natural environment. Instead our actions are both a product and a cause of the environment in which we behave.

Similarly, Schultz suggests that, in a technological society, humans have become alienated from the natural environment of their evolution[2]. For many, almost all of their lives are now spent enclosed within a built environment. Cars and aircraft exemplify such alienation. It appears that, for a person to be concerned about global issues, they need to experience an emotional connectedness with other living beings[3].

Oskamp[4] raises the issue of how things have gone so badly wrong:

> Was it a flaw in evolved human nature, which can only be remedied through eons of natural selection processes? Or is it due to patterns of learned human behaviour, which can be modified by systematic

application of principles of learning and attitude and behaviour change?*

Of course, if we focus on the first possibility, the prospects are depressing indeed, since we simply don't have eons of time available to evolve into something less sensitive to immediate and environmentally-damaging material rewards. We are inevitably stuck with the evolved human 'designs' that we see around us today.

An answer to the question of the possible "flaw" that Oskamp identifies is that we are living now in an environment very different from that in which we evolved. In Skinnerian terms, reward-based processes that delivered adaptive behaviour in our early environment are now triggering maladaptive patterns. Rule-governing processes are simply not up to the job of restraining the reward-processes in adaptive ways. We are being asked to bring present behaviour, with its inherent reinforcement for gross overconsumption, under the control of a distant and remote contingency. This is of the form that actions taken now might be followed by destruction of all life on earth, of course, this being the first such experience of the contingency in the history of life on earth. A Skinnerian perspective allows the problem to be seen in its starkest terms[5].

The tragedy of the commons

The problem that the world confronts is described by the term 'tragedy of the commons'[6] and it lends itself well to Skinnerian analysis. The expression 'commons' refers to the common land available to people of a parish on which they could allow their cattle to graze. Suppose that there are 20 families in the parish and each has one cow. The land available will support just 20 cows and no more. Now suppose that one parishioner decides to invest in an extra cow so that 21 are now grazing the land. There is insufficient food for this number and so the cows suffer slightly, as do the parishioners, except the one who has two cows. He has a net advantage relative to everyone else and hence can better feed his family with milk. The tragedy is that both evolution and reinforcement might seem to conspire to undermine the collective good of those using the commons[7].

---

*Readers who think in Darwinian terms might see the notion of a 'flaw' as implying a purposive ('design') element in evolution. Without us needing to get involved in such considerations, suffice it to note that Oskamp raises an interesting issue.

Evolution would presumably favour strategies for maximizing nutrient yield, which, on an individual basis, might form a powerful source of positive reinforcement (though see Chapter 11 for a complication and glimmer of hope here).

Social traps

The expression 'trap' conveys the meaning that people tend to get trapped in courses of action that are, in the long term, unpleasant or even lethal, with there being no obvious escape route. We first met one-person traps in the discussion of addictions in Chapter 3 and we now extend this to traps that involve the individual and society at large: the 'social trap'[8]. The short-term advantage of the course of action to the individual keeps behaviour going, even though it is to the collective disadvantage. In each social trap the positive reinforcement is both rapid and acts at an individual level, whereas the punishing consequence is long-term and collective.

Consider the example of the decline of railways, while each individual switches to using a private car. The comfort of the car is immediate and personal, whereas, to many people, the discomfort of the loss of a railway is only long-term and collective. As the railways decline, still more people switch to cars with the net effect of closing the railway and creating traffic gridlock on the roads. The punishing effects of public transport are usually up-front in the form of fares, whereas those of motoring are often more delayed, e.g. yearly maintenance costs, insurance etc.[9]. Conversely, the rewards for using public transport, such as taking more exercise, tend to be remote, as compared with the immediate comfort of the private car. Ideally, costs should reflect long-term real costs to the environment, in which case cars would become very expensive indeed as compared to public transport[10]. Cheap flights would become a thing of the past whereas trains and metro systems would suddenly become very cheap, if not free of charge.

A Skinnerian analysis is relevant here because behaviour tends to be more strongly influenced by immediate ('positively reinforcing') consequences than by long-term ('punishing') consequences. It is more useful to explain such phenomena in terms of maladaptive reinforcement that emerges in groups rather than as 'collective irresponsibility' or 'social evil'[11]. The former suggests solutions that can be tried.

Another form of social trap that Platt[12] describes can be termed the problem of the 'missing hero'. The scene is played out on a Sunday evening in summer as cars are streaming back from Cape Cod. A mattress falls from a station wagon into one lane of the road. All of the traffic in one direction is delayed as each car in turn slowly negotiates its way round the mattress, avoiding cars coming in the opposite direction. Platt asks "Now who moves the mattress?" and apparently the answer is that most often no one does. People way back in the queue do not know what the problem is but, when they are near enough to see it, they don't leave their cars but just drive on, avoiding still further delay and possible injury to themselves. Occasionally, in such a situation, a hero emerges to push the mattress to the side of the road. Platt reports a conversation with an Englishman, who claimed that the mattress problem is a peculiarly American one, since all it would have taken to solve it is for one Englishman (or Englishwoman?!) to have been stuck in the queue. This was on the grounds that the English are trained to assume leadership. The present author, duly flattered, will none-the-less pass by this observation without further comment! It might also have been solved, according to Platt, for there to have been one Mormon in the queue (presumably of any nationality), since this group is also trained to be moved to self-sacrifice by the collective good. Platt[13] concludes:

> We need continuing positive reinforcers for brave and intelligent initiative to help keep up our "character" in cases of this kind...

Research effort needs to focus on how to get a reversal of reinforcers, so that ecologically desirable actions are immediately reinforced at an individual level. Conversely, ecologically unsound actions need to have immediate punishing effects. In addition, superordinate authorities are needed to allocate scarce resources such as petrol and to lower speed limits.

Politicians get caught in social traps[14]. In democratic societies, they need to get re-elected every four to five years or so and therefore tend to appeal to short-term feel-good factors for voters (e.g. tax cuts) even at the expense of long-term ecological harm (e.g. by not introducing green taxes).

The problem of consumerism

Some basic behavioural controls are being triggered into activity in ways that are incompatible with long-term survival. Amongst other factors, commercial messages make us dissatisfied with our current lot in life and urge us to resolve this by consuming more[15]. Some messages work by means of Pavlovian associations: for example, a particular scent or car might be associated with a beautiful and sexy person. Estimates suggest that, as a daily average, each citizen of the U.S.A. is exposed to some 3,000 commercial advertisements[16]. As a conservative estimate, this amounts to some 50 minutes of exposure each day to a message "equating happiness with consumption". Much advertising appears to work by means of negative reinforcement: it persuades people to make purchases that will give only a temporary lift to their negative emotional state. Consider the statement by Nancy Shalek, the president of the Shalek agency:[17]

> Advertising at its best is making people feel that without their product, you're a loser. Kids are very sensitive to that...You open up emotional vulnerabilities, and it's very easy to do with kids because they're the most emotionally vulnerable.

Skinner[18] speculates on what a waste-free society would be like:

> It would be a world in which people produced the goods they needed, not because of contingencies arranged by a business or industry but simply because they were "goods" and hence directly reinforcing.

This is problematic. Surely anything that sells must be reinforcing in some sense to those people who are prepared to pay money to obtain it. What Skinner appears to be implying is that so many things that are reinforcing to purchase are of no long-term benefit. Rather, advertising simply persuades people to buy particular products and hence helps to establish their reinforcement potential.

Kasser presents evidence that concern for the environment is incompatible with, and is undermined by, materialistic concerns[19]. Individuals who pursue materialist goals generally tend to have little concern for the environment. Furthermore, materialism is bad for one's happiness and health.

Although the terms used by Kasser are very different from those of Skinnerian behaviourism, the conclusions drawn are remarkably similar. This is particularly so when it comes to diagnosing the ills of a materialist society and the over-exploitation of resources. Both perspectives urge the abandonment of materialist goals and the finding of happiness in simple pursuits that are intrinsically rewarding, such as outdoor nature-related activities.

Both Skinner and Kasser see the futility of the pursuit of material goods in terms of its abject failure to deliver individual human satisfaction and its disastrous ecological effects. Indeed, Kasser[20] argues in terms that could have come straight from Skinner:

> What is required is that people pursue activities for what the activities themselves have to offer, not for rewards or praise.

Kasser reviews evidence on the merely transient satisfactions of materialism, e.g. people feel persuaded to purchase goods since the purchase tends to trigger a very brief reduction in self-doubt and a boost to self-esteem. Alas, the nervous system tends to link the purchase with these transient positive effects rather than with the long-term failure of the purchase to produce any durable sense of well-being. This links to the work of Kent Berridge on the possible dissociation between wanting and liking (Chapter 5).

Towards sustainability: the broad context

The physical environment has an effect on behaviour, sometimes, it would appear, acting at an unconscious level[21]. An environment can have important effects on well-being and thereby social harmony. Alas, the environment is most often in the news these days in terms of its destruction.

If humans live in a way involving symbiosis with nature and emotional attachment to it, they are likely to want to protect nature. Emotional affinity with nature arises from *experience* in nature, e.g. observing animals in their natural environment[22]. The following argument would surely have met with Skinner's approval, in its urging that people be helped to move away from[23]:

> ...modern madness, characterized by pressure-filled occupations, dehumanized urban centres, and lack of contact with nature...

and they should be helped to:

> ...move *toward* a way of life that focuses on connections between past and future generations, as well as feelings of connection with all of life...

There is very nearly universal acceptance that, if life on earth has a chance of survival, we must change drastically our ways of living. The changes might need to be as profound as those of the agricultural and industrial revolutions[24]. For survival, we must act now for a future of *sustainability*, rather than one in which we continue to plunder the earth's resources. This is perhaps the most serious challenge that humankind has ever faced and radical action is long overdue. Clearly, the challenge is in part a technological one but, perhaps even more fundamentally, it is a *behavioural* one.

Acting in an environmentally friendly way and in the interests of others would appear to be an instance of the broader class of altruistic ('other directed') behaviour[25]. Indeed, there is a correlation between sympathy for others ('actively caring') and environmental concern[26]. A feeling of personal control was also found to be correlated with environmental concern. In developing these ideas, Geller attempts to integrate aspects of Skinnerian behaviourism (e.g. reinforcement of environmentally-friendly behaviour) with motivational concepts arising from within humanistic psychology (e.g. self-transcendence in helping others).

How can we change direction?

How do we change the behaviour of humans in ways that are compatible with sustainability and thereby survival? How do we limit the growth in the world's population[27]?

A range of perspectives

The issue of the conservation of energy brings into the picture the range of the controls of behaviour that have been introduced in earlier chapters. The case to be advanced in this chapter is that we need to exploit every available insight (For an excellent book that looks at what psychology can contribute, see Winter and Koger[28]). It will be suggested that the processes described by Skinner need to be seen as embedded within other processes. Once we do that, it becomes somewhat clearer as to how we might use psychology to help to rescue the dire situation. Bandura[29] emphasizes learning that takes one of two forms: (i) direct experience of rewarding or punishing consequences of actions and (ii) other people in the role of social models. A social learning perspective would urge behavioural modelling by influential people, e.g. city mayors and government representatives taking up cycling and bus use[30]. Television soaps can be exploited to promote ecological messages, e.g. to limit family size. Actors ('models') can be used to demonstrate rewarding and punishing consequences of behaviour[31].

The importance of the notion of a prior commitment to conservation is sometimes emphasized, e.g. buying a yearly season ticket for using public transport[32], though how this first commitment arises remains somewhat open to speculation.

Avoiding false leads

In a collection of readings largely dedicated to Skinner and with frequent references to the environment, Chance[33] perceptively observes:

> As a society, we try to change behaviour more or less as the Romans did 2,000 years ago: We threaten, we instruct, and we implore. We warn people not to waste gasoline. We teach them about safe sex. And we implore them to "say no to drugs".

The author argues that these are relatively weak ways of changing behaviour. Rather, we need to employ a scientific understanding. We are still dealing with our problems by producing messages of the kind "Give a hoot. Don't pollute".

Nevin[34] notes the frequently-expressed argument that, in order to secure the future of the environment, people need to:

> ...achieve a new holistic vision of themselves as part of the natural world rather than as its exploiters.

Such visions might indeed play some role but reality suggests the more viable way forward of small piece-meal changes, which in sum-total could represent a holistic vision. It might be an error to see the holistic vision as a precondition, part of the causal sequence leading to a better environment.

Simply providing people with information (e.g. campaigns on how to save energy) has a limited effect on their behaviour, as compared to social modelling[35]. In keeping with a Skinnerian perspective, changing people's *attitudes* towards conservation and environmental protection correlates poorly with changes in the corresponding *behaviour*[36]. People are being asked to make a change now, based on what will happen apparently very far into the future[37]. Alas, Katzev and Johnson note that what they call "cognitive strategies" dominate the scene[38]. In spite of the evidence, vast sums of money are spent in trying to change attitudes as a prerequisite to changing behaviour[39]. Behaviourists argue that behaviour needs to be targeted rather than suggested internal causes of behaviour and this is true in the present context[40].

The application of Skinnerian principles

Basic points

Combating environmental degradation would seem to be pre-eminently a challenge for which Skinnerian principles are highly applicable. Not only was Skinner concerned with how to change behaviour but he was particularly engaged with the issue of designing a viable culture in which sustainability was at centre-stage. Indeed, as we have seen already, he was amazingly prescient in his arguments on this issue, being one of the world's first 'greens'. *Walden Two* exemplified a culture that had survival value, as measured by criteria of ecological viability[41].

A change in the *immediate consequences* of behaviour, e.g. to attain frequent rewards for environmentally-sustainable behaviour, is needed[42]. The reinforcers that are maintaining current unsustainable practices need to be removed, while devising reinforcers for ecologically-valid behaviour[43]. Some green initiatives fit rather obviously to behavioural principles, e.g. a deposit system on bottles, which thereby helps to reinforce recycling behaviour[44].

In keeping with the 'small is beautiful' message of *Walden Two*, local initiatives on energy conservation can be particularly effective[45]. This strategy can be summed up by 'Think globally, act locally'. The efficacy of interpersonal factors, such as behaviour modelling, might be greatest at this level. At first, small local goals concerning conservation can be introduced, goals that have a good chance of being reached can be set[46], feedback given and goal achievement can be celebrated locally[47]. Large and apparently overwhelming tasks can be broken down into manageable chunks. In undertaking local initiatives, people can cooperate with others whom they already know. Feelings of self-efficacy and empowerment arise in such a context[48].

Feedback on actions can sometimes be very useful in achieving conservation[49]. There is potential in the techniques of 'self-monitoring' and 'self-control' in producing energy conservation[50]. For example, people can be taught to monitor their behaviour and to reward themselves for energy-conservation in the way of treats. It hardly needs saying that the treat itself ('self reinforcement') should be ecologically-viable! Self-statements can be modified and people can be taught to bring the long-term negative consequences of energy waste to conscious awareness and behavioural decision-making.

It appears that external rewards and aversive stimuli have various effects on behaviour, some of which can be characterized in the basic terms of reinforcement and punishment. However, in addition, there are cognitive factors that might appear anomalous in terms of behavioural principles but which also need consideration[51]. One is that introducing an external reward can undermine the rewarded activity if the reward is later removed (though see Flora[52] for a critique of such ideas). Temporary external rewards for conservation, such as free rail tickets, might produce only a temporary shift to ecologically better behaviour. Behaviour might then revert once the external prop is removed. Sometimes, when rewards have been introduced and then removed, behaviour promptly returns to baseline following reward removal[53]. The period of reward might have been insufficient to allow natural rewards (e.g. improvements in the environment) to take over.

Link with Kasser's work

Entirely compatible with a Skinnerian approach, Kasser[54] suggests that we can carefully monitor our behaviour and moods. For example, observe whether so-called 'shopping therapy' really works in the long run or, as is highly likely, any lift of mood is only very transient. Ask yourself whether the pursuit of material goods is part of the *cause* of the problem, rather than its solution. Find other activities, which are not energy-consuming, are incompatible with the pursuit of wealth and will fill time previously spent in shopping malls. These include such things as socializing, helping the disadvantaged, cross-country trekking, jogging or visiting an art gallery. After introducing changes and allowing them about a month to take effect, review your level of satisfaction with life[55].

Carefully observe any relationship that you are in. Is the pursuit of material wealth having a long-term beneficial or harmful effect upon it? Are there joint pursuits that could better consolidate the relationship than does the pursuit of wealth? It is necessary to consider the next generation of high spenders and how they are being taught the values of materialism. If you have children, it could be worthwhile to try to undermine some of the more toxic influences of materialism to which they will doubtless have daily exposure (see Kasser[56] for advice). The evidence suggests that if children are not brought up in a climate that fosters self-worth, they are more likely to seek their worth in life from acquiring material possessions[57].

Positive rather than negative controls

As a general principle in keeping with Skinnerian philosophy, environmental interventions that involve positive actions are more desirable than those involving punishment of undesirable action[58]. In one of his last published works, which appeared after his death, Skinner wrote on the subject of organizations that are dedicated to the prevention of war and environmental destruction[59]:

> ...the principal modus operandi of these organizations is to frighten people rather than to offer them a world to which they will turn because of the reinforcing consequences of doing so.

Geller[60] emphasizes the value of positive reinforcement for ecologically-sound actions:

> ...when positive recognition is delivered correctly, it does more than increase the frequency of the behaviour it follows. It also increases the likelihood that other desirable behaviours will occur and that positive recognition will be used more often to benefit both behaviour and attitude.

This exemplifies the point made in Chapter 3 that positive reinforcers have a wider range of effects than simply to increase the future probability of the responses that immediately preceded them. Positively reinforced actions allow for the perception of personal freedom. Punishment of undesirable actions can be associated with the arousal of general negative emotion, such that compliance with desired behaviour might only be shown when the punishing agent is perceived to be present. Also there might be only a very limited generalization of restraint from the punished behaviour to other forms of undesirable behaviour. Alas, in practice, greater weight has been placed on telling people what not to do rather than what to do, yet research indicates that polite urges suggesting what people *can do* are more effective. Indeed, telling someone what not to do can trigger a counter-reaction of non-compliance[61].

A highly catastrophic presentation of the global crisis could be ineffective at best or even counter-productive in trying to meet the goal of causing people to change behaviour[62]. Fear appears not to be a good motivator of positive action in this situation. It tends to increase statements of commitment to change without actual behavioural change. This would probably not have surprised Skinner in the least. A strong threat of punishment for engaging in an activity can actually have less effect than a mild threat.

As the chapter has shown, a Skinnerian analysis not only allows us to understand much better how we got to the present situation but it also suggests viable solutions. This completes the specialist topics. It is now time to bring things together.

13 Conclusions

When looking back to the preceding twelve chapters, some general conclusions on the influence of Skinner can be suggested, as follows.

- The principle of reinforcement might well have been known to circus-trainers for centuries but Skinner put it on a scientific footing and articulated its parameters, more than any other investigator.
- Skinner's writing leads us to examine the possibility that subtle reinforcement might be hidden within a given instance of person-environment interaction.
- The control exerted by partial reinforcement schedules was demonstrated by Skinner.
- The disadvantages of punitive controls were clearly articulated.
- Skinner urged us to study behaviour itself and to have a healthy scepticism towards theories. The latter might lead us astray, as in the implicit assumption that seemingly aversive interventions just have to produce desirable ends.
- The use of Skinnerian methods in such areas as clinical psychology and education has been considerable but the future potential is much greater still.
- The Skinner box was an invention of enormous importance to psychology.
- The teaching machine and its modern variant, the personal computer as a teaching device, have proven extremely valuable to many students and teachers.
- Time-out from positive reinforcement is a humane intervention advanced by Skinner.
- Skinner presented a utopian vision of how we might build an ecologically-viable society and hence has given us an intellectual framework for bringing psychology to the issue of climate change.

The principle of reinforcement

The principle of reinforcement, as described by Skinner, is alive and well, in much the same way as are the principles of gravity and of evolution by natural selection. Skinner carefully observed and documented this fundamental property of the living world. We ignore this at our peril. Knowledge of the principle of reinforcement can help us greatly to understand our own behaviour and that of others. Those making decisions that affect others, e.g. managers, teachers and law-enforcement agencies, can benefit by greater insights into this principle and its application. Skinner articulated how reinforcement-governed behaviour and rule-governed behaviour can, in combination, account for a great deal of human behaviour. However, the argument of the present book is that the principle of reinforcement can be best understood when it is examined in the context of a range of additional processes that also play a role in the control of behaviour.

Revisiting the possible compromise

Suppose that we accept the centrality of the principles *affirmed* by Skinner. We might thereby choose to 'buy the whole package' and reject that which was centrally *rejected* by Skinner, e.g. the value of studying cognition and consciousness. However, we might alternatively follow the compromise position developed through Chapters 1–12:

- There are processes underlying the control of behaviour *in addition* to those articulated by Skinner and they have a cognitive flavour (e.g. goal-seeking and thereby producing novel behaviours).
- There are alternative ways of describing/explaining behaviour, e.g. lever-pressing in a Skinner box. A Skinnerian account in terms of reinforcement might be compatible with an account in terms of cognition. That is to say, taking an 'outside perspective', the term 'reinforcement' can be used to describe a procedure that changes behaviour. From an 'inside perspective', reinforcement can (i) strengthen some direct controls and (ii) form cognitions of the kind that a particular action by the animal leads to a particular consequence. Whether one favours the Skinnerian or cognitive account can depend upon the purpose of the study.

- Some therapists exemplify the benefits of an approach that takes features of both Skinnerian and cognitive perspectives.
- Humans might gain conscious insight into reinforcement conditions and act in idiosyncratic ways as a result. This suggests a hierarchy of controls that jointly determines behaviour.

Beyond freedom and dignity?

The discussion of Skinner in the preceding chapters inevitably means confronting a series of nested paradoxes that are at the core of the study of human behaviour and consciousness:

- Is our behaviour determined or not?
- Does the notion of free will have any value?
- Why do people *want* to believe either that we have free will or that we are determined?
- Does it make any difference what we believe on the issue of free will?

The issue of free will and determinism might end up in a compromise position, in which humans are seen as having some degree of autonomy but also a strong deterministic feature in their make-up. The position that we adopt might need to reflect pragmatic considerations as much as anything else. Whether, it makes any difference what people believe on this issue would seem to be a question open to experimental investigation. Limited experimental evidence suggests that what one believes does indeed appear to make a difference to behaviour.

The argument that behaviour is deterministically controlled by genetic and environmental factors is profoundly shocking to many people, who see it as undermining any meaning of life[1]. The suggestion seems to be quite counter to common sense and the evidence of our own experience. Even if the argument is correct, it is a difficult philosophy by which to live one's life by day-to-day. Harcum[2] articulates the fear and resentment that Skinner's rejection of freedom and dignity triggers in some. He suggests that, in trying to 'sell' his message, Skinner miscalculates the effects that such ideas are likely to have in that people want to believe that they have free will and agency. Their self-worth is tied up in such notions:

> Pity the poor salesman who begins his sales pitch by insulting his intended customer with a blow to the self-esteem.

It remains a daunting challenge to develop a philosophy that is true to the evidence and yet is not too bitter a pill to swallow. We might simply have to live with the dilemma of free will and determinism, taking a pragmatic stance towards it.

Friends and critics of Skinner

Certain critics have been unfair to Skinner. Some of them still associate his approach with the centrality of the stimulus-response connection[3], even though Skinner distanced himself from this explanatory device early in his career. A number of otherwise well-informed psychologists persist in giving Skinner the 'stimulus-response' label[4]. Skinner advanced the idea that operant behaviour increases in frequency as a result of its *consequences*, not that it is triggered automatically by particular stimuli.

Skinner was quite unfairly accused of promoting methods of punishment, when in reality his whole approach was involved with designing a culture that shunned this tool. For example, one grant application was turned down with the dismissive comment[5]:

> "We don't want him putting babies in boxes and shocking them.

Some eminent psychologists[6] acknowledge that Skinner made profound discoveries but add that he suffered from the failings of parochialism. Skinnerian fundamentalists could be accused of setting up a cult and thereby cutting themselves off from the rest of psychology. However, some psychologists coming from a Skinnerian angle have been prepared to offer the hand of friendship and integration to psychologists of other persuasions, e.g. humanistic psychology[7] (Chapter 12 of the present book).

Critics regret Skinner's refusal to compromise and his reluctance to see that anything useful could be gained by building bridges between his perspective and those of others. For example, biological psychologists might offer some useful insights into the bases of reinforcement.

One is led to entertain the paradoxical notion that Skinner could himself have been a considerably better Skinnerian. That is to say, Skinner failed to shape the behaviour of his fellow psychologists by reinforcing their moves in a direction of compromise. A close observation of the behaviour of these psychologists over the years might have revealed that the harshness and rejecting tone of the Skinnerian message was punishing to the good behaviour of those that it needed to positively reinforce.

Success and failure

Behaviour analysts working in a Skinnerian tradition can claim some very significant successes[8]. For example, parents can be taught how to deal with head-banging in autistic children. Therapists have been helped to lower the frequency of hallucinations in schizophrenic patients. Severely retarded people have been helped to dress themselves. Chance[9] writes:

> They have, in other words, persuaded a select population to use a narrow range of behavioural techniques to help them cope with a few carefully defined behavioural problems. But they have seldom attempted to persuade policymakers or the public at large that the functional approach can help solve society's great problems. It is ironic that those who know so much about how to modify behaviour have done so little to modify the public's views of their work...

Chance goes on to suggest that the behaviour analysts need to employ the tools of their trade to advance a better understanding of the principles of behaviour analysis. The public perception needs to be altered. It is somewhat ironical that, even though Skinner's book *Beyond Freedom and Dignity* topped the best-seller charts, its message seems to have been taken to heart by relatively few people. So, a principal challenge for 21th century admirers of Skinner is to bring the techniques of behaviourism into much greater public awareness and acceptance. Amongst others, politicians, teachers, industrialists, ecologists and planners need to be familiar with what a Skinnerian approach has to offer.

Skinner, the man

John Mills[10] applies to Skinner the expression first coined by Winston Churchill: "he was a riddle wrapped in a mystery inside an enigma". To Baars[11], the enigma consisted in Skinner's "double life". On the one hand, Skinner was a man of great erudition with a wide appreciation of the arts, literature and music. One can only speculate that there existed a rich subjective world of conscious experience. On the other hand, Skinner denied that a science of psychology should concern itself very much with such subjective worlds.

The second volume of Skinner's autobiography was entitled *The Shaping of a Behaviorist*. So, in summary, what might have been the crucial factors that shaped him into America's best-known scientist? Skinner himself played down any element of planning in his life's events, emphasizing chance and good luck, as in the example of when he made an important discovery simply as a result of running out of food pellets. Yet, paradoxically, the society that he came to advocate was based on a technology of behavioural planning, even down to its tiniest details. Similarly, to some observers, Skinner's own life seems to be imbued with purpose, the ultimate one, the distant objective, being that of saving the world by means of a science of psychology equipped with operant conditioning[12]. To meet this end, it was necessary to achieve sub-goals such as the completion of his books and their successful promotion.

Early experience of making gadgets put him in a good position to invent laboratory equipment, as in the Skinner box itself. Happening upon the works of Bertrand Russell and John Watson must have exerted a decisive role.

Growing up in a Puritan culture dominated by the Protestant work ethic had a massive shaping role. Skinner had a life-long ambivalence and ambiguity about his background. Occasionally, in so-called 'high society', he was embarrassed by his parents. Surely an important factor in the abhorrence of aversive control was the early experience of punishment and negative reinforcement. The young Fred was required to act so as to avoid both eternal damnation and the disapproval expressed by "What will people think?" However, reflecting the two cultures between which Skinner moved uncomfortably, the relative safety and ecological viability of life in

Susquehanna doubtless helped to inspire *Walden Two*. Although turning his back on the religion of previous generations of Skinners, it was precisely this element which provided so much of the glue holding together society. Indeed, on the hero of the story of *Walden Two*, Skinner wrote[13]:

> It seems to me that Frazier represents the confluence of a Judeo-Christian or protestant Ethic culture and Western science reaching at last human behavior.

In Skinner's writings, Mills[14] detects a distrust of emotions. The utopian society of *Walden Two* could be engineered to avoid the excesses of emotion, particularly those of a negative kind. This needs to be viewed in the context of Skinner's own powerfully-expressed emotional reactions, as detailed in Chapter 2 of the present book. Might this distrust be a reaction to his own excessive psychological pain?

In his excellent biography, Daniel Bjork attributes some significance to the trauma of young Fred witnessing first hand the death of both his brother and grandfather[15]. One moment there was a behaving organism and the next moment extinction – no behaviour – apparently nothing. Having rejected religion, might Skinner's coping strategy have been one of trying to promote a detached matter-of-fact attitude? Could this have instilled the idea "that there might be nothing more to an organism than its behavior"?

References and Notes

Chapter 1

1. Agnew, S. (1972) Agnew's blast at behaviourism: "A new kind of despotism…What arrogance! What contempt!" *Psychology Today*, pp.4, 84, 87.
2. Skinner, B.F. (1983) *A Matter of Consequences*. Alfred A. Knopf, New York, p.323.
3. See page 23 of Platt, J.R. (1973) The Skinnerian revolution. In *Beyond the Punitive Society – Operant Conditioning: Social and Political Aspects* (ed. H. Wheeler), Wildwood House, London, pp.22–56.
4. Kagan, J. (1974) Foreword. In Carpenter, F. *The Skinner Primer: Behind Freedom and Dignity*. The Free Press, New York.
5. Baum, W.M. (1994) *Understanding Behaviorism: Science, Behavior, and Culture*. HarperCollins, New York.
6. *Ibid.*
7. Nye, R.D. (1979) *What is B.F. Skinner Really Saying?* Prentice-Hall, Englewood Cliffs.
8. Flora, S.R. (2004) *The Power of Reinforcement*. State University of New York Press, Albany.
9. This is discussed in Robinson, T.E. and Berridge, K.C. (1993) The neural basis of drug craving: an incentive-sensitization theory of addiction. *Brain Research Reviews*, 18, 247–291.
10. Skinner, B.F. (1953) *Science and Human Behavior*. The Free Press, New York.
11. Flora, S.R. (2004) *op. cit.*
12. Nye, R.D. (1979) *op. cit.*
13. *Ibid.*
14. Jones, S.L. (1988) A religious critique of behavior therapy. In *Behavior Therapy and Religion: Integrating Spiritual and Behavioral Approaches to Change* (eds. W.R. Miller and J.E. Martin), Sage Publications, Newbury Park, pp.139–170.
15. Flora, S.R. (2004) *op. cit.*
16. *Ibid.*; Swinson, J. and Harrop, A. (2005) An examination of the effects of a short course aimed at enabling teachers in infant, junior and secondary schools to alter the verbal feedback given to their pupils. *Educational Studies*, 31, 115–129.
17. Harcum, E.R. (1994) *A Psychology of Freedom and Dignity: The Last Train to Survival*. Praeger Publishers, Westport, CT.
18. Skinner, B.F. (1983) *op. cit.*, p.121.
19. Skinner, B.F. (2005) *Walden Two*. Hackett Publishing Co., Indianapolis (this is the latest reprint of the original book).
20. See p.113 of Toynbee, A. (1973) Great expectations. In *Beyond the Punitive Society – Operant Conditioning: Social and Political Aspects* (ed. H. Wheeler), Wildwood House, London, pp.113–120.
21. Skinner, B.F. (2002) *Beyond Freedom and Dignity*. Hackett Publishing Co., Indianapolis (this is the latest reprint of the book).

22. See p.16 of Wheeler, H. (1973) Introduction: A nonpunitive world? In *Beyond the Punitive Society – Operant Conditioning: Social and Political Aspects* (ed. H. Wheeler), Wildwood House, London, pp.1–21.
23. Platt, J.R. (1973) *op. cit.*, p.34.
24. Richelle, M.N. (1993) *B.F. Skinner: A Reappraisal*. Lawrence Erlbaum Associates, Hove, p.ix.
25. Harcum E.R. (1994) *A Psychology of Freedom and Dignity: The Last Train to Survival*. Praeger Publishers, Westport, CT.
26. *Ibid.*
27. *Ibid.*

Chapter 2

1. Skinner, B.F. (1976) *Particulars of My Life*. Jonathan Cape, London.
2. Bjork, D.W. (2002) *B.F. Skinner: A Life*. American Psychological Association, Washington, p.14.
3. *Ibid.*, p.7.
4. Skinner, B.F. (1979) *The Shaping of a Behaviorist*. Alfred A. Knopf, New York, p.278.
5. *Ibid.*, p.296.
6. *Ibid.*, p.142.
7. Bjork, D.W. (2002) *op. cit.*, p.21.
8. Skinner, B.F. (1976) *op. cit.*, p.60.
9. *Ibid.*, p.198.
10. *Ibid.*, p.199.
11. *Ibid.*, p.223.
12. Skinner, B.F. (1983) *A Matter of Consequences*. Alfred A. Knopf, New York, p.313.
13. Skinner, B.F. (1979) *op. cit.*, p.137.
14. Skinner, B.F. (1976) *op. cit.*, p.221.
15. Bjork, D.W. (2002) *op. cit.*, p.116.
16. Skinner, B.F. (1979) *op. cit.*, p.70.
17. Skinner, B.F. (1953) *Science and Human Behavior*. The Free Press, New York.
18. Sagal, P.T. (1981) *Skinner's Philosophy*. University Press of America, Washington.
19. Baum, W.M. (1994) *Understanding Behaviorism: Science, Behavior, and Culture*. Harper-Collins, New York.
20. Carpenter, F. (1974) *The Skinner Primer: Behind Freedom and Dignity*. The Free Press, New York.
21. Bjork, D.W. (2002) *op. cit.*, p.113.
22. Skinner, B.F. (1979) *op. cit.*, p.80.
23. *Ibid.*, p.80.
24. *Ibid.*, p.80.
25. *Ibid.*, p.80.
26. *Ibid.*, p.95.
27. Skinner, B.F. (1953) *op. cit.*
28. Skinner, B.F. (1979) *op. cit.*, p.102.
29. Skinner, B.F. (1953) *op. cit.*
30. *Ibid.*
31. Skinner, B.F. (1979) *op. cit.*
32. *Ibid.*, p.334.
33. Skinner, B.F. (1983) *op. cit.*, p.284.
34. Skinner, B.F. (1953) *op. cit.*, p.319.

35. Vaughan, M. (1987) Rule-governed behavior and higher mental processes. In *B.F. Skinner: Consensus and Controversy* (eds. Modgil, S. and Modgil, C.). Falmer Press, New York, pp.257–264.
36. Skinner, B.F. (1979) *op. cit.*
37. *Ibid.*, p.287.
38. Nye, R.D. (1979) *What is B.F. Skinner Really Saying?* Prentice-Hall, Englewood Cliffs.
39. Skinner, B.F. (1979) *op. cit.*, p.292.
40. Matson, F.W. (1973) Humanistic theory: The third revolution in psychology. In *Without/Within: Behaviorism and Humanism* (ed. F.W. Matson), Brooks/Cole Publishing Company, Monterey, pp.11–22.
41. Skinner, B.F. (1979) *op. cit.*, p.296.
42. *Ibid.*, p.346.
43. Richelle, M.N. (1993) *B.F. Skinner: A Reappraisal*. Lawrence Erlbaum Associates, Hove.
44. Sagal, P.T. (1981) *op. cit.*, p.1.
45. Bjork, D.W. (2002) *op. cit.*
46. Bethlehem, D. (1987) Scolding the carpenter. In *B.F. Skinner: Consensus and Controversy* (eds. Modgil, S. and Modgil, C.). Falmer Press, New York, pp.89–97.
47. Bjork, D.W. (2002) *op. cit.*
48. *Ibid.*
49. Skinner, B.F. (1983) *op. cit.*, p.53.
50. *Ibid.*, p.56.
51. *Ibid.*, p.64.
52. *Ibid.*, p.297.
53. Bjork, D.W. (2002) *op. cit.*
54. Skinner, B.F. (1980) *Notebooks*. Prentice-Hall, Englewood Cliffs, p.66.
55. Skinner, B.F. (1983) *op. cit.*, p.150; For an account of Fromm, see Thomson, A. (2009) *Erich Fromm*. Palgrave Macmillan, Basingstoke.
56. Carpenter, F. (1974) *op. cit.*
57. Skinner, B.F. (1983) *op. cit.*, p.179.
58. Parrott, A.C. (1999) Does cigarette smoking *cause* stress? *American Psychologist*, 54, 817–820.
59. Skinner, B.F. (1983) *op. cit.*, p.180.
60. *Ibid.*, p.219.
61. *Ibid.*, p.247.
62. *Ibid.*, p.255.
63. *Ibid.*, p.265.
64. *Ibid.*, p.270.
65. Rutherford, A. (2000) Radical behaviourism and psychology's public: B.F. Skinner in the popular press, 1934–1990. *History of Psychology*, 3, 371–395.
66. Nye, R.D. (1979) *op. cit.*
67. Slater, L. (2004) *Opening Skinner's Box*. W.W. Norton, New York. p.28.
68. Bjork, D.W. (2002) *op. cit.*, p.193.
69. Nye, R.D. (1979) *op. cit.*, p.86.
70. Bjork, D.W. (2002) *op. cit.*, p.220.
71. Rutherford, A. (2000) *op. cit.*, p.384.
72. See p. 84 of Agnew, S. (1972) Agnew's blast at behaviourism: "A new kind of despotism…What arrogance! What contempt!" *Psychology Today*, pp.4, 84, 87.
73. Rutherford, A. (2000) *op. cit.*
74. Kagan, J. (1974) Foreword. In Carpenter, F. *The Skinner Primer: Behind Freedom and Dignity*. The Free Press, New York.
75. Rutherford, A. (2000) *op. cit.*
76. Nye, R.D. (1979) *op. cit.*

77. Skinner, B.F. (1983) *op. cit.*, p.329.
78. Bjork, D.W. (2002) *op. cit.*, p.212.
79. Rutherford, A. (2000) *op. cit.*
80. Meichenbaum, D. (1977) *Cognitive-Behavior Modification: An Integrative Approach.* Plenum Press, New York.
81. Carpenter, F. (1974) *op. cit.*
82. Slater, L. (2004) *op. cit.*
83. Richelle, M. (1993) *op. cit.*, p.xii.
84. anonymous obituary in (1991) In memoriam. *Zygon*, 26, 189–194.

Chapter 3

1. Nisbett, R.E. and Wilson, T.D. (1977) Telling more than we can know: Verbal reports on mental processes. *Psychological Review*, 84, 231–259.
2. Wilson, T.D. (2002) *Strangers to Ourselves: Discovering the Adaptive Unconscious.* The Belknap Press of Harvard University Press, Cambridge.
3. Described in Bargh, J.A. and Ferguson, M.J. (2000) Beyond behaviourism: On the automaticity of higher mental processes. *Psychological Bulletin*, 126, 925–945.
4. Wilson, T.D. (2002) *op. cit.*
5. *Ibid.*
6. *Ibid.*, p.212.
7. *Ibid.*, p.212.
8. Brewer, W.F. (1974) There is no convincing case for operant or classical conditioning in humans. In *Cognition and the Symbolic Process* (ed. W.B. Weimer and D.S. Palermo), Lawrence Erlbaum, Hillsdale, pp.1–42.
9. For details of Fromm's life, See Thomson, A. (2008) *Erich Fromm.* Palgrave Macmillan.
10. Lowe, C.F. (1983) Radical behaviourism and human psychology. In *Animal Models of Human Behavior: Conceptual, Evolutionary, and Neurobiological Perspectives* (ed. G.C.L. Davey), John Wiley, Chichester, pp.71–93.
11. Powers, W. (1973) *Behaviour: The Control of Perception.* Wildwood House, London.
12. Bandura, A. (1974) Self-reinforcement: Theoretical and methodological considerations. *Behaviorism*, 4, 133–155.
13. Brewer, W.F. (1974) *op. cit.*
14. Skinner, B.F. (1983) *A Matter of Consequences.* Alfred A. Knopf, New York, p.317.
15. Platt, J.R. (1973) The Skinnerian revolution. In *Beyond the Punitive Society – Operant Conditioning: Social and Political Aspects* (ed. H. Wheeler), Wildwood House, London, pp.22–56, p.35.
16. *Ibid.*, p.35.
17. See p.217 of Patterson, G.R. (2008) A comparison of models for interstate wars and for individual violence. *Perspectives on Psychological Science*, 3, 203–223.
18. *Ibid.*, p.218.
19. Cited by Nye, R.D. (1979) *What is B.F. Skinner Really Saying?* Prentice-Hall, Englewood Cliffs, p.31.
20. Watson, D.L. and Tharp, R.G. (1997) *Self-Directed Behavior: Self-Modification for Personal Adjustment.* Brooks/Cole Publishing, Pacific Grove, p.207.
21. Skinner, B.F. (1953) *Science and Human Behavior.* The Free Press, New York.
22. Ferster, C.B., Culbertson, S. and Boren, M.C.P. (1975) *Behavior Principles* (2nd edition), Prentice-Hall, Englewood Cliffs, p.145.
23. Skinner, B.F. (1953). *op. cit.*; Nye, R.D. (1979) *op. cit.*
24. White, R.W. (1959) Motivation reconsidered: The concept of competence. *Psychological Review*, 66, 297–333.

25. Zimbardo, P.G. and Miller, N.E. (1958) The facilitation of exploration by hunger in rats. *Journal of Comparative and Physiological Psychology*, 51, 43–46.

26. White, R.W. (1959) *op. cit.*, p.320.

27. Lyons, C. (1991) Application: smoking. In *Human Behavior in Today's World* (ed. W. Ishaq), Praeger, New York, pp.217–230.

28. Baker, T.B., Japuntich, S.J., Hogle, J.M., McCarthy, D.E. and Curtin, J.J. (2006) Pharmacologic and behavioural withdrawal from addictive drugs. *Current Directions in Psychological Science*, 15, 232–236.

29. Discussed by Flora, S.R. (2004) *The Power of Reinforcement*. State University of New York Press, Albany.

30. Robins, L.N., Helzer, J.E. and Davis, D.H. (1975) Narcotic use in Southeast Asia and afterward. *Archives of General Psychiatry*, 32, 955–961.

31. Alexander, B.K. and Hadaway, P.F. (1982) Opiate addiction: The case for an adaptive orientation. *Psychological Bulletin*, 92, 367–381.

32. Flora, S.R. (2004) *op. cit.*

33. *Ibid.*

34. *Ibid.*

35. *Ibid.*

36. Nevin, J.A. (1991) Behavior analysis and global survival. In *Human Behavior in Today's World* (ed. W. Ishaq), Praeger, New York, pp.39–49.

37. Kubey, R. and Csikszentmihalyi, M. (2002) Television addiction is no mere metaphor. *Scientific American*, 286(2), 74–81.

38. Wood, P.B., Gove, W.R., Wilson, J.A. and Cochran, J.K. (1997) Nonsocial reinforcement and habitual criminal conduct: An extension of learning theory. *Criminology*, 35, 335–366.

39. *Ibid.*

40. Wood, P.B., Cochran, J.K., Pfefferbaum, B. and Arneklev, B.J. (1995) Sensation-seeking and delinquent substance use: An extension of learning theory. *Journal of Drug Issues*, 25, 173–193.

41. Akers, R.L. and Jensen, G.F. (2003) *Social Learning Theory and the Explanation of Crime*. Transaction Publishers, New Brunswick. Gottfredson, M.R. and Hirschi, T. (1990) *A General Theory of Crime*. Stanford University Press, Stanford.

42. Carlson, M., Charlin, V. and Miller, N. (1988) Positive mood and helping behavior: A test of six hypotheses. *Journal of Personality and Social Psychology*, 55, 211–229.

43. Skinner, B.F. (1953) *op. cit.*, p.320.

44. Flora, S.R. (2004) *op. cit.*

45. *Ibid.*, p.15.

46. *Ibid.*

47. *Ibid.*, p.31.

48. Carpenter, F. (1974) *The Skinner Primer: Behind Freedom and Dignity*. The Free Press, New York.

49. Baum, W.M. (1994) *Understanding Behaviorism: Science, Behavior, and Culture*. Harper-Collins, New York.

50. Sidman, M. and Ishaq, W. (1991) Beware of coercion. In *Human Behavior in Today's World* (ed. W. Ishaq), Praeger, New York, pp.51–69.

51. Rachlin, H. (1980) *Behaviorism in Everyday Life*. Prentice-Hall, Englewood Cliffs.

52. Richelle, M.N. (1993) *B.F. Skinner: A Reappraisal*. Lawrence Erlbaum Associates, Hove.

53. Skinner, B.F. (1953) *op. cit.*

54. Barkley, R.A. (1997) Behavioural inhibition, sustained attention, and executive functions: constructing a unified theory of ADHD. *Psychological Bulletin*, 121, 65–94; Meichenbaum, D. (1977) *Cognitive-Behavior Modification: An Integrative Approach*. Plenum Press, New York; Watson, D.L. and Tharp, R.G. (1997)

Self-Directed Behavior: Self-Modification for Personal Adjustment. Brooks/Cole Publishing, Pacific Grove.

55. Jeannerod, M. (1997) *The Cognitive Neuroscience of Action*, Blackwell, Oxford.

Chapter 4

1. Winter, D.D. and Koger, S.M. (2004) *The Psychology of Environmental Problems* (2nd Edition). Lawrence Erlbaum, Mahwah, p.89.
2. Miller, G.A., Galanter, E. and Pribram, K.H. (1960) *Plans and the Structure of Behavior.* Holt, Rinehart and Winston, New York; Powers, W. (1973) *Behaviour: The Control of Perception.* Wildwood House, London; Tolman, E.C. (1932) *Purposive Behaviour in Animals and Men.* The Century Co., New York.
3. Mills, J.A. (1998) *Control: A History of Behavioral Psychology.* New York University Press, New York; Tolman, E.C. (1932) *Purposive Behaviour in Animals and Men.* The Century Co., New York.
4. Dickinson, A. and Balleine, B. (1992) Actions and responses: the dual psychology of behaviour. In *Problems in the Philosophy and Psychology of Spatial Representation* (eds. N. Eilan, R.A. McCarthy and M.W. Brewer), Blackwell, Oxford, pp.277–293.
5. *Ibid.*
6. Crespi, L.P. (1942) Quantitative variation of incentive and performance in the white rat. *The American Journal of Psychology*, 55, 467–517.
7. Skinner, B.F. (1980) *Notebooks.* Prentice-Hall, Englewood Cliffs, p.77.
8. Dickinson, A. (1980) *Contemporary Animal Learning Theory.* Cambridge University Press, Cambridge.
9. Skinner, B.F. (1953) *Science and Human Behavior.* The Free Press, New York, p.57.
10. Berridge, K.C. (2004) Motivation concepts in behavioral neuroscience. *Physiology and Behavior*, 81, 179–209; Bindra, D. (1978) How adaptive behaviour is produced: a perceptual–motivational alternative to response-reinforcement. *The Behavioral and Brain Sciences*, 1, 41–91; Toates, F. (1986) *Motivational Systems.* Cambridge University Press.
11. Rachlin, H. (1980) *Behaviorism in Everyday Life.* Prentice-Hall, Englewood Cliffs, p.163.
12. Baum, W.M. (1994) *Understanding Behaviorism: Science, Behavior, and Culture.* Harper-Collins, New York.
13. *Ibid.*, p.78.
14. *Ibid.*, p.78.
15. *Ibid.*, p.83.
16. *Ibid.*, p.83.
17. *Ibid.*, p.83.
18. Mills, J.A. (1998) *Control: A History of Behavioral Psychology.* New York University Press, New York.
19. Lacey, H. and Schwartz, B. (1987) The explanatory power of radical behaviorism. In *B.F. Skinner: Consensus and Controversy* (eds. Modgil, S. and Modgil, C.). Falmer Press, New York, pp.165–176, p.171.
20. May, R. (1979) *Psychology and the Human Dilemma.* W.W. Norton, New York.
21. Meichenbaum, D. (1977) *Cognitive-Behavior Modification: An Integrative Approach.* Plenum Press, New York.
22. Bargh, J.A. and Ferguson, M.J. (2000) Beyond behaviourism: On the automaticity of higher mental processes. *Psychological Bulletin*, 126, 925–945.
23. *Ibid.*
24. *Ibid.*, p.938.

25. Bargh, J.A. (2008) Free will is un-natural. In *Are We Free? The Psychology of Free Will* (eds. J. Baer, J. Kaufman and R. Baumeister), Oxford University Press, New York, pp.128–154, p.142.

26. Skinner, B.F. (1957) *Verbal Behavior*. Appleton-Century-Crofts, New York.

27. Chomsky, N. (1959) Review of Verbal Behaviour by B.F. Skinner. *Language*, 35, 26–58.

28. Andresen, J. (1991) Skinner and Chomsky 30 years later or: The return of the repressed. *The Behavior Analyst*, 14, 49–60.

29. Baum, W.M. (1994) *op. cit.*

30. Flora, S.R. (2004) *The Power of Reinforcement*. State University of New York Press, Albany.

31. Chomsky, N. (1959) *op. cit.*, p.57.

32. Richelle, M.N. (1993) *B.F. Skinner: A Reappraisal*. Lawrence Erlbaum Associates, Hove. Overskeid, G. (2007) Looking for Skinner and finding Freud. *American Psychologist*, 62, 590–595. For an account of Freud, see Stevens, R. (2008) *Freud*. Palgrave Macmillan, Basingstoke.

33. Nye, R.D. (1979) *What is B.F. Skinner Really Saying?* Prentice-Hall, Englewood Cliffs.

34. Overskeid, G. (2007) *op. cit.*, p.592.

35. Richelle, M.N. (1993) *op. cit.*

36. Nye, R.D. (1979) *op. cit.*

37. Richelle, M.N. (1993) *op. cit.*

38. Nye, R.D. (1979) *op. cit.*

39. *Ibid.*

40. Skinner, B.F. (1953) *op. cit.*, p.370.

41. *Ibid.*, p.373.

42. *Ibid.*, p.379.

43. Skinner, B.F. (1980) *op. cit.*, p.291.

44. Carpenter, F. (1974) *The Skinner Primer: Behind Freedom and Dignity*. The Free Press, New York, p.182.

45. Skinner, B.F. (1953) *op. cit.*

46. Nye, R.D. (1979) *op. cit.*

47. Ryan, R.M. and Deci, E.L. (2000) Self-determination theory and the facilitation of intrinsic motivation, social development, and well being. *American Psychologist*, 55, 68–78.

48. Flora, S.R. (2004) *op. cit.*

49. Ryan, R.M. and Deci, E.L. (2000) *op. cit.*, p.68.

50. *Ibid.*, p.69.

51. Flora, S.R. (2004) *op. cit.*

52. Ryan, R.M. and Deci, E.L. (2000) *op. cit.*, p.70.

53. Kasser, T. (2002) *The High Price of Materialism*. The MIT Press, Cambridge.

54. *Ibid.*, p.74.

55. Ryan, R.M. and Deci, E.L. (2000) *op. cit.*, p.70.

56. Flora, S.R. (2004) *op. cit.*

57. *Ibid.*

58. Ryan, R.M. and Deci, E.L. (2000) *op. cit.*, p.74.

59. Seligman, M.E.P. and Csikszentmihalyi, M. (2000) Positive psychology. *American Psychologist*, 55, 5–14, 5.

Chapter 5

1. Spread throughout Skinner's writing is the implicit or explicit assumption that the study of behaviour is in essence a part of biological sciences.

2. Richelle, M. (1987) Variation and selection: The evolutionary analogy in Skinner's theory. In *B.F. Skinner: Consensus and Controversy* (eds. Modgil, S. and Modgil, C.). Falmer Press, New York, pp.127–137.

3. Edelman, G.M. (1987) *Neural Darwinism*. Oxford University Press, Oxford.

4. Platt, J.R. (1973) The Skinnerian revolution. In *Beyond the Punitive Society – Operant Conditioning: Social and Political Aspects* (ed. H. Wheeler), Wildwood House, London, pp.22–56, p.28.

5. Comfort, A. (1973) Skinner's new broom. In *Beyond the Punitive Society – Operant Conditioning: Social and Political Aspects* (ed. H. Wheeler), Wildwood House, London, pp.199–211, p.200.

6. Lorenz, K.Z. (1981) *The Foundations of Ethology*, Springer-Verlag, New York.

7. Berkowitz, L. (1973) Simple views of aggression. In *Man and Aggression* 2nd ed. (ed. A. Montagu), Oxford University Press, New York, pp.39–52; Montagu, A. (1973) The new litany of "innate depravity", or original sin revisited. In *Man and Aggression* 2nd ed. (ed. A. Montagu), Oxford University Press, New York, pp.3–18.

8. Eisenberger, L. (1973) The *human* nature of human nature. In *Man and Aggression* 2nd ed. (ed. A. Montagu), Oxford University Press, New York, pp.53–69.

9. Montagu, A. (1973) *op. cit.*, p.14.

10. Berkowitz, L. (1973) *op. cit.*, p.50.

11. *Ibid.*; Crook, J.H. (1973) The nature and function of territorial aggression. In *Man and Aggression* 2nd ed. (ed. A. Montagu), Oxford University Press, New York, pp.183–220; For a consideration of the conditions under which aggression can be reinforcing, see Azrin, N.H., Hutchinson, R.R. and McLaughlin, R. (1965) The opportunity for aggression as an operant reinforcer during aversive stimulation. *Journal of the Experimental Analysis of Behavior*, 8, 171–180; This issue is discussed in Toates, F. (2007) *Biological Psychology*. Pearson Education, Harlow.

12. *Ibid.*

13. Baum, W.M. (1994*) Understanding Behaviorism: Science, Behavior, and Culture*. Harper-Collins, New York.

14. Dubos, R. (1973) Man's nature and social institutions. In *Man and Aggression* 2nd ed. (ed. A. Montagu), Oxford University Press, New York, pp.84–91.

15. Skinner, B.F. (1953) *Science and Human Behavior*. The Free Press, New York, p.373.

16. Tooby, J. and Cosmides, L. (1990) The past explains the present. *Ethology and Sociobiology*, 11, 375–424.

17. Pinker, S. (2002) *The Blank Slate: The Modern Denial of Human Nature*. Penguin Books, London.

18. Richelle, M.N. (1993) *B.F. Skinner: A Reappraisal*. Lawrence Erlbaum Associates, Hove.

19. *Ibid.*; Skinner, B.F. (1979) *The Shaping of a Behaviorist*. Alfred A. Knopf, New York, p.166.

20. Sagal, P.T. (1981) *Skinner's Philosophy*. University Press of America, Washington.

21. Norman, D.A. and Shallice, T. (1986) Attention to action – willed and automatic control of behaviour. In *Consciousness and Self- regulation: Advances in Research and Theory*, Vol.4 (eds. R.J. Davidson, G.E. Schwartz and D. Shapiro), Plenum Press, New York, pp.1–18; F. Toates (1998) The interaction of cognitive and stimulus-response processes in the control of behaviour. *Neuroscience and Biobehavioural Reviews*, 22, 59–83; F. Toates (2006) A model of the hierarchy of behaviour, cognition and consciousness. *Consciousness and Cognition*, 15, 75–118; F. Toates (2009) An integrative theoretical framework for understanding sexual motivation, arousal and behaviour. *Journal of Sex Research*, 46, 168–193.

22. Skinner, B.F. (1980) *Notebooks*. Prentice-Hall, Englewood Cliffs, p.341.
23. *Ibid.*, p.4.
24. Raine, A., Buchsbaum, M. and LaCasse, L. (1997) Brain abnormalities in murderers indicated by positron emission tomography. *Biological Psychiatry*, 42, 495–508; Wallace, J.F. and Newman, J.P. (2008) RST and psychopathy: associations between psychopathy and the behavioural activation and inhibition systems. In *The Reinforcement Sensitivity Theory of Personality* (ed. P.J. Corr), Cambridge University Press, Cambridge, pp.398–414.
25. Brugger, P., Dowdy, M.A. and Graves, R.E. (1994) From superstitious behavior to delusional thinking: The role of the hippocampus in misattributions of causality. *Medical Hypotheses*, 43, 397–402.
26. Berridge, K.C. (2001) Reward learning: Reinforcement, incentives, and expectations. In *The Psychology of Learning and Motivation* (Vol.40) (ed. D.L. Medin), Academic Press, pp.223–278.
27. Rolls, E.T. (2005) *Emotion Explained*. Oxford University Press, Oxford.
28. Rilling, J.K., Gutman, D.A., Zeh, T.R., Pagnoni, G., Berns, G.S. and Kilts, C.D. (2002) A neural basis for social cooperation. *Neuron*, 35, 395–405.
29. Bachner-Melman, R., Gritsenko, I., Nemanov, L., Zohar, A.H., Dina, C. and Ebstein, R.P. (2005) Dopaminergic polymorphisms associated with self-report measures of human altruism: a fresh phenotype for the dopamine D4 receptor. *Molecular Psychiatry*, doi: 10.1038/sj.mp.4001635, pp.1–3.
30. Rilling, J.K. *et al.* (2002), *op. cit.*, p.400.
31. Fricchione, G. (2007) Altruistic love, resiliency, health, and the role of medicine. In *Altruism and Health: Perspectives from Empirical Research* (ed. S.G. Post), Oxford University Press, New York, pp.351–370.
32. *Ibid.*; Brown, S.L., Brown, R.M., Schiavone, A. and Smith, D.M. (2007) Close relationships and health through the lens of selective investment theory. In *Altruism and Health: Perspectives from Empirical Research* (ed. S.G. Post), Oxford University Press, New York, pp.299–313.
33. Olds, J. and Milner, P. (1954) Positive reinforcement produced by electrical stimulation of septal area and other regions of rat brain. *Journal of Comparative and Physiological Psychology*, 47, 419–427.
34. Panksepp, J. (1981) Hypothalamic integration of behavior: Rewards, punishments, and related psychobiological process. In *Handbook of the Hypothalamus*, Vol.3, Part A. *Behavioral Studies of the Hypothalamus*. P.J. Morgane and J. Panksepp (eds.). New York: Marcel Dekker, pp.289–487.
35. Berridge, K.C. (2001) *op. cit.*; Rideout, H.J. and Parker, L.A. (1996) Morphine enhancement of sucrose palatability: analysis by the taste reactivity test. *Pharmacology Biochemistry and Behaviour*, 53, 731–734; This topic is described in introductory terms in Toates, F. (2007) *Biological Psychology*. Pearson Education, Harlow.
36. Kozlowski, L.T., Wilkinson, A., Skinner, W., Kent, C., Franklin, T. and Pope, M. (1989) Comparing tobacco cigarette dependence with other drug dependencies. *Journal of the American Medical Association*, 261, 898–901.
37. Balfour, D.J.K. (2004) The neurobiology of tobacco dependence: A preclinical perspective on the role of the dopamine projections to the nucleus. *Nicotine and Tobacco Research*, 6, 899–912.
38. Robinson, T.E. and Berridge, K.C. (1993) The neural basis of drug craving: an incentive-sensitization theory of addiction. *Brain Research Reviews*, 18, 247–291.
39. Ellinwood, E.H. and Escalante, O. (1970) Chronic amphetamine effect on the olfactory forebrain. *Biological Psychiatry*, 2, 189–203, 189.

Chapter 6

1. Chomsky, N. (1973) The case against B.F. Skinner. In *Without/Within: Behaviorism and Humanism* (ed. F.W. Matson), Brooks/Cole Publishing Company, Monterey, pp.58–79.
2. Wright, J. (1987) B.F. Skinner: The pragmatic humanist. In *B.F. Skinner: Consensus and Controversy* (eds. Modgil, S. and Modgil, C.). Falmer Press, New York, pp.79–87.
3. Skinner, B.F. (1953) *Science and Human Behavior*. The Free Press, New York, p.20.
4. May, R. (1979) *Psychology and the Human Dilemma*. W.W. Norton, New York, p.175.
5. *Ibid.*, p.174.
6. E.R. Harcum (1994) *A Psychology of Freedom and Dignity: The Last Train to Survival*. Praeger Publishers, Westport, CT.
7. Skinner, B.F. (1953) *op. cit.*, p.115.
8. Wegner, D.M. (2002) *The Illusion of Conscious Will*. The MIT Press, Cambridge.
9. Nye, R.D. (1979) *What is B.F. Skinner Really Saying?* Prentice-Hall, Englewood Cliffs.
10. F. Toates (2006) A model of the hierarchy of behaviour, cognition and consciousness. *Consciousness and Cognition*, 15, 75–118; Zhu, J. (2004) Is conscious will an illusion? *Disputatio*, 16, 58–68.
11. Toynbee, A. (1973) Great expectations. In *Beyond the Punitive Society – Operant Conditioning: Social and Political Aspects* (ed. H. Wheeler), Wildwood House, London, pp.113–120, p.119.
12. Carpenter, F. (1974) *The Skinner Primer: Behind Freedom and Dignity*. The Free Press, New York; Harcum, E.R. (1994) *op. cit.*
13. Baum, W.M. (1994) *Understanding Behaviorism: Science, Behavior, and Culture*. HarperCollins, New York.
14. Harcum, E.R. (1994) *op. cit.*
15. Richelle, M.N. (1993) *B.F. Skinner: A Reappraisal*. Lawrence Erlbaum Associates, Hove.
16. Harcum, E.R. (1994) *op. cit.*, p.6.
17. *Ibid.*, p.29.
18. Carpenter, F. (1974) *op. cit.*
19. Harcum, E.R. (1994) *op. cit.*
20. Carpenter, F. (1974) p.101.
21. *Ibid.*
22. Flora, S.R. (2004) *The Power of Reinforcement*. State University of New York Press, Albany.
23. Carpenter, F. (1974) *op. cit.*
24. Nettler, G. (1959) Cruelty, dignity, and determinism. *American Sociological Review*, 24, 375–384.
25. Shapiro, D.H. (1978) *Precision Nirvana*. Prentice-Hall, Englewood Cliffs, p.112.
26. Harcum, E.R. (1994) *op. cit.*
27. Skinner, B.F. (1953) *op. cit.*
28. Bethlehem, D. (1987) Scolding the carpenter. In *B.F. Skinner: Consensus and Controversy* (eds. Modgil, S. and Modgil, C.). Falmer Press, New York, pp. 89–97, p.96.
29. Carpenter, F. (1974) *op. cit.*, p.115.
30. *Ibid.*, p.115.
31. Vohs, K.D. and Schooler, J.W. (2008) The value of believing in free will. *Psychological Science*, 19, 49–54.
32. Harcum, E.R. (1994) *op. cit.*, p.1.

33. *Ibid.*, p.2.
34. *Ibid.*, p.5.
35. Nye, R.D. (1979) *op. cit.*
36. Fontana, D. (1984) Perspectives on the wider educational applications of behaviourism. In *Behaviourism and Learning Theory in Education* (ed. D. Fontana), pp.192–195, p.194.
37. Toynbee, A. (1973) *op. cit.*, p.120.
38. Neal, F.W. (1973) Questions? In *Beyond the Punitive Society – Operant Conditioning: Social and Political Aspects* (ed. H. Wheeler), Wildwood House, London, pp.170–176.
39. Fontana, D. (1984) *op. cit.*
40. Pirages, D.C. (1973) Behavioral technology and institutional transformation. In *Beyond the Punitive Society – Operant Conditioning: Social and Political Aspects* (ed. H. Wheeler), Wildwood House, London, pp.57–70. p.57.
41. Neil, F.W. (1973) *op. cit.*
42. *Ibid.*, p. 172.
43. Wheeler, H. (1973) Introduction: A nonpunitive world? In *Beyond the Punitive Society – Operant Conditioning: Social and Political Aspects* (ed. H. Wheeler), Wildwood House, London, pp.1–21, p.14.

Chapter 7

1. Watson, D.L. and Tharp, R.G. (1997) *Self-Directed Behavior: Self-Modification for Personal Adjustment*. Brooks/Cole Publishing, Pacific Grove.
2. Shapiro, D.H. (1978) *Precision Nirvana*. Prentice-Hall, Englewood Cliffs.
3. Skinner, B.F. (1953) *Science and Human Behavior*. The Free Press, New York.
4. Winter, D.D. and Koger, S.M. (2004) *The Psychology of Environmental Problems* (2nd Edition) Lawrence Erlbaum, Mahwah.
5. Watson, D.L. and Tharp, R.G. (1997) *op. cit.*
6. *Ibid.*
7. Nye, R.D. (1979) *What is B.F. Skinner Really Saying?* Prentice-Hall, Englewood Cliffs, p.173.
8. Rachlin, H. (1980) *Behaviorism in Everyday Life*. Prentice-Hall, Englewood Cliffs.
9. Ferster, C.B., Culbertson, S. and Boren, M.C.P. (1975) *Behavior Principles* (2nd edition), Prentice-Hall, Englewood Cliffs, p.677.
10. Rachlin, H. (1980) *op. cit.*
11. *Ibid.*
12. *Ibid.*
13. *Ibid.*
14. Kubey, R. and Csikszentmihalyi, M. (2002) Television addiction is no mere metaphor. *Scientific American*, 286(2), 74–81.
15. Rachlin, H. (1980) *op. cit.*
16. Nye, R.D. (1979) *op. cit.*
17. *Ibid.*, p.159.
18. Baum, W.M. (1994) *Understanding Behaviorism: Science, Behavior, and Culture*. HarperCollins, New York.
19. Rachlin, H. (1980) *op. cit.*
20. Nye, R.D. (1979) *op. cit.*
21. *Ibid.*
22. Watson, D.L. and Tharp, R.G. (1997) *op. cit.*
23. *Ibid.*, p.120.
24. *Ibid.*

25. Discussed by Flora, S.R. (2004) *The Power of Reinforcement*. State University of New York Press, Albany.
26. *Ibid.*
27. Nye, R.D. (1979) *op. cit.*
28. Watson, D.L. and Tharp, R.G. (1997) *op. cit.*, p.139.
29. Carpenter, F. (1974) *The Skinner Primer: Behind Freedom and Dignity*. The Free Press, New York, p.28.
30. Kasser, T. (2002) *The High Price of Materialism*. The MIT Press, Cambridge, p.89.
31. Rachlin, H. (1980) *op. cit.*, p.161.
32. Skinner, B.F. (1953) *Ibid.*
33. Flora, S.R. (2004) *op. cit.*
34. Nye, R.D. (1979) *op. cit.*
35. *Ibid.*, p.164.
36. Baum, W.M. (1994) *op. cit.*

Chapter 8

1. Skinner, B.F. (1983) *A Matter of Consequences*. Alfred A. Knopf, New York, p.320.
2. Carpenter, F. (1974) *The Skinner Primer: Behind Freedom and Dignity*. The Free Press, New York.
3. Richelle, M.N. (1993) *B.F. Skinner: A Reappraisal*. Lawrence Erlbaum Associates, Hove, p.203.
4. Pirages, D.C. (1973) Behavioral technology and institutional transformation. In *Beyond the Punitive Society – Operant Conditioning: Social and Political Aspects* (ed. H. Wheeler), Wildwood House, London, pp.57–70, p.67.
5. Skinner, B.F. (1983) *op. cit.*, p.305
6. Slater, L. (2004) *Opening Skinner's Box*. W.W. Norton, New York, p.29.
7. Platt, J.R. (1973) The Skinnerian revolution. In *Beyond the Punitive Society – Operant Conditioning: Social and Political Aspects* (ed. H. Wheeler), Wildwood House, London, pp.22–56, p.22.
8. Wheeler, H. (1973) Introduction: A nonpunitive world? In *Beyond the Punitive Society – Operant Conditioning: Social and Political Aspects* (ed. H. Wheeler), Wildwood House, London, pp.1–21, p.1.
9. Pirages, D.C. (1973) *op. cit.*
10. Rozynko, V., Swift, K., Swift, J. and Boggs, L.J. (1973) Controlled environments for social change. In *Beyond the Punitive Society – Operant Conditioning: Social and Political Aspects* (ed. H. Wheeler), Wildwood House, London, pp.71–100, p.83.
11. Skinner, B.F. (1980) *Notebooks*. Prentice-Hall, Englewood Cliffs.
12. *Ibid.*, p.287.
13. Skinner, B.F. (1980) *op. cit.*, p.27.
14. Skinner, B.F. (1983) *op. cit.*, p.355.
15. *Ibid.*, p.355.
16. Platt, J.R. (1973) *op. cit.*, p.41
17. Discussed by Flora, S.R. (2004) *The Power of Reinforcement*. State University of New York Press, Albany (see citations in here).
18. *Ibid.*
19. Skinner, B.F. (1983) *op. cit.*, p.307.
20. Cited by Strobel, L. (2004) *The Case for a Creator: A Journalist Investigates Scientific Evidence That Points Toward God*. Zondervan, Grand Rapids, p.256.
21. *Ibid.*, p.256.

22. Patterson, G.R. (2008) A comparison of models for interstate wars and for individual violence. *Perspectives on Psychological Science*, 3, 203–223.
23. Nevin, J.A. (1991) Behavior analysis and global survival. In *Human Behavior in Today's World* (ed. W. Ishaq), Praeger, New York, pp.39–49.
24. Carpenter, F. (1974) *op. cit.*

Chapter 9

1. Bowlby, J. (2005) *A Secure Base*. Routledge, London (this is the latest printing of the book).
2. Skinner, B.F. (1979) *The Shaping of a Behaviorist*. Alfred A. Knopf, New York, p.297.
3. Harlow, H.F. and Harlow, M.K. (1962) Social deprivation in monkeys. *Scientific American*, 207, No.5, 136–146.
4. Skinner, B.F. (1953) *Science and Human Behavior*. The Free Press, New York, p.80.
5. *Ibid.*, p.310.
6. Kasser, T., Ryan, R.M., Zax, M. and Sameroff, A.J. (1985) The relations of maternal and social environments to late adolescents' materialistic and prosocial values. *Developmental Psychology*, 31, 907–914; van Lange, A.M., Otten, W., de Bruin, E.M.N. and Joireman, J.A. (1997) Development of prosocial, individualistic, and competitive orientations: Theory and preliminary evidence. *Journal of Personality and Social Psychology*, 73, 733–746.
7. Bowlby, J. (2005) *A Secure Base*. Routledge, London (this is the latest printing of the book).
8. Baum, W.M. (1994) *Understanding Behaviorism: Science, Behavior, and Culture*. HarperCollins, New York.
9. Piaget, J. and Inhelder, B. (1972) *The Psychology of the Child*. Basic Books, New York.
10. See description in Toates, F. (1998) The interaction of cognitive and stimulus-response processes in the control of behaviour. *Neuroscience and Biobehavioral Reviews*, 22, 59–83.
11. Ferster, C.B., Culbertson, S. and Boren, M.C.P. (1975) *Behavior Principles* (2nd edition). Prentice-Hall, Englewood Cliffs, p.143.
12. Fordyce, W.E. (1976) *Behavioral Methods for Chronic Pain and Illness*. Mosby, St. Louis.
13. Flora, S.R. (2004) *The Power of Reinforcement*. State University of New York Press, Albany.
14. Peterson, C., Maier, S.F. and Seligman, M.E.P. (1996) *Learned Helplessness: A Theory for the Age of Personal Control*. Oxford University Press, New York; Seligman, M.E.P. (1998) *Learned Optimism*. Free Press, New York.
15. Flora, S.R. (2004) *op. cit.*
16. *Ibid.*, p.32.
17. Carpenter, F. (1974) *The Skinner Primer: Behind Freedom and Dignity*. The Free Press, New York.
18. *Ibid.*, p.193.
19. Skinner, B.F. (1983) *A Matter of Consequences*. Alfred A. Knopf, New York, p.145.
20. Flora, S.R. (2004) *op. cit.*, p.147.
21. Baum, W.M. (1994) *op. cit.*
22. Writing in Evans, R.I. (1968) *B.F. Skinner: The Man and his Ideas*. E.P. Dutton, New York, p.70.
23. Bjork, D.W. (2002) *B.F. Skinner: A Life*. American Psychological Association, Washington, p.170.

24. Hallam, S. and Rogers, L. (2008) *Improving Behaviour and Attendance at School*. Open University Press, Maidenhead.
25. Swinson, J. and Harrop, A. (2005) An examination of the effects of a short course aimed at enabling teachers in infant, junior and secondary schools to alter the verbal feedback given to their pupils. *Educational Studies*, 31, 115–129, 124.
26. *Ibid.*, p.119.
27. *Ibid.*, p.120.
28. Hallam, S. and Rogers, L. (2008) *op. cit.*
29. Wheldall, K. and Merrett, F. (1984) The behavioural approach to classroom management. In *Behaviourism and Learning Theory in Education* (ed. D. Fontana), pp.15–42.
30. Fontana, D. (1984) Behaviourism and learning theory in the classroom. An overview. In *Behaviourism and Learning Theory in Education* (ed. D. Fontana), pp.107–114.
31. Wheldall, K. and Merrett, F. (1984) *op. cit.*
32. Fontana, D. (1984) *op. cit.*, p.108.
33. Richelle, M.N. (1993) *B.F. Skinner: A Reappraisal*. Lawrence Erlbaum Associates, Hove.
34. Light, P. (1997) Annotation: Computers for learning: psychological perspectives. *Journal of Child Psychology and Psychiatry*, 38, 497–504.
35. Richelle, M.N. (1993) *op. cit.*
36. Light, P. (1997) *op. cit.*, p.497.
37. Mercer, N. and Littleton, K. (2007) *Dialogue and the Development of Children's Thinking*. Routledge, London, p.79.
38. Light, P. (1997) *op. cit.*
39. Mercer, N. and Littleton, K. (2007) *op. cit.*
40. discussed in Flora, S.R. (2004) *op. cit.*
41. *Ibid.*
42. Burland, R. (1984) Behaviourism in the closed community: The token economy and performance contracting. In *Behaviourism and Learning Theory in Education* (ed. D. Fontana), pp.117–135.
43. *Ibid.*
44. Patterson, G.R. (2008) A comparison of models for interstate wars and for individual violence. *Perspectives on Psychological Science*, 3, 203–223.
45. Patterson, G.R., Reid, J.B. and Dishion, T.J. (1992) *A Social Interactional Approach*. Vol.4. *Antisocial Boys*. Castalia Publishing Company, Eugene.
46. *Ibid.*
47. *Ibid.*
48. Patterson, G.R. (2008) *op. cit.*
49. Patterson, G.R. *et al.* (1992) *op. cit.*, p. 22.

Chapter 10

1. Richelle, M.N. (1993) *B.F. Skinner: A Reappraisal*. Lawrence Erlbaum Associates, Hove.
2. Alexander, B.K. and Hadaway, P.F. (1982) Opiate addiction: the case for an adaptive orientation. *Psychological Bulletin*, 92, 367–381.
3. Peterson, C., Maier, S.F. and Seligman, M.E.P. (1996) *Learned Helplessness: A Theory for the Age of Personal Control*. Oxford University Press, New York.
4. Richelle, M.N. (1993) *op. cit.*, p.156.
5. *Ibid.*

6. Franks, C.M. and Barbrack, C.R. (1991) Behavior therapy with adults: An integrative perspective for the nineties. In *The Clinical Psychology Handbook* (2nd Edition) (eds. M. Hersen, A.E. Kazdin and A.S. Bellack), Pergamon Press, New York, pp.551–566.

7. Lazarus, A.A. (1977) Has behavior therapy outlived its usefulness? *American Psychologist*, 32, 550–554.

8. Nye, R.D. (1979) *What is B.F. Skinner Really Saying?* Prentice-Hall, Englewood Cliffs.

9. *Ibid.*

10. Truax, C.B. (1966) Reinforcement and nonreinforcement in Rogerian psychotherapy. *Journal of Abnormal Psychology*, 71, 1–9.

11. Skinner, B.F. (1953) *Science and Human Behavior*. The Free Press, New York.

12. Flora, S.R. (2004) *The Power of Reinforcement*. State University of New York Press, Albany.

13. Zimbardo, P.G. (2004) Does psychology make a significant difference in our lives? *American Psychologist*, 59, 339–351.

14. *Ibid.*, p.342.

15. Melzack, R. and Wall, P.D. (1965) Pain mechanisms: a new theory. *Science*, 150, 971–979.

16. Fordyce, W.E. (1976) *Behavioral Methods for Chronic Pain and Illness*. Mosby, St. Louis.

17. *Ibid.*

Chapter 11

1. Dawkins, R. (1976) *The Selfish Gene*. Oxford University Press, Oxford.

2. Post, S.G. (2007) *Altruism and Health: Perspectives from Empirical Research*. Oxford University Press, New York.

3. Wilson, D.S. and Csikszentmihalyi, M. (2007) Health and the ecology of altruism. In *Altruism and Health: Perspectives from Empirical Research* (ed. S.G. Post), Oxford University Press, New York, pp.314–331.

4. Boehm, C. (2007) A short natural history of altruism and healing. In *Altruism and Health: Perspectives from Empirical Research* (ed. S.G. Post), Oxford University Press, New York, pp.332–350.

5. van Lange, A.M., Otten, W., de Bruin, E.M.N. and Joireman, J.A. (1997) Development of prosocial, individualistic, and competitive orientations: Theory and preliminary evidence. *Journal of Personality and Social Psychology*, 73, 733–746.

6. Skinner, B.F. (1991) Why we are not acting to save the world. In *Human Behavior in Today's World* (ed. W. Ishaq), Praeger, New York, pp.19–29, p.26.

7. Penner, L.A., Dovidio, J.F., Piliavin, J.A. and Schroeder, D.A. (2005) Prosocial behavior: Multilevel perspectives. *Annual Review of Psychology*, 56, 365–392.

8. Singer, T., Seymour, B., O'Doherty, J., Kaube, H., Dolan, R.J. and Frith, C.D. (2004) Empathy for pain involves the affective but not sensory components of pain. *Science*, 303, 1157–1162.

9. Post, S.G. (2007) *op. cit.*

10. Koenig, H.G. (2007) Altruistic love and physical health. In *Altruism and Health: Perspectives from Empirical Research* (ed. S.G. Post), Oxford University Press, New York, pp.422–441.

11. Oman, D. (2007) Does volunteering foster physical health and longevity? In *Altruism and Health: Perspectives from Empirical Research* (ed. S.G. Post), Oxford University Press, New York, pp.15–32; Post, S.G. (2007) *op. cit.*

12. Schwartz, C. (2007) Altruism and subjective well-being: Conceptual model and empirical support. In *Altruism and Health: Perspectives from Empirical Research* (ed. S.G. Post), Oxford University Press, New York, pp.33–42.

13. van Lange, A.M. (1997) *op. cit.*

14. Kasser, T., Ryan, R.M., Zax, M. and Sameroff, A.J. (1985) The relations of maternal and social environments to late adolescents' materialistic and prosocial values. *Developmental Psychology*, 31, 907–914.

15. Wilson, D.S. and Csikszentmihalyi, M. (2007) *op. cit.*

16. Penner, L.A., Dovidio, J.F., Piliavin, J.A. and Schroeder, D.A. (2005) Prosocial behavior: Multilevel perspectives. *Annual Review of Psychology*, 56, 365–392; Post, S.G. (2007) *op. cit.*

17. Jones, S.L. (1988) A religious critique of behavior therapy. In *Behavior Therapy and Religion: Integrating Spiritual and Behavioral Approaches to Change* (eds. W.R. Miller and J.E. Martin), Sage Publications, Newbury Park, pp.139–170.

18. Ishaq, W. (1991) Behavior analysis across cultures. In *Human Behavior in Today's World* (ed. W. Ishaq), Praeger, New York, pp.257–277.

19. Skinner, B.F. (1953) *Science and Human Behavior*. The Free Press, New York.

20. Baum, W.M. (1994) *Understanding Behaviorism: Science, Behavior, and Culture*. HarperCollins, New York.

21. *Ibid.*, p.162.

22. *Ibid.*, p.164.

23. Carpenter, F. (1974) *The Skinner Primer: Behind Freedom and Dignity*. The Free Press, New York.

24. Miller, W.R. and Martin, J.E. (1988) Spirituality and behavioral psychology. In *Behavior Therapy and Religion: Integrating Spiritual and Behavioral Approaches to Change* (eds. W.R. Miller and J.E. Martin), Sage Publications, Newbury Park, pp.13–23.

25. Skinner, B.F. (1976) *Particulars of My Life*. Jonathan Cape, London.

26. Skinner, B.F. (1980) *Notebooks*. Prentice-Hall, Englewood Cliffs.

27. Skinner, B.F. (1983) *A Matter of Consequences*. Alfred A. Knopf, New York, p.246.

28. Skinner, B.F. (1980) *op. cit.*, p.38.

29. *Ibid.*, p.33.

30. Pattison, E.M. (1988) Behavioral psychology and religion: A cosmological analysis. In *Behavior Therapy and Religion: Integrating Spiritual and Behavioral Approaches to Change* (eds. W.R. Miller and J.E. Martin), Sage Publications, Newbury Park, pp.171–186, p.172.

31. *Ibid.* p.173.

32. Skinner, B.F. (1983) *A Matter of Consequences*. Alfred A. Knopf, New York, p.402.

33. Novak, M. (1973) Is he really a grand inquisitor? In *Beyond the Punitive Society – Operant Conditioning: Social and Political Aspects* (ed. H. Wheeler), Wildwood House, London, pp.230–246, p.237.

34. Skinner, B.F. (1980) *op. cit.*, p.80.

35. *Ibid.*, p.81.

36. Pattison, E.M. (1988) *op. cit.*

37. Skinner, B.F. (1983) *op. cit.*, p.62.

38. Jones, S.L. (1988) *op. cit.*

39. Harcum, E.R. (1994) *op. cit.*, p.160.

40. Needless to say, the implications of such debate are enormous and would stretch the discussion beyond the brief of the present book. It is hoped, though, that the relevance of a Skinnerian perspective to the debate will be evident.

41. Jones, S.L. (1988) *op. cit.*

42. Witvliet, C.V.O. and McCullough, M.E. (2007) Forgiveness and health: A review and theoretical exploration of emotion pathways. In *Altruism and Health: Perspectives*

from Empirical Research (ed. S.G. Post), Oxford University Press, New York, pp.259–276.

43. Cunningham, M.R., Steinberg, J. and Grev, R. (1980) Wanting to and having to help: Separate motivations for positive mood and guilt-induced helping. *Journal of Personality and Social Psychology*, 38, 181–192; Zhong, C-B. and Liljenquist, K. (2006) Washing away your sins: Threatened morality and physical cleansing. *Science*, 313, 1451–1452.

44. Novak, M. (1973) *op. cit.*

45. Jeeves, M.A. (1976) *Psychology and Christianity: The View both Ways.* Inter-Varsity Press, Leicester; MacKay, D.M. (1974) *The Clockwork Image: A Christian Perspective on Science.* Intervarsity Press, London; Stannard, R. (2003) *Why? Why Evil? Why Suffering? Why Death?* Lion Publishing, Oxford.

46. Clement, P.W. (1988). Integrating behavioral theory and training with personal faith. In *Behavior Therapy and Religion: Integrating Spiritual and Behavioral Approaches to Change* (eds. W.R. Miller and J.E. Martin), Sage Publications, Newbury Park, pp.37–42, p.40.

47. Witvliet, C.V.O. and McCullough, M.E. (2007) *op. cit.*

48. Harcum, E.R. (1994) *op. cit.*, p.160.

49. Bergin, A.E. (1988) Three contributions of a spiritual perspective to psychotherapy and behavior change. In *Behavior Therapy and Religion: Integrating Spiritual and Behavioral Approaches to Change* (eds. W.R. Miller and J.E. Martin), Sage Publications, Newbury Park, pp.25–36.

50. Platt, J.R. (1973) The Skinnerian revolution. In *Beyond the Punitive Society – Operant Conditioning: Social and Political Aspects* (ed. H. Wheeler), Wildwood House, London, pp.22–56, p.35.

51. MacKay, D.M. (1979) *Human Science and Human Dignity.* Hodder and Stoughton, London.

52. *Ibid.*, p.74.

53. Epstein, R. (2006) Giving psychology away: A personal journey. *Perspectives in Psychological Science*, 1, 389–400.

54. Burhoe, R.W. (1954) Religion in the age of science. *Science*, 120, 522–524, 523.

Chapter 12

1. Winter, D.D. and Koger, S.M. (2004) *The Psychology of Environmental Problems* (2nd Edition). Lawrence Erlbaum, Mahwah, p.119.

2. Schultz, P.W. (2002) Inclusion with nature: The psychology of human-nature relations. In *Psychology of Sustainable Development* (eds. P. Schmuck and W.P. Schultz), Kluwer Academic Publishers, Boston, pp.61–78.

3. Schmuck, P. and Schultz, P.W. (2002) Sustainable development as a challenge for psychology. In *Psychology of Sustainable Development* (eds. P. Schmuck and W.P. Schultz), Kluwer Academic Publishers, Boston, pp.3–17.

4. Oskamp, S. (2002) Summarizing sustainability issues and research approaches. In *Psychology of Sustainable Development* (eds. P. Schmuck and W.P. Schultz), Kluwer Academic Publishers, Boston, pp.301–324, p.308.

5. Ishaq, W. (1991) *Human Behavior in Today's World.* Praeger, New York.

6. Hardin, G. (1968) The tragedy of the commons. *Science*, 162, 1243–1248.

7. Nevin, J.A. (1991) Behavior analysis and global survival. In *Human Behavior in Today's World* (ed. W. Ishaq), Praeger, New York, pp.39–49.

8. Platt, J. (1973) Social traps. *American Psychologist*, 28, 641–651.

9. Geller, E.S., Winett, R.A. and Everett, P.B. (1982) *Preserving the Environment: New Strategies for Behavior Change*. Pergamon Press, New York.
10. Winter, D.D. and Koger, S.M. (2004) *op. cit.*
11. Platt, J. (1973) *op. cit.*
12. *Ibid.*
13. *Ibid.*, p.645.
14. Winter, D.D. and Koger, S.M. (2004) *op. cit.*
15. Osbaldiston, R. and Sheldon, K.M. (2002) Social dilemmas and sustainability: Promoting peoples' motivation to "cooperate with the future". In *Psychology of Sustainable Development* (eds. P. Schmuck and W.P. Schultz), Kluwer Academic Publishers, Boston, pp.37–57.
16. Gladwin, T.N., Newburry, W.E. and Reiskin, E.D. (1997) Why is the northern elite mind biased against community, the environment, and a sustainable future? In *Environment, Ethics, and Behavior* (eds. M.H. Bazerman, D.M. Messick, A.E. Tenbrunsel and K.A. Wade-Benzoni), The New Lexington Press, San Francisco, pp.234–274.
17. Kasser, T. (2002) *The High Price of Materialism*. The MIT Press, Cambridge, p.91.
18. Skinner, B.F. (1991) Why we are not acting to save the world. In *Human Behavior in Today's World* (ed. W. Ishaq), Praeger, New York, pp.19–29, p.26.
19. Kasser, T. (2002) *op. cit.*
20. *Ibid.*, p.77.
21. Kaplan, S. (1995) The restorative benefits of nature: Toward an integrative framework. *Journal of Environmental Psychology*, 15, 169–182.
22. Kals, E. and Maes, J. (2002) Sustainable development and emotions. In *Psychology of Sustainable Development* (eds. P. Schmuck and W.P. Schultz), Kluwer Academic Publishers, Boston, pp.97–122.
23. Osbaldiston, R. and Sheldon, K.M. (2002) *op. cit.*, p.54.
24. Schmuck, P. and Schultz, P.W. (2002) *op. cit.*
25. Geller, E.S. (1995) Actively caring for the environment: An integration of behaviorism and humanism. *Environment and Behavior*, 27, 184–195.
26. Allen, J.B. and Ferrand, J.L. (1999) Environmental locus of control, sympathy, and proenvironmental behavior: A test of Geller's actively caring hypothesis. *Environment and Behavior*, 31, 338–353.
27. Bandura, A. (2002) Environmental sustainability by sociocognitive deceleration of population growth. In *Psychology of Sustainable Development* (eds. P. Schmuck and W.P. Schultz), Kluwer Academic Publishers, Boston, pp.209–238; McKenzie-Mohr, D. (2002) The next revolution: sustainability. In *Psychology of Sustainable Development* (eds. P. Schmuck and W.P. Schultz), Kluwer Academic Publishers, Boston, pp.19–33.
28. Winter, D.D. and Koger, S.M. (2004) *op. cit.*
29. Bandura, A. (2002) *op. cit.*
30. Geller, E.S., Winett, R.A. and Everett, P.B. (1982) *Preserving the Environment: New Strategies for Behavior Change*. Pergamon Press, New York.
31. *Ibid.*
32. Katzev, R.D. and Johnson, T.R. (1987) *Promoting Energy Conservation: An Analysis of Behavioral Research*. Westview Press, Boulder.
33. Chance, P.B. (1991) The sky is falling. In *Human Behavior in Today's World* (ed. W. Ishaq), Praeger, New York, pp.31–38, p.34.
34. Nevin, J.A. (1991) Behavior analysis and global survival. In *Human Behavior in Today's World* (ed. W. Ishaq), Praeger, New York, pp.39–49, p.48.
35. Katzev, R.D. and Johnson, T.R. (1987) *op. cit.*; Winter, D.D. and Koger, S.M. (2004) *op. cit.*

36. Degenhardt, L. (2002) Why do people act in sustainable ways? Results of an empirical survey of lifestyle pioneers. In *Psychology of Sustainable Development* (eds. P. Schmuck and W.P. Schultz), Kluwer Academic Publishers, Boston, pp.123–147; Geller *et al.* (1982) *op. cit.*; Katzev, R.D. and Johnson, T.R. (1987) *op. cit.*

37. Geller, E.S. (1995) *op. cit.*

38. Katzev, R.D. and Johnson, T.R. (1987) *op. cit.*

39. McKenzie-Mohr, D. (2002) *op. cit.*

40. Winter, D.D. and Koger, S.M. (2004) *op. cit.*

41. Skinner, B.F. (2005) *Walden Two*. Hackett Publishing Co., Indianapolis (this is the latest reprint of the original book)

42. Geller, E.S. (1995) *op. cit.*

43. Winter, D.D. and Koger, S.M. (2004) *op. cit.*

44. Geller, E.S. *et al.* (1982) *op. cit.*

45. Katzev, R.D. and Johnson, T.R. (1987) *op. cit.*

46. Eigner, S. and Schmuck, P. (2002) Motivating collective action: Converting to sustainable energy sources in a German community. In *Psychology of Sustainable Development* (eds. P. Schmuck and W.P. Schultz), Kluwer Academic Publishers, Boston, pp.241–256; Geller, E.S. *et al.* (1982) *op. cit.*

47. Geller, E.S. (1995) *op. cit.*

48. *Ibid.*

49. *Ibid.*

50. Katzev, R.D. and Johnson, T.R. (1987) *op. cit.*

51. *Ibid.*

52. Flora, S.R. (2004) *The Power of Reinforcement*. State University of New York Press, Albany.

53. Geller, E.S. (2002) The challenge of increasing proenvironmental behaviour. In *Handbook of Environmental Psychology* (eds. R.B. Bechtel and A. Churchman), Wiley, New York, pp.525–540.

54. Kasser, T. (2002) *op. cit.*

55. *Ibid.*

56. *Ibid.*

57. Ryan, R.M., Sheldon, K.M., Kasser, T. and Deci, E.L. (1996) All goals are not created equal: An organismic perspective on the nature of goals and their regulation. In *The Psychology of Action: Linking Motivation to Behavior* (eds. P.M. Gollwitzer and J.A. Bargh), The Guilford Press, New York, pp.7–26.

58. Geller, E.S. (1995) *op. cit.*; Geller, E.S. *et al.* (1995) *op. cit.*

59. Skinner, B.F. (1991) *op. cit.*, p.28.

60. Geller, E.S. (2002) *op. cit.*, p.528.

61. Geller, E.S. *et al.* (1982) *op. cit.*

62. Kals, E. and Maes, J. (2002) Sustainable development and emotions. In *Psychology of Sustainable Development* (eds. P. Schmuck and W.P. Schultz), Kluwer Academic Publishers, Boston, pp.97–122; Osbaldiston, R. and Sheldon, K.M. (2002) *op. cit.*

Chapter 13

1. Nye, R.D. (1979) *What is B.F. Skinner Really Saying?* Prentice-Hall, Englewood Cliffs.

2. Harcum, E.R. (1994) *A Psychology of Freedom and Dignity: The Last Train to Survival*. Praeger Publishers, Westport, CT, p.84.

3. *Ibid.* p.17.

4. Jeeves, M.A. (1976) *Psychology and Christianity: The View both Ways*. Inter-Varsity Press, Leicester.
5. Skinner, B.F. (1983) *A Matter of Consequences*. Alfred A. Knopf, New York, p.332.
6. Pribram, K.H. (1973) Operant behaviourism: Fad, fact-ory, and fantasy? In *Beyond the Punitive Society – Operant Conditioning: Social and Political Aspects* (ed. H. Wheeler), Wildwood House, London, pp.101–112.
7. Geller, E.S. (1995) Actively caring for the environment: An integration of behaviorism and humanism. *Environment and Behavior*, 27, 184–195.
8. Chance, P.B. (1991) The sky is falling. In *Human Behavior in Today's World* (ed. W. Ishaq), Praeger, New York, pp.31–38.
9. *Ibid.*, p.35.
10. Mills, J.A. (1998) *Control: A History of Behavioral Psychology*. New York University Press, New York, p.123.
11. Baars, B.J. (2003) The double life of B.F. Skinner: Inner conflict, dissociation and the scientific taboo against consciousness. *Journal of Consciousness Studies*, 10, 5–25.
12. Carpenter, F. (1974) *The Skinner Primer: Behind Freedom and Dignity*. The Free Press, New York.
13. Bjork, D.W. (2002) *B.F. Skinner: A Life*. American Psychological Association, Washington, p.153.
14. Mills, J.A. (1998) *op. cit.*
15. Bjork, D.W. (2002) *op. cit.*, p.59.

Index